The Art of Metal

The Art of Metal

FIVE DECADES OF HEAVY METAL ALBUM COVERS, POSTERS, T-SHIRTS, AND MORE

CONSULTANT EDITORS: MARTIN POPOFF & MALCOLM DOME

Voyageur Press

First published in 2013 by Voyageur Press, an imprint of MBI Publishing Company, 400 First Avenue North, Suite 400, Minneapolis, MN 55401 USA

Copyright © Elephant Book Company Limited 2013

www.elephantbookcompany.com

This 2013 edition published by Voyageur Press by arrangement with Elephant Book Company Ltd.

Voyageur Press titles are also available at discounts in bulk quantity for industrial or sales-promotional use. For details write to Special Sales Manager at MBI Publishing Company, 400 First Avenue North, Suite 400, Minneapolis, MN 55401 USA.

To find out more about our books, visit us online at www.voyageurpress.com

ISBN: 978-0-7603-4493-4

Editorial director: Will Steeds
Project manager: Judith John
Executive editors: Laura Ward and Chris McNab
Book design and cover artwork: Paul Palmer-Edwards, www.gradedesign.com
Production: Alastair Gourlay
Picture editor and image licensing manager: Joanna St. Mart
Picture research: Olivia Airey

Printed in China

10 9 8 7 6 5 4 3 2 1

Contents

A Word from Lemmy

Hello everybody. How are you? Oh I'm OK, thanks. In the studio as I write this.

Anyway, what a splendid book this is, eh? Some of the best images and artwork from almost every type of metal you could wish for—well, we couldn't do them all. There's just so much to cover. But I reckon what's here is a very comprehensive overview of what we've all been doing forever. And you've gotta love the Motörhead content!

It makes you realize just how important art has been to the music since it all began. And it's about time those designers and artists who've worked away behind the scenes for so long got some attention.

Hope you can afford this book. Things being the way they are at the moment. And if you can't, well you know what I always say: if you can't, ask one of your mates to get it for you! It's worth having.

Happy staring!

Los Angeles.
February 2013

6

Introduction

MALCOLM DOME

Welcome to the first comprehensive book ever put together to celebrate the artwork that's been part of the metal scene ever since . . . well, it first began. You don't have to think very hard to realize that the first impression that will spring to mind for any band is an image. Let's try it. So . . .

Motörhead—Oh, the Snaggletooth symbol

Iron Maiden—Eddie

Metallica—The logo

Megadeth—Vic Rattlehead

See what I mean? They are as important to the bands' heritage and legacy as any of their iconic songs. These help to define what the band is all about, and give them their own niche in the zone of rock 'n' roll. And while it's disingenuous to suggest that no other form of music appreciates artwork the way that metal does, nonetheless can any of these other styles claim to have such diversity?

You want fantasy? How about the remarkable paintings of Frank Frazetta. You want weirdness? Look no further than Hipgnosis. You want blood? Then check out the Cannibal Corpse album covers. You want overtly erotic scenes? The photos by Helmut Newton will do the trick. You want science fiction vistas? Hugh Syme can fulfil your needs.

Everywhere you look, the world of metal is stuffed with some of the most phantasmagorical, elevated, and downright sinister images to be seen. Some of them are so iconic that they stand in their own right, without the need to connect them to any band or album. And we will be celebrating every nook, cranny, and head popped up over the parapet since metal first began to stir its multidimensional hind legs, got up onto its limbs, and bounded into the future. That was back in the 1960s, at a time when music as a whole was just starting to get the hang of this thing called the album.

It is astonishing to think that it took a further fifteen years after the introduction of the LP format for anyone to realize what it had given to music. The format was introduced in 1948 at a press conference by Columbia Records. However, instead of musicians immediately seeing the increased opportunities for recording, it took fifteen years, and the arrival of a certain Bob Dylan, before eyes were opened, jaws dropped, and the world became sonically more colorful.

Now, while Dylan's 1963 album *The Freewheelin' Bob Dylan* might not mean anything in the context of this book, it was the first record to really exploit the extra grooves and space available on what was a 33 1/3rpm format. But not only did Dylan use the resource to record more than just a couple of new songs, he also ensured that the album photo—of himself and his girlfriend—was interesting.

To put this into context—and it's important for what was to follow—at this time, record labels filled up most albums with pointless covers. Even bands like the Beatles and the Rolling Stones failed to appreciate what the technology of the time had to offer. Their earliest LPs were packed with filler songs that showed no interest in showcasing the growing song writing talents of the bands. What's more, the photos on the sleeves were prosaic and deficient, adding little sparkle or lustre to their images.

Yet, by the time the Who released *A Quick One* in 1966, things were changing on the artwork front. The album cover was designed by the pop artist Alan Aldridge, and displayed an enthusiasm for engaging the fans in the visual as well as the audio. This was the start of a revolution that would make the 12" LP format the perfect vehicle for encouraging a sense of visual artistry that could be seen by millions. While the art gallery remained the province of the elite, now young painters had a different medium within which to express themselves, as well as complementing the music of a fresh generation who were prepared to push the envelope.

In 1960s San Francisco, poster artists like Rick Griffin, Stanley Mouse, and Alton Kelley created a series of concert posters that were rich in color and patterns, making them far more than advertising vehicles for gigs or festivals. They are still outstanding even today.

While the likes of Jefferson Airplane, the Quicksilver Messenger Service, and the Doors on the US West Coast were exhibiting signs and signals as a result of paying attention to visuals almost as much as to musical expression, across America another type of band was doing similarly impressive and far-reaching work. The MC5 and the Stooges (later Iggy and the Stooges) in Detroit were far earthier and confrontational in their music, something they also encouraged in the packaging used for their albums. The cover photo by Joel Brodsky used for the former's *Kick Out the Jams* in 1969 was a mind-bending collage of shapes and colors, designed to disorientate. And the same photographer was also responsible for the cover photo used by the latter for *The Stooges* album in the same year. The photo expressed an insouciant, sneering dishevelment about the Stooges, which became a blueprint for many subsequent photo shoots with metal bands.

Of course, while one can appreciate the visual approaches used by the likes of Cream and Jimi Hendrix—which have retained their cachet—the real birth of metal began in 1969 with the release of the self-titled, debut album from Black Sabbath. It is here that everything being preached on all levels by Blue Cheer, the Kinks, and Iron Butterfly—to name but three pioneers—finally coalesced. It was the birth of what we would later term heavy metal, but back then was known as underground or heavy rock.

The imagery used on that sleeve was to become as much a part of metal folklore as the music. However, it was to be years before people understood what designer Marcus Keef had created. In many respects, he laid the groundwork for all that follows in this book.

Just how much detail was put into this cover can be understood by realizing the original gatefold release not only had an inverted cross as the centerfold, but there was a poem inscribed inside the cross: "Still falls the rain, the veils of darkness shroud the blackened trees, which, contorted by some unseen violence, shed their tired leaves, and bend their boughs towards a grey earth of severed bird wings. Among the grasses, poppies bleed before a gesticulating death, and young rabbits, born dead in traps, stand motionless, as though guarding the silence that surrounds and threatens to engulf all those that would listen. Mute birds, tired of repeating yesterday's terrors, huddle together in the recesses of dark corners, heads turned from the dead, black swan that floats upturned in a small pool in the hollow. There emerges from this pool a faint sensual mist, that traces its way upwards to caress the chipped feet of the headless martyr's statue, whose only achievement was to die too soon, and who couldn't wait to lose. The cataract of darkness forms fully, the long black night begins, yet still, by the lake a young girl waits. Unseeing she believes herself unseen, she smiles, faintly at the distant tolling bell, and the still falling rain."

In one swoop, Keef managed to capture the imaginings of metal fans and musicians over the next forty-five years. The ominous nature of his work still sends shivers down the spine.

So, this is where it all began. Barely three years after album cover artwork was first given creative credence, Black Sabbath were already grinding it forward to a new era.

In the first chapter, we explore the way in which a handful of artistic prophets gave metal flesh and bone, as it was shaped into something vibrant and different. The differentiation between this genre and many others was first brought to fruition in this era, when there were no rules. The record industry itself was still finding its feet and setting its own allusions and illusions.

When the New Wave of British Heavy Metal (NWOBHM) took root and flight in 1979, things were taken to another level. It was at this juncture that the term heavy metal was embraced and absorbed by bands, fans, and the media. Suddenly, it all made sense.

In reality, NWOBHM was a very disparate scenario, taking in such a diversity of bands and styles. It was also the only time in the history of the genre when music was geographically so specific. But that was the only unifying factor for a range of names from Iron Maiden to Def Leppard to Diamond Head.

This seeming disparity in the musical movement also took in the artwork. So, while Maiden developed the character of Eddie, Leppard went for an altogether more oddball approach, thanks to the attentions of design group Hipgnosis. But what was also apparent as we moved into the 1980s was that a striking, unique band-specific image was very profitable.

TOP LEFT The cover of the 1978 self-titled, debut album (Epic) from southern rockers Molly Hatchet is actually a 1973 painting from American fantasy and science fiction artist Frank Frazetta. It was called *The Death Dealer*, and was the first in a series of similar paintings that were used for the covers of novels and comic books, as well as for statues and action figures.

MIDDLE LEFT This is one of the covers for Sleep's album *Jerusalem*. The album caused controversy because it was just one long track. The artwork shown was the cover for an unauthorized version released in 1999 by Rise Above. The design was by Doug Ebright of Visual Flight, who also worked on *Dopesmoker* (The Music Cartel, 2003), which was the same album under a new title.

BOTTOM LEFT *Fair Warning* (Warner Bros., 1981) was the fourth Van Halen album. The cover is actually a part of a painting called *The Maze*, by the Canadian artist William Kurelek. Painted in 1952, while the artist was actively seeking psychiatric help at the Maudsley Hospital, London, it depicts Kurelek's representation of his own tormented mind.

ABOVE RIGHT The figure of Eddie has long been used by Iron Maiden as the sole image when it comes to marketing. This was the poster designed by Melvyn Grant for the band's 2011 tour, and was also used on the cover of the tour program. As Maiden bassist Steve Harris once said of Eddie: "He is the face of the band, and has become the most recognized figure in metal."

While the idea of patches and T-shirts had come into vogue during the end of the 1970s, as far as protometal fans were concerned, it was the explosion of interest when NWOBHM took hold of the charts and record stores that really brought them into sharp focus. The allegiance and alliance of fans to their favorite bands was now not just about purchasing the albums and singles, but also about wearing the insignia. So, you had the impressive sight of fans at festivals and gigs in denim jackets that exploded with patches. Each of these patches had the identifiable logo of its band, and that's why, in this era, a logo became far more than merely an insignia on an album sleeve.

In fact, the same could be said of the LP covers themselves. The images were used on T-shirts and other such paraphernalia, as the likes of Maiden realized that the strong visual connections they had to their own records was actually worth so much more to them than merely being a way of housing the music. So, it was with the advent of NWOBHM that the art of metal became commercially viable in its own right.

This was all taken to another level when the hair metal regime took hold, starting in America and then spreading itself out across the planet. Now, here was a moment when metal truly connected with masses, whatever gender or creed they might have been. It was a fascinating time, because what had been the main guiding force of the genre up until that moment was a state of tribal embrace. Metal was locked in its own mores and attitudes, forever believing that by cutting off the outside world and remaining steadfastly underground, it would survive.

But the arrival of bands like Bon Jovi, Mötley Crüe, and Poison changed everything. Following in the wake of Van Halen—who sketched the blueprint for this type of presentation—these bands went for sexier, more overtly suggestive images and artwork. The idea was to attract women as well as men.

Whereas the artwork for NWOBHM, for instance, was aimed firmly at male interests and attitudes, what the hair metal bands wanted to do was embrace the feminine audience, while not alienating their male fans. You can see in the way the artwork associated with such bands and their albums was presented that it ran a fine line between sex and sexism, a line which was occasionally crossed. But, as was seen by the way Guns N' Roses tackled the situation, this provocative artwork brought a lot of ingenuity into the arena.

It was also a style of music that had its own coterie of female stars. People like Lita Ford, for example, openly espoused their female attributes, while avoiding the image clichés. The result was that of the artwork from the hair metal movement being stylized, glamorous, yet also able to get grit under the fingernails.

More than any type of metal, it had to appeal to everyone. And, at its best, did precisely that, which is why the art it encouraged hasn't dated.

By contrast, doom and stoner metal was built on the outer limits of the genre. It was seemingly influenced by drugs, even if the protagonists themselves weren't actually indulging. The music was a slow, sedate drive, wherein the musicians and bands elevated the craft of extending the basic song structures with a pliable sense of jamming. It was almost like being on the border between the conscious and subconscious. The accompanying artwork is simply astonishing. All you have to do is to drink in the art that adorns the covers of albums from early pioneers Atomic Rooster, followed by Pentagram and Sleep, to see the way in which this music has inspired remarkable imagery.

The likes of Robert Crumb and Gilbert Shelton (who created the *Fabulous Furry Freak Brothers*) laid the template for stoner artwork, which has been taken to a new level. If you look at the astonishingly intricate and ornate artwork associated with Cathedral, or the remarkably individual strokes of John Baizley (who is also a member of Baroness), then you are truly seeing paintings that are as much self-contained genius as they are vessels to house music. Here is art for art's sake.

By the end of the twentieth century, metal had once again undergone a transformation, with the arrival of what was termed nu metal. Bands such as Korn, System of a Down, Limp Bizkit, Deftones, and Linkin Park brought new influences into their music, ranging from industrial to hip-hop right through to Armenian folk. As a result, the genre was again expanded technically and artistically.

Inevitably, the artwork that was spawned at the time also had a new, fresh feel. As we hit the twenty-first century, the album covers for so many bands of this ilk reflected lyrics that spoke to teenagers about being disenfranchised, abused, and alone. You sensed in the artwork that these bands were talking directly to a growing generation who feared and hated the world in which they were closeted. While the art of so many other metal genres was very much the embodiment of the larger-than-life character of the music, here were a set of performers and related artists who were carefully sifting through not the rebellious nature of youth, but the mental and physical damage their fans were facing. It was a somber, yet very crucial period.

At the start of the 1990s, another, sinister form of metal rose up and snapped with barely disguised blackness. It was the formal arrival of the appropriately named black metal movement, which began in Norway and spread across the world.

In reality, this style of music—dedicated to satanic rituals and rites, and never disguising a disgust with Christianity—had existed

since the start of the '80s when Venom had released their *Black Metal* (1982) album, yet it was only with the arrival of Emperor, Mayhem, Darkthrone, and other like-minded malcontents that black metal took root and blossomed.

Now, it's inevitable that satanic and demonic imagery plays its role in the artwork associated with black metal. But that is just the tip of this dark iceberg. Artists like Joachim Luetke and Kristian Wåhlin have ensured that there is a diversity of stunning art augmenting what has become a deeply sophisticated musical regime.

But black metal really grew out of the thrash and death metal area. And it was with these styles that artwork took a definite turn toward more explicit and gory representations. In fact, no other genre of metal can claim to have had as much artwork banned and censored as has been the case with these gruesome genres. One only has to think of Slayer, Kreator, and Cannibal Corpse, all of whom have suffered at the hands of the authorities.

But it is the very extremity of art tied in with thrash and death, which makes it so intriguing. Artists such as Ed Repka and Pushead, not to mention Michel "Away" Langevin of Voivod, have ensured that a high degree of creativity and quality is maintained.

One can argue that the thrash/death axis reflects horror movie history, running the gamut from the intelligent, thought-provoking releases, to the more over the top, underground gorefests. But it is certainly never dull!

Of course, in comparison, prog metal has come to represent a much more sophisticated, intricate, and intellectually challenging form of music and art. Bands such as Rush and Queensrÿche took on the progressive mantle of Yes, Genesis, et al., and married it to a more vigorous, riff-laden approach. Similarly, their artwork was also a representation of something altogether more exhaustive.

In more recent times, we have seen the rise of such bands as Dream Theater, Mastodon, Tool, Coheed and Cambria, and Meshuggah, all of whom apply an individual twist on the overall blueprint. But what they share is a desire to explore and push the envelope musically. Moreover, each band uses imagery to create an atmosphere that very much connects to them personally. It is a triumph of art—both audio and visual—representing both complexity and aggression.

So, this is what awaits you in this enthralling and engrossing book. What you have here is a uniquely informative guide to the remarkable and wonderfully evocative artwork that has become such a central part of the metal scene. And without the images created by so many artists with an insight and gift for visually augmenting and compounding the pounding of the music, metal would be incomplete.

That's enough from me; on with the show!

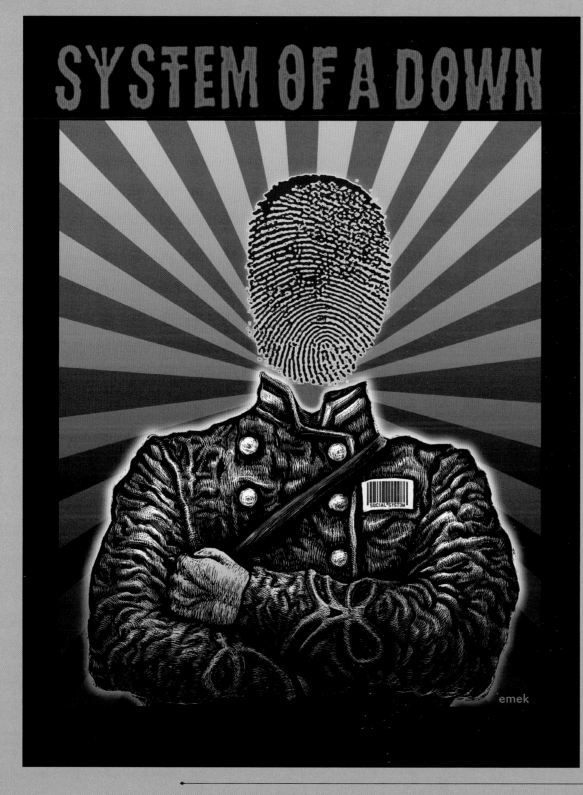

ABOVE LEFT System of a Down have long had a militant and highly politicized viewpoint, which is reflected in their art as well as the music. This poster uses the fingerprint motif in place of a head to emphasize that we are all individuals, but all too often we submerge this individuality in pursuit of the flock mentality, as represented by the uniform.

TOP RIGHT The cover for the ninth album from black metal pioneers Bathory. Called *Blood on Ice* (Black Mark, 1996), this is a concept album, and this concept is reflected in the cover artwork by Kristian Wåhlin. It tells the tale of a young survivor of a village raid, and how he takes revenge drawing on Norse mythology and supernatural powers.

MIDDLE RIGHT This is the cover for Megadeth's 1990 album *Rust in Peace* (Capitol). Created by Ed Repka, it shows band mascot Vic Rattlehead holding court alongside the five major world leaders of the time (left to right): British Prime Minister John Major, Japanese Prime Minister Toshiki Kaifu, German President Richard von Weizsacker, Russian General Secretary Mikhail Gorbachev, and American President George W. Bush.

BOTTOM RIGHT The artwork for this album was created by wood carver AJ Fosik, as part of his remit for work on the 2011 Mastodon album *The Hunter* (Reprise). Here's what Mastodon drummer Brann Dailor told *Alternative Press* about Fosik's involvement: "We were going to use something that was already there. But he wanted to use something that was brand new. [It] was his idea." Fosik also designed the backdrop for the band's live show.

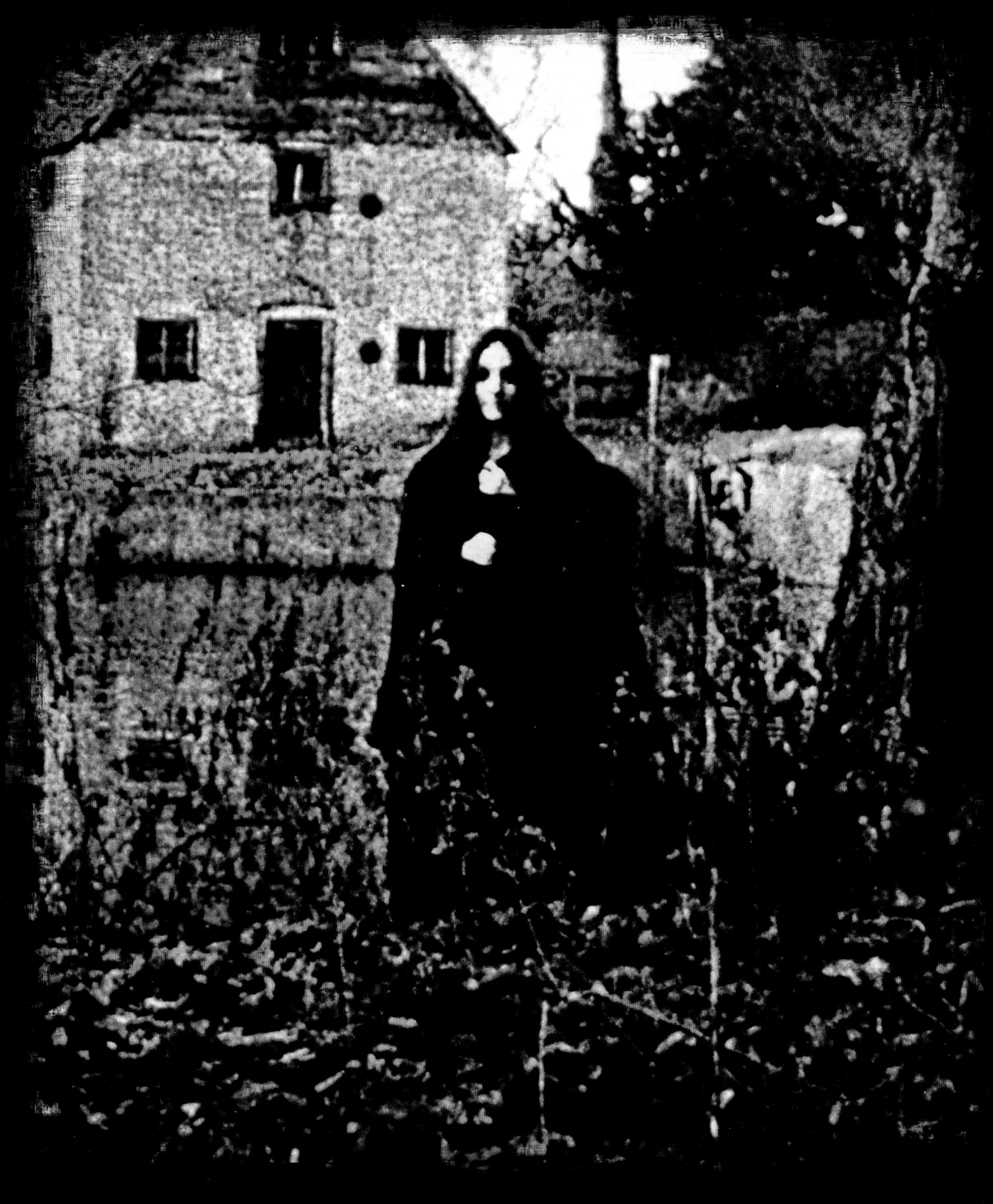

CHAPTER 1

Origins: Traditional Metal

"WE DIDN'T HAVE ANYTHING TO DO WITH THE COVER, BUT MARCUS KEEF
DEFINITELY MANAGED TO CAPTURE THE ESSENCE OF THE BAND. THE FIRST TIME WE
SAW THE INVERTED CRUCIFIX WAS WHEN WE OPENED THAT ALBUM. NOW IT HAS
BECOME SOMETHING THAT IS SYNONYMOUS WITH THE BAND. WE LOVED IT."

—Jim Simpson, Black Sabbath, first manager

Born to be Wild

KYLIE OLSSON

Artwork—whether it be albums, flyers, poster art, or merchandising—is part of the emotional connection we have with music. Without it, our whole musical experience would be a very different one. Just by mentioning a particular album, we can, by virtue of its cover art, conjure up an emotional image—a bit like the music itself.

As the sound of the '50s was coming to an end, a new dawn was breaking, and out of the sunrise a whole new sound arose that would shape the very world we live in today.

This sound was loud, gritty, and dark; it had never been heard before. Along with the change in music came a dramatic shift in the accompanying artwork. The days of the perfect nuclear family—with Mom in a cocktail dress, Dad in a tie, and the kids looking clean with well-ironed clothes—were being pushed aside, making way for the likes of the Beatles, the Rolling Stones, the Who, Led Zeppelin, and many more. All of a sudden, and for the first time, album artwork started to depict a real image of our society. It went from the very simple to telling an entire story that could be read in a single glance.

As teenagers swung their way into the 1960s, the realization dawned that they no longer had to be like their parents. Pushing away from the previous generations, so marked by war, young people wanted to create their own future and stop living in the past. National service was abolished, a man walked on the moon, the pill gave sexual liberation to women, and rather than go to college to learn how to be a mechanic or carpenter, teens had a new institution known as the art college. All of this had dramatic effects on society. Suddenly anything was possible.

Music played an integral part in this new liberation that was spreading over the world, and a new breed of artists, photographers, and designers was forming. One of the pivotal albums was the Beatles' *Sgt. Pepper's Lonely Hearts Club Band* (1967). It was one of the first packaged vinyls to create an emotional connection outside the music, coming complete with inserts and an album cover pioneering of design, which was created by Peter Blake, the godfather of the British pop art movement, and his then-wife, artist Jann Haworth. What with the paper cutouts of famous people, mannequins, and a doll wearing a T-shirt emblazoned with "Welcome the Rolling Stones, Good Guys," at that moment there was an obvious divergence between pop and rock. Until then, youth music was mainly seen as pop. *Sgt. Pepper* made people realize there was genuinely such a thing as rock.

Album artwork began to grow and develop from this stage. Record labels and musicians themselves started to market to specific demographics and groups. Graphics became more inventive, and famous artists were commissioned to add their expertise to the evolving world of album cover art. Bands began to include more lyrics, band pictures, and production notes in the album sleeves. Subsequently, many controversial, provocative, and famous album covers were produced from the late '60s onward.

Mention must be made here of the early American pioneers of psychedelic rock Blue Cheer; their 1968 debut album *Vincebus Eruptum* is considered one of the first metal records, and the cover showed a photo of the trio in a blue haze. Soon after, graphic designer Barney Bubbles took us to space when he designed and came up with the album title of Hawkwind's *In Search of Space* in '71. Along with this came a twenty-four-page booklet called *The Hawkwind Log*, produced by space-age poet Robert Calvert. Bubbles then continued the same theme/concept over the next two albums he designed for the band (*Doremi Fasol Latido*, 1972, and *The Hall of the Mountain Grill*, 1974). Space rock had begun. In contrast, in America Ted Nugent's over-the-top persona was reflected in his

> ## "THEY DISCUSSED A WHOLE RANGE OF ISSUES, BUT HOWEVER VARIED THEIR INTERESTS, THEY REMAINED COMPLETELY STEADFAST IN THEIR COVER REQUIREMENTS. SHADES OF [GERMAN EROTIC PHOTOGRAPHER] HELMUT NEWTON, BUT NOT."—Storm Thorgerson, designer

sleeve artwork. Ted Nugent avoided themes and stayed away from using imagery and art, opting for photos of himself, as on his seminal '77 release *Cat Scratch Fever*. However, this was not the traditional smiling portrait, instead showing a wild-looking—indeed, a slightly out-of-his-head-looking—Nugent.

The English band Deep Purple showed their self-confidence (and sense of humor) by sticking their faces on the American monument Mount Rushmore on their 1970 breakthrough album *In Rock*.

In London, the work of Hapshash and the Coloured Coat, a partnership between Michael English and Nigel Waymouth in the mid-'60s, should also be noted. They were both influential designers of psychedelic posters and musicians. As the latter, they released *Featuring the Human Host and the Heavy Metal Kids* (1967), which predates Steppenwolf's "Born to Be Wild" anthem by two years—and is claimed to be the first time the term "heavy metal" was used in a musical context!

Flipping back to the end of the '60s, the leaders of a new, more underground musical movement were being established and beginning to influence a whole new school of fans. The birth of metal had begun.

One of its most famous offspring was a band unprecedented in style, sound, and vision. That band was Black Sabbath.

They said it all in their self-titled debut album cover art, which conjured up an image of solitude, doom, and gloom, demanding that listeners sit down and listen—if they dared. Both visually and musically, it was like nothing else that had been seen or heard before—it was eerie and sparse, and the use of false color (infrared) photography by Marcus Keef, then the in-house photographer at Vertigo Records, reflected the mood of the album perfectly. This was also one of the first times a scary format had been used in sleeve art. Led Zeppelin had been linked to the occult before, but Black Sabbath were wearing it on their sleeves, in more ways than one.

Keef really captured the essence of Sabbath's music in their self-titled album *Black Sabbath* (1970) with the bare trees, blacked-out windows of the mill (Mapledurham Watermill in Oxfordshire, England), and an eerie figure in black peering from the undergrowth with hollow eyes, pale skin, and a cloak. The image is both evocative and truly creepy. Sabbath bassist Geezer Butler said of the artwork: "The album cover did a brilliant job in representing our music. When I first saw it, I did think, 'What the hell is this?' But the more I saw it, the more I became convinced it was visually just right. It's haunting, eerie, and a little scary. That's what we were after on the album. I don't think you could pick up the album and think you were getting a collection of Christmas songs."

The floodgates were now open, and artists and designers such as the Hipgnosis team—initially the influential duo Storm Thorgerson and Aubrey Powell—became known for their surrealist work, creating many weird and wonderful images. One in particular that transported us to the twenty-first century was Black Sabbath's *Technical Ecstasy* (1976), which depicts two robots having sex—or, as Ozzy Osbourne once said, "Two robots screwing on an escalator." Storm then flipped the new wave of artwork on its head by taking us back in time with an updated nuclear family image on Led Zeppelin's *Presence* (1976). Hipgnosis also designed every UFO album cover from 1974 to 1981, on which their skewed and surreal depictions of reality both amuse and unsettle.

The Scorpions, from Germany, then took Storm's surreality to a sexual level when they asked him to design the cover for their *Lovedrive* album in 1979. Their requirements were to the point; they stated that he could do what he wanted as long as it had sex and a woman in it and was a bit strange. Storm said, "They discussed a whole range of issues, but however varied their interests, they remained completely steadfast in their cover

"WHEN I WAS AT CBS, RECORD COVERS WERE AS IMPORTANT AS MINISKIRTS AND HOCKNEY PAINTINGS . . . IT WAS A NEW DESIGN, AND NOTHING HAD BEEN SEEN LIKE THIS BEFORE. IT WAS ALL COMING TOGETHER AT THE SAME TIME. THERE WAS A CHANCE FOR EVERYBODY TO SHINE AND BE KNOWN. WITH *STAINED CLASS*, I REALLY WANTED TO MOVE AWAY FROM THE CROWD, SO I JUST CAME UP WITH THIS IMAGE AND PRESENTED IT TO THE BAND, AND THIS WAS A TIME WHEN YOU ACTUALLY GOT TO SPEAK TO THE BAND YOU WERE DESIGNING FOR."
—Roslaw Szaybo, CBS Creative Director

requirements. Shades of [German erotic photographer] Helmut Newton, but not." (Newton would shoot the cover for the band's 1984 album *Love at First Sting*.)

As far as album artwork goes, the Scorpions were probably one of the most controversial bands out there during the '70s. Their 1975 release, *In Trance*, shot by photographer Michael von Gimbut, was censored for clearly showing the cover model's exposed breast—this was the first of many Scorpions releases to be censored.

However, their most contentious sleeve was for their 1976 release *Virgin Killer*, which features a nude ten-year-old girl with a shattered glass effect obscuring her genitalia; this was also shot by von Gimbut, and it definitely gained a lot of notoriety for the band. Their album artwork was all about pushing boundaries, repeatedly going "over the edge"; they were never afraid of offending people. This was a far cry from the 1950s; the Scorpions' artwork could be described as controversial even by today's standards, but this just goes to show both how famous and infamous sleeve artwork became during this period.

Logos started to play a big part in a band's visual image; the logo quickly became a way to brand a band for merchandising and for the fans to instantly recognize them. Judas Priest were one of the first to do this, under the guidance of Roslaw Szaybo, the Creative Director at CBS, the band's label. He moved them away

from their gothic script logo of earlier releases and created what was to become their classic logo, first seen on the sci-fi-themed *Stained Class* in 1978.

"When I was at CBS, record covers were as important as miniskirts and Hockney paintings," says Szaybo. "It was a new design, and nothing had been seen like this before. It was all coming together at the same time. There was a chance for everybody to shine and be known. With *Stained Class*, I really wanted to move away from the crowd, so I just came up with this image and presented it to the band, and this was a time when you actually got to speak to the band you were designing for."

Several other bands took this route, including AC/DC, Motörhead, the Scorpions, and even the Rolling Stones with their iconic tongue, originally designed by Ernie Cefalu.

This was a unique time period, signaling an evolution of a hugely influential art form—from the simplicity of the early 1960s to the extravagance, artistic self-indulgence, and gatefold sleeve excesses that were a by-product of the heady era of metal in the late '60s and '70s. The art of heavy metal, much like any other art form, depicts the many cultural aspects and changes we have gone through in our society. Fashion, politics, social values, racial views, lifestyles—it's all there, reflecting back to us our cultural development through the marvelous world of album artwork.

TICKETS SAN FRANCISCO: City Lights Bookstore; Bally Lo (Union Square); S F State College (Hut T-1); The Town Square (1318 Polk); Fertile Earth (723 Irv- ing); The Haight Ashbury Store (1538 Haight); HAYWARD: Matsuri. SAN MATEO: Town & Country Records. PALO ALTO: Dana Morgan M... SAUS- ALTO: The Tides. BERKELEY: Discount Records, Shakespeare & Co. SAN RAFAEL: Record King, REDWOOD CITY: Redwood...

LEFT A poster for a gig at the famous East Coast American venue, Fillmore East, which took place on August 27–29, 1969. Performers included Steppenwolf, Staple Singers, Grateful Dead, and Santana. The poster was created by artist Lee Conklin, who was based in San Francisco and was active as a poster artist only from 1968 to 1970.

"OUR GUITAR PLAYER, PETER HESSLEIN, LIKED TO DRAW, SO HE SCRIBBLED DOWN A FEW IDEAS AND GAVE IT TO THE LABEL, AND THIS WAS WHAT THEY CAME BACK WITH. THE TALL GUY WAS A WAITER, AND THEN WE THOUGHT 'WHAT ABOUT IF WE GOT A MINUTE GUY TO STAND NEXT TO HIM?' THE WHOLE THING WAS SHOT IN HAMBURG."
—John Lawton, Lucifer's Friend vocalist

TOP LEFT Design/photography by Juligan Studio. This is the self-titled debut from the German band Lucifer's Friend (Philips, 1970), who are cited as one of the early practitioners of heavy metal. It was presented as a gatefold that when opened showed a brick wall with a photo of each band member on it. The wall itself was an extension of a small part of the wall on the front cover.

BOTTOM LEFT The blazing cover evokes the fiery music on the album. *Fun House* (Elektra, 1970) was the Stooges' second album and their first to re-create their powerhouse live sound on record. Under the art direction of Greg Allen and Robert L. Heimall, photographer Ed Caraeff did the cover photo. He was renowned for shooting the famed photo on Captain Beefheart's *Trout Mask Replica* (Straight/Reprise, 1969).

BOTTOM RIGHT *High Time* (Atlantic, 1971) was the last album from MC5 and musically their best—it's tight and streamlined and offers the "real" MC5. They used artist Gary Grimshaw, who was high school friends with Rob Tyner, for many of their covers—this one, with a battered clock that references the back cover of "Let It Bleed," was also burned in places, hinting at the fact that the band were "on fire" at that stage of their career.

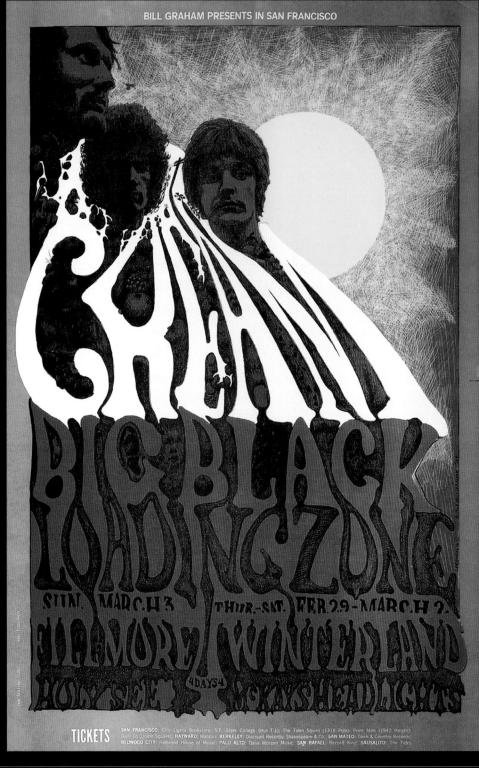

BILL GRAHAM PRESENTS IN SAN FRANCISCO

TICKETS
SAN FRANCISCO: City Lights Bookstore; S.F. State College (Hut T-1); The Town Squire (1318 Polk); Print Mint (1542 Haight); Bally Lo (Union Square); HAYWARD: Matsuri; BERKELEY: Discount Records; Shakespeare & Co.; SAN MATEO: Town & Country Records; REDWOOD CITY: Redwood House of Music; PALO ALTO: Dana Morgan Music; SAN RAFAEL: Record King; SAUSALITO: The Tides

TOP LEFT This iconic image was based on a famous live black-and-white photo of Jimi Hendrix taken by photographer Linda Eastman (later McCartney). Artist Martin Sharp used this photograph to create a colorful explosion in 1967.

BOTTOM LEFT Photography by Bob Whitaker (known for his work on several of the Beatles albums) and cover art created by Australian artist—and at the time, housemate of Eric Clapton—Martin Sharp. The cover of Cream's *Disraeli Gears* (Reaction, 1967) was a lot more psychedelic than that of their debut album, reflecting the sound that came to define the band.

ABOVE RIGHT Cream broke into America in 1967 after their performance at the famous Fillmore venue. In 1968 they were invited back to San Francisco by promoter Bill Graham to perform a three-day gig, but this time to play the slightly bigger West Coast venue Fillmore Winterland. This poster portrays the band as golden gods and shows that expectations were high. Cream exceeded

"ERIC ASKED ME TO DESIGN THE COVER FOR *DISRAELI GEARS*. I LOVED RECORD COVER ART AND WAS VERY HAPPY TO DO IT. I COMMISSIONED MY EX–STUDIO MATE, BOB WHITAKER, TO TAKE SOME PHOTOS, WHICH WERE USED IN A COLLAGE ON THE BACK COVER. I BELIEVE THE PHOTO USED ON THE COVER WAS A PUBLICITY SHOT THAT I GOT FROM ERIC. I WAS USING FLUORESCENT PAINTS AT THE TIME. IT WAS THE HEIGHT OF PSYCHEDELIA. SOME OF THE INGREDIENTS IN THE COVER ARE MADE UP FROM VICTORIAN DECORATIVE ENGRAVINGS. IT WAS DONE IN BLACK-AND-WHITE FIRST AND THEN PAINTED WITH FLUORESCENT COLORS. I TRIED TO CAPTURE THE WARM JOYFUL LIVELINESS OF CREAM'S SONGS. I LATER WENT ON TO DESIGN THE COVER FOR *WHEELS OF FIRE* FOR CREAM."—Martin Sharp, artist

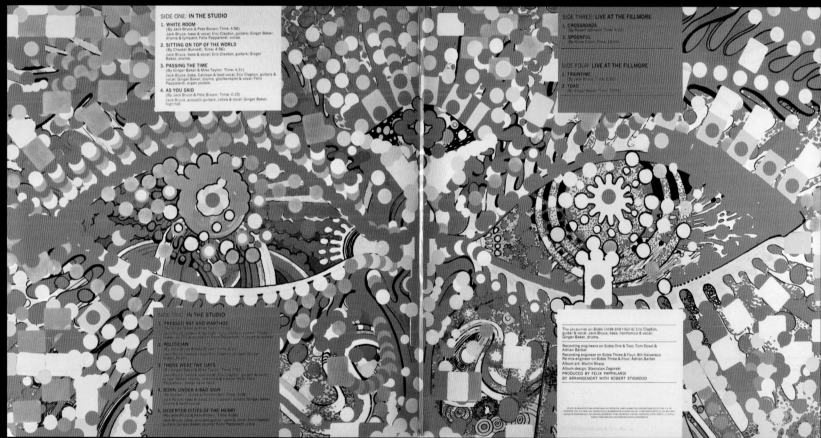

TOP LEFT For the follow-up to *Disraeli Gears*, *Wheels of Fire* (Polydor, 1968), famed Australian designer Martin Sharp again created the artwork as on their previous album; Jim Marshall was the photographer. The album was also released as two separate records, "Wheels of Fire (In the Studio)" and "Wheels of Fire (Live at the Fillmore)," which were released together.

ABOVE This is the gatefold of the *Wheels of Fire* (Polydor, 1968) album; as on *Disraeli Gears* (Reaction, 1967), Martin Sharp contrasts stark black-and-white imagery with an explosion of color. This combination is disorienting, almost evoking an acid trip.

Ernie Cefalu & the Golden Age of Album Artwork

Fresh out of art school in 1969, Ernie Cefalu moved from California to New York with great expectations of becoming an ad man. Working his way up the ladder on Madison Avenue, he quickly made his mark by designing the iconic *Jesus Christ Superstar* (1970) album art. Then, during an interview for a job at Craig Braun Inc., he found himself designing the most iconic and recognized logo of all time: the Rolling Stones tongue (later adapted by John Pasche). As you might expect it landed him the job, and he went on to help pioneer one of the most elaborate art forms in sleeve note history, which became known as Custom Packaging. The golden age of album artwork had arrived.

The whole music industry was starting to move to LA, so Craig Braun asked Ernie and his Vice President, Tony Grabois, to set up shop for him there. However, it didn't go as planned: "At this point I was living with Tony, and we had become pretty good friends, so one night we decided to drop some mescaline. I ended up sharing with him that I was going to leave Craig. So it was on that night, at the end of 1971, on a mescaline trip, that Tony and I decided to set up our own company, Pacific Eye & Ear."

During this period there was only a handful of indie design groups. The record label was king, and their art departments were churning out cover after cover each week. However, this impersonal approach left room for boutique agencies like Pacific Eye & Ear to really focus on the musicians and build a bridge between music and image.

"Before I got out to LA I knew I wanted to work on Alice Cooper's *School's Out* [1972]. I was really attracted to Alice and his show; he was so mysterious. So I had this comp with me that I had already designed for Cooper, and he just so happened to be in town making some last touches to his album. Tony and I called Alice's manager, Shep Gordon, and said, 'You have no idea who we are, but we designed the *Jesus Christ Superstar* album and the tongue logo for the Stones, and we would like to show you an idea we have for you. No commitment.' We showed them my school desk concept, and Alice and Shep loved it.

"Shep had already made loads of these panties that they were going to throw out into the audience, so when I showed him the school desk, he took the record and put a pair of panties over it and said, 'This is how we should do it.' So that started my relationship with Alice, and ended my relationship with Craig Braun."

Pacific Eye & Ear set themselves apart from other design companies with their elaborate designs—for example the previously mentioned Custom

Packaging, which from 1970 to 1984 evolved into a distinct genre, with Ernie as the godfather. "It came along out of necessity. It became a whole new way to go beyond just the front and the back or an open-up album. It gave fans the chance to interact. It got people involved, and everyone loved it."

Ernie sees it this way: "Musicians are delivering messages to their fans through their music, and they are making an emotional connection. Most companies didn't understand that; we did. We were the link between the musician and his audience. And with stills, not moving images, I needed to catch someone's eye, in an ocean of album covers, which best conveyed the message that this artist was trying to convey with his music. And that emotional connection was key."

CEFALU

TOP RIGHT Ernie working at his desk in Pacific Eye & Ear in Beverley Hills, 1980. The woman in the background is Ernie's wife, Bonnie, who was also Pacific Eye & Ear's bookkeeper. Says Ernie of his business persona, "I didn't look like an ad man; I had a big beard and long hair. I looked more like Jesus."

"WE HAD TO BE CONTROVERSIAL, BECAUSE WHEN YOU WENT INTO A RECORD STORE ALL YOU SAW WAS AN OCEAN OF RECORDS. COVER AFTER COVER AFTER COVER. THEY WERE ALL SQUARE AND ALL THE SAME SIZE. SO IN THOSE DAYS YOU HAD TO DO SOMETHING THAT JUMPED UP AND YELLED, 'LOOK AT ME!' I DID A ROUND COIN FOR GRAND FUNK RAILROAD, *E PLURIBUS FUNK* [1971]. I SPENT TWO WEEKS WITH THIS OLD CRAFTSMAN CREATING THE EMBOSSING PLATES THAT FEATURED THE BAND MEMBERS' PROFILES. IT WAS A PAINSTAKING PROCESS USING DENTIST TOOLS ETCHING INTO THE METAL, BUT THAT'S HOW YOU DID ARTWORK BACK IN THOSE DAYS." —Ernie Cefalu, Creative Director and designer

OPPOSITE, BOTTOM LEFT The iconic *Jesus Christ Superstar* (Decca/MCA, 1970) logo was created by Ernie while he was working at the Norman Levitt Agency—the pitch secured them the Decca account. The album came as a gatefold and on the inside featured a drawing of the cast.

OPPOSITE, BOTTOM RIGHT This image was created for the backstage pass of Alice Cooper's 1978 tour "From the Inside," by Pacific Eye & Ear staff illustrator Bill Garland, with lettering designed by Ernie. Garland went on to win multiple awards, and has painted poster images for films from *Mad Max* to comedies such as *Monty Python's the Meaning of Life* and *Brazil*.

TOP LEFT *E Pluribus Funk* (Capitol, 1971) stood out from the crowd quite literally as it was a round cover, designed by Ernie and covered in a metalic-silver film to resemble an actual coin. On the back was a die-cast picture of Shea Stadium to commemorate Grand Funk Railroad's feat of breaking the Beatles' record by selling out in just seventy-two hours.

BOTTOM LEFT The logo used on Alice Cooper's album *Billion Dollar Babies* (Warner Bros., 1973) was a giant green wallet. On the original design, the naked baby girl featured on the back cover was deemed too shocking by the sensitive distributors, so Ernie responded by strategically placing a fig leaf cut out from a $100 bill to protect her modesty. Job done!

BOTTOM RIGHT The *Dolls Alive* image that helped inspire the Rolling Stones' iconic tongue logo. Ernie on that iconic image: "So then I saw the album come out, and it didn't have my logo on it. Marshall took it to the Stones; Mick knew Pasche, and he did a variation of my logo. Pasche took my logo and breathed life into it."

"OUT OF THE 214 COVERS I'VE DONE, I PROBABLY ONLY DID A HANDFUL FOR RECORD COMPANIES; EVERYTHING ELSE WAS FOR THE BANDS. THE LABELS HATED US—WE WERE THE REDHEADED STEPCHILD. WE WERE TAKING AWAY WORK FROM THEM, AS THEY HAD THEIR OWN ART DEPARTMENT. THE BAND UNDERSTOOD THE VALUE, DEDICATION, HONESTY, AND LOYALTY WE GAVE TO THEM."

—Ernie Cefalu, Creative Director and designer

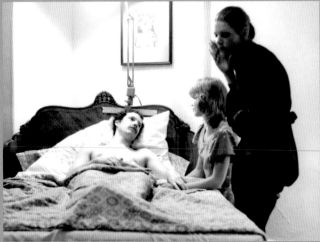

Building a reputation for himself, it was only a matter of time before designers started to flock to Pacific Eye & Ear: "It started out with me; I was the art department, and my friend, Tony, was the sales department. We lived in a little one-bedroom house up in the Hollywood Hills by Capitol Records. Then I hired a production artist named Dean Marriot, and artists started coming to me. Joe Garnet, Bill Strazen, Bill Garland, Carl Ramsey, and the now legendary illustrator Drew Struzan, who designed all the *Star Wars* illustrations— the first thing he designed for me was Jefferson Airplane."

One of the bands that Pacific Eye & Ear worked closely with were Captain Beyond. "We ended up designing three albums for them, but the *Sufficiently Breathless* [1973] one was amazing, because there was all these characters we created, and the back cover has some more, and on the inside they are all on a flying carpet. We did some crazy-arse stuff with those guys."

From there the floodgates opened and a long list of designs ensued. One in particular was Black Sabbath's *Sabbath Bloody Sabbath* (1973).

"I did some really beautiful lettering for Sabbath," says Ernie, "but at the last minute they cut it out of the cover and put on a black border and some ugly lettering. However, they left some of the lines where the lettering went down behind the skull, on the top of the cover, so if you knew what that was then you would know why those lines were coming left and right into the skull.

"I was thinking about the band and the music, and I had these two pieces of photographic lithos from the turn of the century that this illustrator did of this good man and an evil man both at the split second of their death. I had been given them by my aunt when I got my confirmation in the fifth grade. And I was looking at those images and I thought, 'Sabbath Bloody Sabbath, this is what it's all about.' And listening to the songs, it's about the kinda person you are, what kinda life you live, what your worth is, what your soul looks like. To me, that became exactly that. The front cover is an evil man dying, his family were turning into these demonic-looking creatures. His bed is becoming a trap to engulf him. His pillow is turning into a snake that is choking him to death. It's all done in red, yellows—very much panic colors. Immediate colors.

"Turn over to the back and there you have the good guy, and he is lying there at peace, his lions are sleeping at the end of his bed, the overall arching spirit is above him. His family are turning into angelic beings. When I showed it to the guys, they flipped out; they loved it. Drew did an incredible illustration both front and back, those original pieces are 30 by 40 [inches], huge. He rendered them in acrylic and colored pencil. The model on the left of the cover is Ingrid Haenke, and the other one, on the right of the back cover, is my wife Bonnie. The man in the bed is Drew.

"I couldn't say what one of my favorite covers are, as it would be like saying who is your favorite kid," Ernie says, laughing. "Visually, Cooper is great, as there are so many brand elements to work with. They looked for me to come to them with some crazy stuff—crazier the better—which I did, as we've done eleven covers together. However, if I had to pick one, I would say *Billion Dollar Babies* [1973]. I love the whole idea of it being a big wallet, very decadent with the diamonds around it and the gold coins we created. Carl Ramsey did the illustrations of the wallet. Joe Petagno did the bill on the album."

Ernie made the following observation, "It was a piece of pop art. It was interactive, with punch-out pictures you could put in your wallet, then when you punched that out there was a picture of the group, all in white with all that money and then holding that little baby girl. The label [people] were freaking out about that, as the little girl's vagina was showing. So what we did was take a $100 bill, and where the face was of the president we cut it out into the shape of a fig leaf and put it over her vagina."

What's incredible about Ernie is that he has always, despite his immense success, kept his feet firmly on the ground. "I still use the same T square I got in 1958, when I convinced my parents they should pay for me to go to art classes. When I signed up I got a T square, but after a couple of lessons I decided, 'Screw this,' and went to play baseball instead. I kept the T square all these years to remind myself that I should never get too full of myself and to remind me that my parents always wanted me to be what I wanted to be. So I needed to succeed."

TOP LEFT This was a series of different photographs used by illustrator Drew Struzan as the basis for creating what was to become the back cover of *Sabbath Bloody Sabbath* (Vertigo, 1973). The man kneeling by the bed is Drew and the lady standing behind him is Ingrid Haenke, a friend of Ernie's wife.

OPPOSITE, TOP RIGHT In this, the second of these, never previously published photographs, Ernie's wife, Bonnie, kneels beside the bed, with illustrator Drew Struzan appearing again, this time in the bed with Ingrid standing in the foreground.

TOP LEFT An early version of the cover for *Sabbath Bloody Sabbath*, featuring Ernie's original hand-lettered typography for the band's name at the top. The type was replaced in the final version with the album title; however, some of the black lines that were part of the original are still visible around the skull.

BOTTOM LEFT A close-up of the original artwork for the front cover of the album, showing the detail in Drew Struzan's work.

TOP RIGHT The original 30"x40" colored pencil and acrylic on board illustration, drawn by Drew Struzan, for the front cover of *Sabbath Bloody Sabbath*. "The front cover is an evil man dying; his family are turning into these demonic-looking creatures . . . It's all done in red, yellows—very much panic colors. Immediate colors."—Ernie Cefalu

BOTTOM RIGHT The original 30"x40" back cover illustration, also drawn by Drew Struzan (easily recognizable as the model for the dying man in the bed). Here the good man dies peacefully in the company of sky-blue angels.

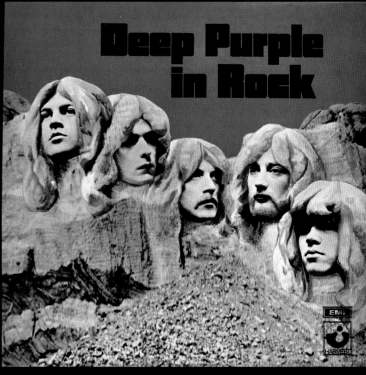

ABOVE LEFT This Halloween poster for a Deep Purple gig at the Grande Cleveland in Ohio (featuring an image of Lon Chaney's *Phantom of the Opera*) was created by the artist and fan of Frank Frazetta, Carl Lundgren. Lundgren's career started in 1967 in Detroit, Michigan, where he created poster art for bands such as the Who and Pink Floyd. His artwork has since become highly collectible.

TOP RIGHT *Deep Purple* (*Deep Purple III*, Harvest, 1969) was the last Deep Purple album with the original lineup. Their US label issued the album in a gatefold sleeve, wrapped with a detail from Hieronymus Bosch's painting *The Garden of Earthly Delights* (mistakenly reproduced in black and white due to a printing error), which was poorly promoted by stockists in the US due to it being wrongly perceived as antireligious.

BOTTOM RIGHT The cover art of *Deep Purple in Rock* (Harvest, 1970) featured an interpretation of the Mount Rushmore monument with the presidents' heads replaced by those of the five band members. The artwork is by Nesbit, Phipps, and Froome, who went on to design the iconic *Burn* album for the band, and cover design is by Edwards Colletta Productions, Purple's management company.

"LOOKING BACK AT OUR COVERS, I HAPPEN TO LIKE THEM BECAUSE THEY'VE BEEN AROUND FOR SO LONG. AND REGARDLESS OF WHAT I THINK OF GAIL—I MEAN, SHE DID SHOOT FELIX—I'M ABLE TO SEPARATE ONE FROM THE OTHER. THEY HAD A THEME RUNNING THROUGH THEM, ALMOST CONCEPTUAL, WHICH WAS PRETTY UNIQUE. YEAH, THEY WERE UNIQUE COVERS FOR A ROCK BAND." —Leslie West, Mountain vocalist-guitarist

TOP LEFT The cover for Deep Purple's *Burn* (EMI, 1974) was photographed by Fin Costello, who worked closely with the band at the time. He came up with the idea of using a candle for each member of the band. "I just thought the idea fitted in with the album title," he said. "The band loved it."

BOTTOM LEFT Talking about their debut album cover art for *Climbing!* (Windfall, 1970): "Gail, Felix Pappalardi's wife, designed it. The woman she put in front of the mountain was her—she put herself in the picture! I didn't have anything to do with the covers; she designed them, Felix produced the albums, and I did the music. It was a little bit like Yoko Ono and the Beatles. Felix was always pushing her—to write, make the covers."—Leslie West

BOTTOM RIGHT *Nantucket Sleighride* (Sony, 1971) is the second album from the band. Released in a gatefold with a lyrics booklet and two glossy photos of the band, this was the second cover designed by Felix Pappalardi's wife, Gail Collins.

COVERS AND LP JACKETS FROM ACROSS THE GLOBE, FOCUSSING ON THE ORIGINAL OZZY ERA 1970–78, BUT I DIDN'T KNOW WHAT TO DO WITH IT, SO I SHOWED IT TO STEVE HAMMONDS FROM THEIR LABEL, WHO SAID IT WOULD LOOK GREAT IN THE CRUCIFIX BOX. WHAT CRUCIFIX BOX? I THOUGHT THE IDEA OF THIS CROSS-SHAPED BOX WAS A LITTLE OVER THE TOP AT FIRST, BUT IT SOLD OUT INSTANTLY, AND IT'S A NICE ITEM TO HAVE IN MY PORTFOLIO."

—Hugh Gilmour, designer

ABOVE LEFT The *Black Sabbath* (Vertigo, 1970) cover was designed by Marcus Keef. It features a woman standing in front of Mapledurham Mill in Oxfordshire, England, and if you look very closely you can see that the woman in the picture is holding a black cat. The inner gatefold sleeve featured an inverted cross with a poem written inside.

ABOVE RIGHT The "Cross Box" was released in 2010 by the Polydor Group and designed by Hugh Gilmour: "I'm not even sure what its proper title is, other than it's referred to as the 'Black Sabbath Cross Box.'" Once seen, never forgotten!

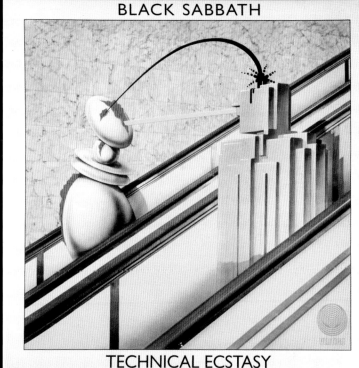

ABOVE LEFT One of a series of Rock-It comics published between mid-1993 and mid-1994. Among their titles were a Metallica biography comic, *Lita Ford: Heavy Metal Queen*, a Pantera comic full of demonic insanity, and companion volumes devoted to Black Sabbath and Ozzy Osbourne. This 1994 issue features the story of Black Sabbath between 1970–79, with interviews from Tony Iommi

TOP RIGHT The artwork on *Never Say Die!* (Vertigo, 1976) is also by Hipgnosis. Formed in 1968 by Thorgerson with Aubrey "Po" Powell (Peter Christopherson joined the team later), Hipgnosis have been hugely influential in British metal illustration, designing covers for (most famously) Pink Floyd and also for Led Zeppelin, AC/DC, Deep Purple, Anthrax, the Scorpions, UFO, and many others.

BOTTOM RIGHT Storm Thorgerson of London's Hipgnosis design team: "*Technical Ecstasy* [Vertigo, 1976] was designed from the title, suggesting something human but not human, or technical but not technical. I imagined two technical beings who might experience ecstasy—instead of exchanging bodily fluids, they exchange lubricating oil or light beams. I thought the image both graphic

JAILBREAK · THIN LIZZY

RED ALERT.
JAIL BREAK!

JIM FITZPATRICK · 76

PHIL LYNOTT   SCOTT GORHAM   BRIAN DOWNEY   BRIAN ROBERTSON

marketed by phonogram

ALBUM 9102 008   CASSETTE 7138 075

ABOVE LEFT Fellow Irishman and friend of the band, Jim Fitzpatrick (creator of the iconic two-tone portrait of Che Guevara in 1968), designed many of Thin Lizzy's album covers and posters. "[We] were both very influenced by H. G. Wells's *War of the Worlds* and American Marvel comics; Philip wanted something that reflected these influences. Together we worked on the imaginary story of 'The Warrior' that Philip had in his mind, and I reworked the roughs to reflect this idea until it all held together."—Jim Fitzpatrick

TOP RIGHT "I was very influenced by Roger Dean at the time, and it shows in the lettering. What no one knows, up until right now, was that the black panther was a silent tribute by both of us to great African Americans like Martin Luther King, Malcolm X, Bobby Smith and John Carlos, Black Power and the Black Panther movement. Philip was meant to be the black panther on the cover. We would have had a real job of explaining that one to the record company!"—Jim Fitzpatrick,

BOTTOM RIGHT "I was very lucky to have a title; usually they didn't have one at this stage. Philip came up with the Chinese idea very early on; he wanted something with a dragon on and lots of burning. I always remember Philip and Scott examining it after I flew over to London with the artwork. Scott had his face right into it, scrutinizing every detail, and said 'Jeez, Jim, you've painted every f***** scale on that dragon.' The only disappointing thing was that I thought the front cover was inferior to the back."—Jim Fitzpatrick on *Chinatown* (Vertigo, 1980)

"WE WERE ALL AWARE THAT WE WERE VERY PRIVILEGED—WE KNEW IT WAS AN EXTRAORDINARY WAY OF SHOWING OFF YOUR ARTWORK. WE HAD VINYL, WHERE YOU HAD GATEFOLDS, WHICH WAS A PERFECT SPACE FOR DESIGNING SOME FANTASTIC CREATIONS—WHICH WE DID."
—Jim Fitzpatrick, artist

TOP LEFT When Led *Zeppelin III* (Atlantic, 1970) was released, the band had a policy of changing their cover artist with each release. "Jimmy came up with the idea that it could be based on a volvelle, so his idea and mine had a meeting point. In making a disc that rotates, you're getting people to participate in the artwork in real time. In a way, it's almost like graphic filmmaking." —Zacron, artist

ABOVE *Houses of the Holy* (Atlantic, 1973) was designed by Aubrey Powell at Hipgnosis. The models were siblings Samantha and Stefan Gates; Stefan later admitted that he found something disturbing about the image, although his sister never had that problem. Like Led Zeppelin's fourth album, neither the band's name nor the album title was printed on the sleeve.

Judas Priest

Sad Wings Of Destiny

"BY THE TIME PRIEST'S SECOND ALBUM *SAD WINGS OF DESTINY* WAS RELEASED, THE GRAPHICS AND THE MUSIC WERE IN PERFECT SYNCHRONICITY . . . [THIS COVER] HAS EVERYTHING THAT A GOOD ALBUM COVER NEEDS: IT HAS A PICTURE [BY PATRICK WOODROFFE] WHICH REFLECTS EMOTIONS FROM GOOD TO BAD. IT'S ANGELIC AND DEMONIC IN EVERY ASPECT . . . IT ALSO HAS THE DEVIL'S TUNING FORK IN IT, THE SYMBOL THAT HAS BEEN PRIEST'S TRADEMARK FOR MANY YEARS."—Pete Alander, designer

ABOVE *Sad Wings of Destiny* (Gull, 1976) is the second album from the band and the last to feature the gothic script logo. Ian Hill of Judas Priest: "The painting was done by a guy named Patrick Woodroffe. It was commissioned for that album. The head of Gull Records actually has the painting on the wall of his office. It is a classic album cover—one of the all-time classics."

"WHEN I FIRST DID [THE] *BRITISH STEEL* COVER, PEOPLE IN MARKETING DIDN'T LIKE IT AT ALL BECAUSE THERE WASN'T ANY CHAINS, MOTOR BIKES, NO HALF-NAKED WOMEN, NO WITCHCRAFT, NO NOTHING. BUT THE BAND WANTED IT SO BADLY THAT THEY SAID THEY WOULD BREAK CONTRACT IF THIS COVER DIDN'T SEE DAYLIGHT."—Roslaw Szaybo, CBS Creative Director

TOP LEFT "A lot of people tried to change this logo. There was a huge debate on the Internet on how this could be changed, but they went back to the original one I designed. I think when something is good you don't need to do it better."—Roslaw Szaybo

BOTTOM LEFT "It was a black mannequin which was lit by certain lights; the face was meant to be someone unusual. The laser lights came from inspiration from the Christmas lights on Oxford Street, and then I painted the shadows and colors on after. It hasn't aged. This was also the first time the band stopped using the gothic logo." —Roslaw Szaybo, on *Stained Class* (CBS, 1978)

BOTTOM RIGHT "Before we had computers you had to really invent everything, and when I had this idea, I had to get friendly with a guy who worked with metal, so I asked him to make a huge blade that was completely real. Then I had to get friendly with a printer who printed everything on the blade, as I didn't want to add it on after, I wanted everything to be on one shot. I think the beauty of it is that there isn't any retouching, no added color, everything is just how it was, but the problem is that it took so long to do. Today, it would be done in a couple of days."—Roslaw Szaybo, on *British Steel* (CBS, 1980)

There Must Have Been Something in the Water

It could have been a scene from Tolkien, reminiscent of Saruman's Isengard. You could hear the sound of the hammer on anvil; you could taste and smell the metal-working factories that helped to intensify the grimness and angry resentment felt by many in the working-class industrial West Midlands.

It was in 1968, in the heart of Birmingham, that a grotty blues clubs called the Pokey Hole witnessed a noise that had never been heard before. With doom-laden lyrics and heavy guitar riffs, it engulfed its audience like no other sound. That band was Earth, and within a year they had changed their name to Black Sabbath. Heavy metal was born, and its birthplace was tucked firmly in the bosom of Birmingham and the West Midlands.

"Birmingham is a working-class, industrial town," says Judas Priest front man Rob Halford. "That led to bands having aggressive attitudes to music. It suited our upbringing and the environment. And that's why metal bands from the area don't write lyrics about flowers. That would not work. Which is why we write about dark and gloomy subjects."

The area gave rise to some of the biggest names in metal, from the founding fathers, Black Sabbath, through the twin guitar attackers Judas Priest, to grindcore founders Napalm Death and Godflesh, plus a whole host of metal junkies.

Music has always been a part of the region's makeup—bands like the Moody Blues and ELO came from the area—but *this* group of artists created a subgenre that really reflected the harsh society around them. Many of the people in these bands had a personal experience of working in the manufacturing industry, which, for most young people growing up in the late '60s and '70s was the only employment option available to them. The significance of the deprivation brought on by this industry became an important factor on the development of their music.

> "LIVERPOOL, THEY LIKED SILLY HAIRCUTS AND HIGH NECK JACKETS. SHEFFIELD/YORKSHIRE MUSICIANS ALWAYS WANTED TO BE HARD AND LOOK LIKE THEY WERE IN GANGSTER MOVIES. BUT BIRMINGHAM PLAYERS JUST PLAYED WELL. THEY TENDED NOT TO ADOPT STYLES. THEY WOULD PLAY MUSIC WELL, REHEARSE WELL, PLAY HARD, HAVE GOOD INFLUENCES AND THEN SIT BACK AND EXPECT THE REST OF THE WORLD TO FIND ITS WAY TO THEIR FRONT DOOR." —Jim Simpson, Big Bear founder

"When I lost the tips of my fingers in an accident while working in a factory," explains Sabbath guitarist Tony Iommi, "I had to learn to play the guitar in a different way. So I downtuned, and the sound got a lot heavier. Which is where the Sabbath sound came from. But this fitted what we wanted and where we came from."

However, without venues the bands wouldn't have had an outlet for their music. But as luck would have it, in Birmingham and the West Midlands in general there was an abundance of underground clubs to support this emerging talent.

Sabbath's first manager, Jim Simpson, ran Henry's Blues House above a pub where Sabbath and Judas Priest played some of their earliest shows, as did local musicians like John Bonham and Robert Plant in pre-Zeppelin days. Then there was the Elbow Room in Ozzy Osbourne's home town of Aston, where Traffic formed.

LEFT "There wasn't any talk about wanting to be millionaires, we just wanted to play well and that is something particularly Birmingham. We viewed it as a job worth doing . . . maybe some of that work ethic came from the hard work we did at the factories." —Jim Simpson

```
MOTHERS....  HAPPENING LIST 18th JULY 69

         RING 021 373 5514 ALL QUERIES.

JULY
   SATURDAY 19th     THE WHO with JOHN PEEL
   SUNDAY   20th     DEEP PURPLE plus CARAVAN plus AMOEBA
   WEDNESDAY 23rd    MICK FARRENS DEVIANTS
   FRIDAY 25th       THE MISUNDERSTOOD
   SATURDAY 26th     THUNDERCLAP NEWMAN + KING CRIMSON
   SUNDAY 27th       THE amazing LIVERPOOL SCENE (Mothers Rag)
   WEDNESDAY 30th    THIRD EAR BAND

FRIDAY AUGUST 1st
                    STEVE MILLER DELIVERY
   SATURDAY 2nd     BONZO DOG BAND
   SUNDAY 3rd       COLOSSEUM
   WEDNESDAY  .      EDGAR BROUGHTON BAND
   FRIDAY 8th       YES
   SATURDAY 9th     SOFT MACHINE
   SUNDAY 10th      KEITH RELF RENAISSANCE
   WEDNESDAY 13th   ALEXIS KORNER
   FRIDAY 15th      JOHN DUMMER BLUES BAND
   SATURDAY 16th    MARSHA HUNT with WHITE TRASH
   SUNDAY 17th      Welcome back to FAIRPORT CONVENTION
   WEDNESDAY 20th   THE DEVIANTS
   FRIDAY 22nd      STEAMHAMMER
   SATURDAY 23rd    THUNDERCLAP NEWMAN + KING CRIMSON
   SUNDAY 24th      THE FAMILY
   WEDNESDAY 27th   EDGAR BROUGHTON BAND


   SATURDAY 30th    LIVERPOOL SCENE

   SAT. SEPT. 6th   INDO JAZZ FUSIONS

   SUNDAY SEPT 7th  FAT MATTRESS

   COMING FROM U.S.A. SATURDAY SEPT 20th. IRON BUTTERFLY
```

One of the most significant clubs—with a lifespan that was sweet but short, as it was open only from 1968 to 1971—was Mothers, in Erdington. It was the first club outside of London that gained such popular status, and fans would queue for hours to get in. Once inside the intimate club, you got to rub shoulders with other like-minded fans, as well as the bands themselves. More than 400 acts performed during the club's short reign, including Black Sabbath, Deep Purple, Jethro Tull, Led Zeppelin, and the Who. John Peel said of its popularity:

"People are amazed to hear that for a few years the best club in Britain was in Erdington."

With a loyal army of devotees, the area had a voice. The new music scene gave them a way to express themselves and break free from their surroundings, which created a whole new genre, one whose roots spread out from the factories that inspired it.

Heavy metal was on the map globally, and its genesis was middle England.

ABOVE LEFT "Half the time we used to do them ourselves but there was also this really interesting place called Arts Lab. They were really creative in their silk screen printing and they used to do your posters in 5 minutes and charge you £2 for it. As long as they had money for their drugs and a glass of wine they didn't care. They did some stunning work."—Jim Simpson

TOP RIGHT A photo of the outside of the famous Mothers club (formerly the Carlton Ballroom). The Mothers club was only open between 1968 and 1971, yet it gained 36,000 members in its short life, who each paid two shillings and six pence (twelve-and-a-half pence in modern currency) for annual membership!

BOTTOM RIGHT An early flyer, listing the many bands performing in July and August 1969 at Mothers. Jim Simpson on the popularity of the local clubs: "Mine [Henry's Blues House] was too small so Mothers was set up because the scene was exploding and we needed more space."

"WE JUST DID NOT KNOW IT WOULD BE A PROBLEM IN AMERICA; IT WAS JUST SEX AND ROCK 'N' ROLL. IT IS ODD THAT IN AMERICA SOME OF THESE COVERS WERE A PROBLEM, BECAUSE IN THE 80s WHEN WE WOULD TOUR HERE, WE ALWAYS HAD BOOBS FLASHED TO US AT THE FRONT OF THE STAGE. NOWHERE ELSE IN THE WORLD, JUST HERE." —Klaus Meine, Scorpions vocalist, on the controversy *Lovedrive* caused in the United States

TOP LEFT The Scorpions liked to create controversy when it came to their album covers. Storm Thorgerson designed the cover for *Lovedrive* (Harvest, 1979) but the naked breast featured was considered too risqué for certain US outlets and was subsequently banned. The year of its release it picked up the accolade for best album sleeve from *Playboy*.

THE BLVE ÖYSTER CVLT
TYRANNY AND MVTATION

OPPOSITE, BOTTOM This scorpion image was created as a "safer" version of the *Lovedrive* cover art and featured on later pressings of the album. The same image (seen here on a T-shirt) was also used for their 1980 British Animal Magnetism Tour.

OPPOSITE, TOP RIGHT The original version of *In Trance* (RCA, 1975), photographed by Michael von Gimbut. Klaus Meine of the Scorpions says, "The idea for the *In Trance* cover came from our label, RCA. And it was Uli Jon Roth, our guitarist, who suggested the guitar be added. On the first printing, one of the girl's breasts was exposed. So for the next run, this was blacked out. It did get some negative comments, but not as many as we got for *Virgin Killer.*"

ABOVE This second release from the group, *Tyranny and Mutation* (Columbia, 1973), is the only album to feature the band's name as The Blue Öyster Cult. The cover was designed by Bill Gawlik, who also created their first album, with photography by Roni Hoffman, who has shot artists such as Iggy Pop and Alice Cooper. The cover features at the center the band's logo, also designed by Gawlik, a stylized version of the astronomical symbol for the planet Saturn.

"YOU DIDN'T HAVE MTV, YOU DIDN'T HAVE COMPUTERS OR ANY OTHER WAY OF GETTING INTO YOUR FANTASY WORLD THAN TO PUT THAT LARGE RECORD ALBUM ON . . . YOU'RE IN YOUR BEDROOM OR YOUR STUDY, AND YOU ARE LOOKING AT THIS ALBUM COVER WHILE IT'S PLAYING, AND THIS WHOLE EFFECT HAPPENS. IT TAKES YOU IN, AND THE COVER BECOMES PART OF YOUR MEMORY OF THE MUSIC. THAT DOESN'T HAPPEN ANYMORE."—Ken Kelly, artist

ABOVE LEFT "It was the second cover I did for KISS, and it came about a year after the *Destroyer* album. I came up with an idea of KISS in an alleyway with a single light above their heads standing in front of a brick wall to a stage entrance door; they were just hanging out there, and there were all girls at their feet/knees, kinda groupie teenagers. But when I showed them the roughs, they said they were much bigger than that, especially Gene, and that they should be on a stage with pillars on it, surrounded by an army of women. So that's how the concept changed from a back alley to a stage."—Ken Kelly, artist (and Frank Frazetta protege) on the gatefold of *Love Gun* (Casablanca, 1977).

TOP RIGHT The inside cover of *Love Gun*—which contained a cardboard "Love Gun" (assembly required)—also painted by Ken Kelly. Kelly says, "When I first saw KISS, I would meet them in an office in New York, and it wasn't a fancy office; it was a little dark place on a side street, with Howard Marks and all the guys coming up with the *Destroyer* album, so I had never seen them in costume. I didn't see them in costume until *Love Gun*, until they were rehearsing, but that was a year later, so my first conception of KISS was just another crazy screaming group."

BOTTOM RIGHT Gene Simmons has admitted that *Meet the Beatles* was a big influence to him, which is evident on this debut album. The cover of *Kiss* (Casablanca, 1974) shows the group positioned against a black background wearing suits, something they have never done since, in a pose visually reminiscent of the Beatles' *With the Beatles* (Parlophone, 1963) album. This was in the early days of their individual images; note Simmons' demon look, much changed today.

TOP LEFT *Highway to Hell* (Atlantic, UK release, 1979) was the first time we saw an actual picture of AC/DC on their album cover. The art direction was by Bob Defrin, who was Head of Art for Atlantic at the time. The photography was by Jim Houghton, who had previously worked with Ted Nugent, Cheap Trick, and the Boys.

TOP RIGHT In Australia, *Highway to Hell* was released (Albert Productions, also 1979) with a slightly different album cover. The photograph of the band was the same as the international release taken by Jim Houghton, while Bob Defrin designed both, but quite differently. With the exception of *Powerage* (Atlantic, 1978), the Australian covers for all Bon Scott-era AC/DC albums were different to those used internationally.

BOTTOM LEFT Guitarist Michael Schenker said of the Hipgnosis designed *Lights Out* (Chrysalis, 1977) cover: "I had no clue what it was about. I was asked to meet at the Battersea Power Station, where Phil Mogg and I took some pictures. I never really analyzed the outcome. I was more focused on the music. Obviously Phil had his ideas. I guess part of his focus in UFO other than lyrics was album covers. I think he used it to express his fantasies."

BOTTOM RIGHT "In March of 1976, I once again joined the band in the recording studio, where they played basic cuts for me ("Back in the Saddle," "Sick as a Dog," and "Rats in the Cellar"). The cuts were more Heavy Metal than their other music, and Joe's guitar was on fire! There was no question we wouldn't use diamonds for the little knobs on the front cover; it's something we thought of straight away."—Ernie Cefalu, Pacific Eye & Ear designer, on *Rocks* (Columbia, 1976)

37

CHAPTER 2

New Wave Of British Heavy Metal

"EQUAL PARTS DISHEVELED AND DEMONIC, IRON MAIDEN'S MAD-EYED MASCOT EDDIE
GLARES OUT FROM THE COVER OF THE BAND'S SELF-TITLED DEBUT ALBUM [EMI, 1980].
IN MANY WAYS EDDIE IS THE MOST-RECOGNIZED 'MEMBER' OF MAIDEN, AND THIS IS
CERTAINLY ONE OF THE GREAT NEW WAVE OF BRITISH HEAVY METAL IMAGES."
—Geoff Barton

Dig the New Wave

GEOFF BARTON

"THE STRAIGHTFORWARD IDEA THAT IT WAS POSSIBLE FOR SOMEONE—*ANYONE*—TO PICK UP A GUITAR, SIT BEHIND SOME DRUMS, GRAB A MIC, RECORD SOME GOD-AWFUL RACKET, AND RELEASE IT WITHOUT RECORD-COMPANY MEGABUCKS . . . STRUCK A SIMPLE BUT STRIDENT CHORD WITH THOUSANDS OF DISAFFECTED YOUNG BRITISH ROCKERS."—Geoff Barton

To many people, the defining image of the New Wave of British Heavy Metal (NWOBHM) is . . . no image. Nothing at all. A blank canvas. Or, to be more accurate, a blank piece of cardboard. Flashback to October 1980. Diamond Head, soon to become one of the NWOBHM's leading bands, have just released their debut album on their own label, Happy Face. Because they had little money, and because the NWOBHM was based—at least initially—on a do-it-yourself ethic, the record came encased in a plain white sleeve with no title. The reason? Diamond Head's manager, Reg Fellows, owned a cardboard factory and could produce rudimentary covers at a very low cost.

Remember the Beatles' so-called *White Album*? Well, *Lightning to the Nations* (as Diamond Head's debut would become known) is the NWOBHM's bargain basement equivalent. The only concession to "artwork" was the scrawled signature of one band member on each of the thousand copies produced.

It seems remarkable that such a brash, vibrant visual medium as NWOBHM should be remembered for the non-image of—as the old joke goes—a polar bear in a snowstorm. But, of course, that didn't last. Once Diamond Head had secured a major record deal, with MCA, they employed popular sci-fi/fantasy artist Rodney Matthews for the sleeve of their second album, *Borrowed Time*, released in March 1982.

In less than eighteen months the NWOBHM had grown into a musical—and artistic—force to be reckoned with.

So what exactly is the NWOBHM? (If you want to say it out loud, pronounce it *ner-wobbum*.) Where did the genre begin and why is it so fondly—no, better make that *loudly*—remembered? Let's travel back to late 1976 or thereabouts. Punk rock is in its

gob-spattered ascendancy. Babylon is burning and a new breed of spiky-haired yob is causing the conflagration. There is, in short, "Anarchy in the UK". The Sex Pistols, the Clash, the Damned, et al. are sweeping the old guard away—and they're using broomsticks tipped with barbed wire.

Behemoth supergroups such as Emerson, Lake & Palmer are being consigned to the dumpster. The carcasses of Led Zeppelin and Yes are being pecked at by scavenging crows at the local dump. Waste containers marked "progressive rock albums, please deposit here" are appearing on street corners alongside glass-and-newspaper-recycling bins.

No doubt about it, punk rock spat in the face of the establishment and upset the timid old gentleman living next door.

Strange as it may seem, punk was also the catalyst for the NWOBHM. It offered the straightforward idea that it was possible for someone—*anyone*—to pick up a guitar, sit behind some drums, grab a mic, record some god-awful racket, and release it without record-company megabucks backing. This mad concept struck a simple but strident chord with thousands of disaffected young British rockers.

Traditionally, rock music had been all about learning your craft, paying your dues, spending a year in a studio perfecting your

material, and eventually releasing a first album, then a second, then a third, by which time your hardcore following had grown to, oh, at least a couple of dozen people . . .

By the time the '70s turned into the '80s, punk rock had already imploded—but its influence remained all-pervasive. Like the Morlocks, the pale-skinned underground dwellers in H. G. Wells's *The Time Machine* (1895), hard 'n' heavy bands made up of gauche young longhairs began to emerge, blinking, from protective bunkers and shadowy alleyways, safe in the knowledge that there were only a handful of people remaining who were likely to hack phlegm at them. From London's East End—Leytonstone, or thereabouts—came Iron Maiden. From Sheffield pounced Def Leppard. From Stourbridge in the English midlands arrived the aforementioned Diamond Head. And from deepest Cheshire stumbled Silverwing . . .

Armed with independent outlooks, total self-belief, and unbridled enthusiasm, this fresh new breed of UK rock band began to break through using the same route to stardom as the punks: *to hell with the big labels who don't understand us; let's make our own records and sell them off our own backs. And if that doesn't work, we'll use the backs of lorries instead.*

Although at the time it was uncool for fans and music critics alike to be into both punk and metal, subconsciously there was an influence. The link was perhaps more in the shared outlook, youthful exuberance and general don't-give-a-damn attitude than in the music itself.

It's true to say that the NWOBHM changed the face of rock music. Looking back, it was a unique era, a fascinating period of musical evolution and the starting point for many of today's stars. Most notably, Metallica. The band's drummer, Lars Ulrich, is famously obsessed with the NWOBHM. Ulrich himself has admitted that Metallica's music is grounded in the genre. No NWOBHM, no Metallica. For a band once known as "Alcoholica," that's a sobering thought, isn't it?

So who helped make the NWOBHM happen? Give a nod to Neal Kay, DJ at the Bandwagon Heavy Metal Soundhouse—a hard-rock discotheque jam-packed with speakers capable of huge power and sound, and situated (believe it or not) in a hall dolled up like a B-movie Wild West whiskey saloon, attached to the side of the Prince of Wales pub at the Kingsbury Circle, London NW9.

When I was a writer for the *Sounds* music weekly, Kay used to phone me up on a regular basis to try and get publicity for the Bandwagon. With his hippy-hangover attitude, gift of the gab, and talent for self-promotion, Kay was extremely difficult—make that *impossible*—to ignore. But even though at that time big American acts such as Aerosmith and Ted Nugent were consistently selling out major venues such as London's Hammersmith Odeon, I couldn't really get my head around the concept of such a quintessentially *British* rock club as the Bandwagon. To be honest, as I slunk into my heavy metal cubicle in the *Sounds* office, the sounds of the latest Lurkers 45 and Vibrators demo resounding in my ears, I was stunned to discover that a place such as the Bandwagon even existed.

"IT'S TRUE TO SAY THAT THE NWOBHM CHANGED THE FACE OF ROCK MUSIC. LOOKING BACK, IT WAS A UNIQUE ERA, A FASCINATING PERIOD OF MUSICAL EVOLUTION, AND THE STARTING POINT FOR MANY OF TODAY'S STARS. MOST NOTABLY, METALLICA."—Geoff Barton

Eventually Kay enticed me up to visit to his home-away-from-home, and I summed up the Bandwagon phenomenon—because phenomenon it most certainly was—in an article headlined "Wednesday Night Fever" in the August 19, 1978 edition of *Sounds*:

"I expected some sort of time-warp populated by scruffy longhairs, a place where head-shaking, imaginary-guitar-playing, peace-sign-flashing and above all blood and thunder reigned supreme," I wrote. "And that was all true apart from the fact that the Bandwagon *ain't no time-warp*."

Kay and his scabby-maned cohorts were very much alive, kicking and fighting back, and doing their level best to mount a rearguard action against the onslaught of punk rock. So I had no choice. I decided to dust off my bright-red-satin Uriah Heep Wonderworld Tour jacket, bring my copy of Deep Purple's *Machine Head* (1971) down from the attic, and join them in their battle.

Matters proceeded apace. Nine months or so later, Kay had outgrown the Bandwagon. Spurred on by the ever-increasing popularity of heavy metal, he decided to go out on a limb and group together three popular 'Wagon live acts under one roof at a major London venue, with himself DJing the whole event.

The date was May 9, 1979, and the place was the Music Machine, a venue that would later metamorphose into the Camden Palace and then become Koko. The three bands on the bill were Angel Witch, Iron Maiden, and Samson. And it was then, according to popular

belief, that the NWOBHM was born. Hell, it had to start somewhere. So that's a taste of the story behind the birth of the NWOBHM. Despite my reservations at the time (and my ongoing obsession with megabuck American bands such as KISS), *Sounds* sensed that it was on to a good thing. The new British rock scene began erupting, and I found myself being dispatched to cover a dizzying array of exciting (and occasionally, if truth be told, not so exciting) new acts.

Meanwhile, the term "NWOBHM" was spawning a whole host of acronyms. Shortly after the Music Machine show, NENWOBHM (North East New Wave of British Heavy Metal) was born. This crazy term had its origins in Wallsend, just down the road from Newcastle-upon-Tyne in northern England, with bands such as Fist, Raven, White Spirit, and the Tygers of Pan Tang making astonishing inroads, despite being on the independent Neat label.

You'll find many of Neat's album covers featured here. Plus sleeves from other small NWOBHM labels such as Heavy Metal Records and Ebony. Apart from a handful of high-profile artists—the aforementioned Rodney Matthews, Iron Maiden's Derek Riggs, and Hipgnosis—the great thing about the art of the NWOBHM is that it's often as basic as the music. There's a naïve intensity to the images that matches the brutal soundtrack to perfection … And that's because a lot of NWOBHM art was done by actual band members, or close associates of the band. They may not have been trained artists, but they knew the music inside out!

"*ACE OF SPADES*—HOW COULD ANYBODY FORGET THAT? EVEN IF PEOPLE DIDN'T LIKE THE SONG . . . IT'S JUST A GOOD TITLE, ISN'T IT? SO ONCE WE'D ALL AGREED ON THE TITLE, WE'RE THINKING, HMM, WELL, HOW CAN WE PORTRAY IT? I THINK I SUGGESTED, WHY DON'T WE HAVE THE ALBUM SLEEVE IN SEPIA, BROWN-AND-WHITE; WE CAN BE GUNFIGHTERS, AND THERE'LL BE A CARD TABLE WITH A DEAD MAN'S HAND ON IT. WE THOUGHT ABOUT THAT . . . *NAH*. THEN WE THOUGHT, HOW ABOUT JUST DRESSING UP AS COWBOYS? I REMEMBER EDDIE [CLARKE, GUITARIST] SAYING: 'I WANT TO BE CLINT EASTWOOD, I WANT TO WEAR A PONCHO!'"—Phil "Philthy Animal" Taylor, Motörhead drummer

LEFT Motörhead wanted to fly to a desert in Arizona to pose for the cover of *Ace of Spades* (Bronze, 1980). But their manager, Doug Smith, knew someone in Barnet, north London, who lived near a sandstone quarry—so that's where the band ended up instead. The bright blue sky was airbrushed in because it was so grey and cloudy when the photo was taken.

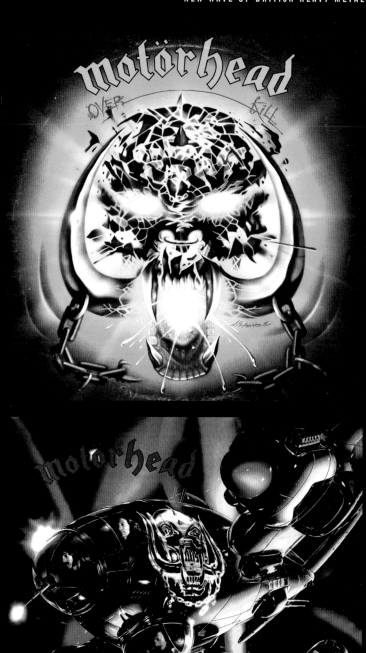

ABOVE LEFT Motörhead's distinctive fang-faced Snaggletooth logo, with its oversized boar's tusks, chains, and spikes, was created by artist Joe Petagno, who worked with Hipgnosis before meeting Lemmy, the band's bassist-vocalist, in 1975. This is the cover to Motörhead's *Stone Deaf Forever!* box set (Castle Music/Sanctuary, 2003).

TOP RIGHT Joe Petagno came up with the Snaggletooth concept after studying drawings of skulls of wild boars, gorillas, and dogs—in a suburban English library, of all places! "When the band saw it, they freaked," he says. "Believe it or not, you couldn't get a decent hotel room wearing a Snag T-shirt in those days; it signaled trouble!" This is the cover to *Overkill* (Bronze, 1979).

BOTTOM RIGHT For *Bomber* (Bronze/Mercury, 1979), the Snaggletooth image is emblazoned on the side of a highly stylized World War II aircraft, based on a German Heinkel 111. The cover is by English commercial artist Adrian Chesterman, who was also responsible for creating cover art for, among others, Chris Rea's *The Road to Hell* (Magnet, 1989). Not very metal, that one . . .

"I ORIGINALLY BASED THE WHOLE DESIGN CONCEPT AROUND THE GOAT OF MENDES THEME. GRA [SCORESBY, DRUMS] DESIGNED THE ORIGINAL, SOMEWHAT MORE ELABORATE ARTWORK FOR USE AS PROMOTIONAL MATERIAL IN THE EARLY DAYS. WHEN WE DECIDED TO SELF-FINANCE THE 'GIVE 'EM HELL' SINGLE [BEFORE THE INVOLVEMENT WITH RONDELET], THE ARTWORK WAS SIMPLIFIED BY THE GIRLFRIEND OF [BASSIST] ANDRO COULTON'S BROTHER, AND THE FINAL IMAGE WAS USED FOR THE 'GIVE 'EM HELL' SINGLE AND ALBUM COVER. I GUESS IT HAS DEVELOPED INTO OUR TRADEMARK IMAGE. I SUPPOSE IT COULD BE CONSIDERED TO BE RATHER EMBARRASSING THESE DAYS WHEN SCRUTINIZED AND COMPARED WITH THE HARD-HITTING, INTENSE IMAGES THAT ARE ASSOCIATED WITH MANY OF OUR CONTEMPORARIES— BUT NEVERTHELESS IT REMAINS AN ICONIC IMAGE."—Montalo, Witchfynde guitarist

LEFT Witchfynde's debut album *Give 'Em Hell* was released on the Rondelet label in 1980; the cover is based on an original design by drummer Gra Scoresby. "People always associate this image with the band," says Montalo, the band's guitarist. "Even when given choices for our merchandise, people always say our fans want the good old goat."

TOP LEFT This image of a sword-wielding barbarian may be crudely rendered, but it's most certainly memorable. Saxon's self-titled debut album was released in 1979 by Carrere, a French label best known for its disco releases. But then singer Biff Byford's band—the so-called "big teasers from Barnsley"—rampaged into town . . .

BOTTOM LEFT Compared to their debut, the cover art for Saxon's fourth album, *Denim and Leather* (Carrere, 1981), is positively minimalist. Along with a denim-effect background, it features the band's now-iconic eagle, which "symbolizes freedom" according to singer Biff Byford. Later the eagle became a massive Saxon stage prop, with a multitude of blazing lights embedded in its wings.

BOTTOM MIDDLE The rudimentary cover of Paralex's "White Lightning" EP (Reddington's Rare, 1980) was designed by David Bower, brother of the band's guitarist Kev "Biffo" Bower. David went on to make a name for himself as the charismatic vocalist in Hell, whose members included brother Kev and Andy Sneap (ex-Sabbat guitarist and now a leading record producer).

TOP RIGHT Angel Witch's self-titled debut album was released by Bronze in 1980. It features a gloomy, doom-drenched painting attributed to John Martin, an English Romantic painter, engraver, and illustrator. The painting, entitled *The Fallen Angels Entering Pandemonium*, was first exhibited in 1841. The original is now on display in London's Tate Gallery.

BOTTOM RIGHT Quartz released their second studio album, *Stand Up and Fight*, on the MCA label in 1980. According to the band, "The idea was designed by a company called Cream who, after hearing the title, came up with a gladiatorial image. We instantly liked it, and over the years the fans seem to have enjoyed it too. We still feel it is a very powerful image."

EDDIE HAS BECOME AN ICON TO IRON MAIDEN'S FANS. WE ARE VERY AWARE OF IT, AND WE USE IT TO THE MAX WHERE WE CAN. IT IS NOT SOMETHING THAT WE PLANNED, THOUGH. YEAH, YOU CAN THINK UP IMAGERY ONCE YOU HAVE AN ALBUM, SINGLE, OR WHATEVER, BUT IT IS NOT SOMETHING THAT WE THOUGHT OF IN THE EARLY DAYS. WE DIDN'T SIT AROUND AND THINK: 'RIGHT, NOW WE NEED AN ICON.'"

—Steve Harris, Iron Maiden bassist

BOTTOM LEFT Iron Maiden's Somewhere on Tour concert tour took place from September 10, 1986 to May 21, 1987. For the tour poster Eddie was depicted as a futuristic being with a laser gun, looking very much like a "terminator," a continuation of the theme explored on the *Somewhere in Time* album cover (EMI, 1986).

BOTTOM MIDDLE "Run to the Hills" (EMI) was released as a single on February 12, 1982. The song is about the Europeans' arrival in the New World, told from the perspective of both the Native Americans and the Anglo-Saxon invaders. The cover art depicts Eddie wrestling a devil in Hell while wielding an axe. Or perhaps it's a tomahawk . . .

TOP RIGHT Iron Maiden's mascot, Eddie the Head, was originally a mask at the back of the stage. Blood capsules were fed through the mouth, often soaking the drummer with fake blood. Artist Derek Riggs based this drawing of Eddie, for Maiden's self-titled debut album (EMI, 1980), on an image of a decapitated head that he saw on a Vietnamese tank.

BOTTOM RIGHT Compared with his brittle, corpse-like appearance on Iron Maiden's debut album, Eddie looked much more muscular and menacing on the cover of follow-up *Killers* (EMI, 1981). He'd obviously been to the gym! The street scene is somewhat similar, but this time the primary lighting source (a street lamp) bathes Eddie in an unpleasant sulfurous yellow.

IRON MAIDEN

"EDDIE IS ENIGMATIC. HE'S THE ULTIMATE MONSTER ANTI-HERO WHO YOU LOVE; HE'D BE THE COOLEST GUY TO HAVE ON THE SCHOOL BUS WITH YOU, BUT YOU WOULDN'T REALLY GO TO DINNER WITH HIM. HE DOES BAD THINGS, BUT ONLY TO PEOPLE WHO DESERVE IT. BUT HE IS AN ENIGMA, AND YOU LOSE THE ENIGMA AT YOUR PERIL, REALLY. YOU LOSE THAT ENIGMATIC THING ABOUT HIM, YOU LOSE THE MYSTERY."—Bruce Dickinson, Iron Maiden vocalist

Edward the Aggressor

Of all the multifarious artwork and images to come out of the New Wave of British Heavy Metal (NWOBHM), the most recognizable and enduring is Iron Maiden's signature character, Eddie. From his humble, coarsely drawn beginnings, Eddie has developed into a worldwide merchandising phenomenon. He's not just a desiccated, disintegrating face on an album sleeve any more. He's a monster of Maiden's making . . .

You know Iron Maiden's pet monster, Eddie? That giant, looming, lurching, stumbling leviathan who fires laser beams from his brow and lightning bolts from his balls, lays waste to all and sundry, scarifies the planet, deforests—er, forests—frightens small children, and causes sundry Maiden members to scuttle for cover behind their monitors?

Well, you wouldn't recognize Eddie tonight.

It's October 1979 and I'm sweating not buckets but *barrels* at the back of London's steamy Kingsbury Bandwagon Heavy Metal Soundhouse; the birthplace of the NWOBHM. As Iron Maiden's live performance reaches its climax, fake blood starts pouring from the mouth of an amateurish-looking, skull-like motif incorporated into a wooden sign dangling precariously above Doug Sampson's drum kit.

This, then, is Eddie in his very earliest guise. More MDF than SMF (which stands for "sick muthafucker," if you don't happen to be a Twisted Sister fan). Who woulda thunk that this clunky chipboard character would ultimately develop into one of the most familiar 'n' fearsome metal mascots of all time?

All credit to artist Derek Riggs for fleshing out the original basic Eddie concept. (Not that there was a *lot* of flesh involved, mind you. Just the odd bit of skin hanging from a shard of mottled bone . . .)

The amazing thing is that Portsmouth, England-born Riggs never got very much feedback from the band about his work. For the first two albums—*Iron Maiden* (1980) (featuring Eddie looking like a disheveled old granny) and *Killers* (1981) (featuring a more muscular Eddie with murder on his mind)—there was no direction from Maiden at all; the pictures were just what Riggs had in mind.

"WHAT DEFINES MAIDEN'S COVERS? I DON'T KNOW, THE FIRST ONE I GUESS; THAT ONE SET THE PLACE FOR EDDIE."
—Derek Riggs, artist

It was only later that a focus was firmly developed for each release. A case in point is the sleeve of *Somewhere in Time* (1986), for which the band told Riggs they wanted a picture of a city like the one in the *Bladerunner* (1982) movie. But the rest was left up to the artist. Sometimes the brief was vague in the extreme. According to Riggs, for *Seventh Son of a Seventh Son* (1988) the band just said, "We want one of your surreal things" and left it at that! Thus Eddie evolved steadily, getting spookier and more spectral with each Maiden release.

Riggs' most celebrated Maiden album cover is *The Number of the Beast* (1982). Band manager Rod Smallwood contacted the artist and said he wanted a picture for a single called "Purgatory," a song about the devil and witchcraft.

Riggs remembered seeing the cover of a *Doctor Strange* comic that depicted an evil villain (possibly a Skrull, sworn enemy of the Fantastic Four) dangling a helpless Master of Mystic Arts on some strings, like a puppet. Riggs used this as the inspiration for his illustration.

The artist spent two days and nights painting it. When he took it into the office, and Smallwood saw the result, he smiled and said: "That will be great for the album." He put it away in a cupboard, locked the door, and asked Riggs to do another one for "Purgatory."

Riggs once told *Classic Rock* magazine: "I don't know if it's the definitive Maiden cover. That's not my call really, that's up to the fans. I did a load of pictures for Maiden; they covered a vast area of subject matter. I am not sure what would make one definitive and another one not. What defines Maiden's covers? I don't know, the first one I guess; that one set the place for Eddie. All the others followed that first one."

LEFT The cover art to Iron Maiden's *Live After Death* (EMI, 1985) appropriately depicts Eddie rising from the grave. Engraved on his tombstone is a quote from iconic horror author H. P. Lovecraft's short story *The Nameless City*, originally published in 1921. Also engraved on the stone is what appears to be Eddie's full name, "Edward T H . . . ," the remainder of which (his surname, "Head") is obscured by a clump of earth.

TOP "It's smashing your brains out, isn't it?" says Derek Riggs about the cover to Iron Maiden's 1988 single "Can I Play with Madness" (EMI). "Eddie's being screwed and there's eggs in his skull, or the idea of scrambled brains/scrambled eggs . . . madness. That's an egg, with a spoon—Eddie the egg cup!"

BOTTOM LEFT "With the Iron Maiden fans, they kind of know what they're going to get," says guitarist Dave Murray. "They hook into the whole package—Eddie, the whole thing. Eddie's certainly an extremely important part of that. He's larger than life in more ways than one—both on our album covers and on stage."

BOTTOM MIDDLE Iron Maiden's *Somewhere Back in Time—The Best of 1980–1989* (EMI, 2008) was released in tandem with their retrospective Somewhere Back in Time World Tour to allow fans to listen to songs that were played during the tour. The cover artwork by Derek Riggs features a double dose of Eddie-ness: the pharaoh Eddie monument from *Powerslave* (EMI, 1984) and cyborg Eddie from *Somewhere in Time* (EMI, 1986).

BOTTOM RIGHT Iron Maiden manager Rod Smallwood had the foresight to recognize Eddie's potential early in the band's career. Shortly after the band secured a recording contract with EMI in December 1979, Smallwood decided that his charges needed "that one figure who utterly stamped his presence and image on the band in a way that was obvious enough to make a good album cover."

THE *WELCOME TO HELL* ALBUM ARTWORK IS MY ILLUSTRATION AND WAS INSPIRED BY THE SIGIL OF BAPHOMET DESIGN, WHICH IS SAID TO HAVE BEEN DESIGNED BY ALEISTER CROWLEY. I WANTED TO CREATE AN ORIGINAL SIGIL FOR VENOM WHILE KEEPING THE SAME STRUCTURE OF (1) THE MAGIC CIRCLE, (2) THE INVERTED PENTAGRAM, AND (3) SATAN'S HEAD. I'VE ALWAYS ADMIRED THE ORIGINAL SIGIL DESIGN AND REALLY JUST WANTED ONE OF MY OWN. I ALWAYS THOUGHT IT WOULD LOOK AMAZING FIFTY [FEET] HIGH ON A STAGE AS A BACKDROP, AS WELL AS AN AWESOME ALBUM SLEEVE. THE LABEL HAD BEEN LOOKING AT OTHER ARTISTS' ARTWORK FOR OUR ALBUM SLEEVE, BUT WEREN'T TOO HAPPY AT THE EXPENSE FOR ARTWORK USAGE RIGHTS, ETC. THE DESIGN STILL STANDS UP TODAY REALLY WELL, AND THE MERCHANDISERS STILL WANT TO PRINT THE SHIRTS, SO THE POPULARITY OF THE DESIGN HAS CERTAINLY NOT BECOME LESS ATTRACTIVE IN ANY WAY OVER THE YEARS, PLUS IT'S NOW INSTANTLY RECOGNIZED AS VENOM."—Cronos, Venom bassist-vocalist

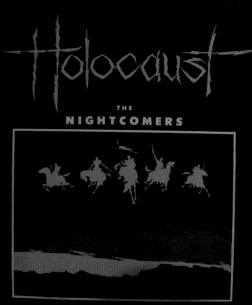

BOTTOM LEFT One of the NWOBHM's most revered and recognizable album covers, Demon's *Night of the Demon* (Carrere, 1981) features a pair of hands emerging from the earth to claw at a tombstone—revealing grisly guts beneath its stony surface. Far from being a black metal band, Demon were actually influenced by the likes of Alex Harvey, Jimi Hendrix, Pink Floyd, the Beatles, and Deep Purple.

TOP RIGHT In his review of Venom's debut album *Welcome to Hell* (Neat, 1981), journalist Geoff Barton called it "an epic of ugliness, a riotous noise, an appalling racket . . . possibly the heaviest record ever allowed in the shops for public consumption." Barton also said the record "had the hi-fi dynamics of a 50-year-old pizza." In other words, he really liked it.

BOTTOM RIGHT *The Nightcomers* is the debut studio album by Scotland's Holocaust, released in 1981 at the apex of the NWOBHM. Issued by the band's own label, Phoenix Record And Filmworks, the simple but effective cover depicts the silhouettes of five mysterious horsemen rampaging across the night sky and into your deepest, darkest dreams . . .

"WHEN WE FIRST STARTED OUT [THE] WHOLE BAND AGREED WE WANTED A RECURRENT TYGER THEME ON THE COVER OF ANY OF OUR RECORD RELEASES. OUR RECORD LABEL AT THE TIME, MCA, SUGGESTED WE USE A COMPANY CALLED CREAM, WHO DID A LOT OF THEIR ALBUM COVERS. WITH INSTRUCTIONS OF A TIGER ON THE COVER THEY CAME UP WITH THE WILD CAT IDEA. THERE WAS AN ORIGINAL OIL PAINTING DONE, AND A PHOTO OF THIS WAS USED FOR THE COVER. AT THE TIME, AND EVEN NOW, THE COVER STANDS OUT AND CATCHES YOUR EYE ON THE RACKS IN RECORD SHOPS (IF YOU CAN FIND ONE). I THINK IT'S QUITE ICONIC AND REMAINS ONE OF MY FAVORITE COVERS OF ALL TIME!"—Robb Weir, Tygers of Pan Tang guitarist

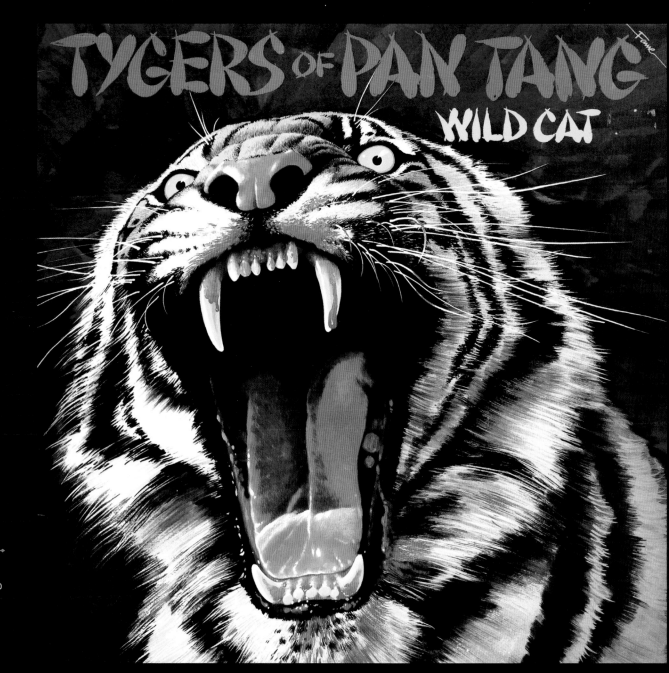

RIGHT The Tygers of Pan Tang's debut album *Wild Cat* was painted by Ricardo di Tommaso and came out on MCA in 1980. "As for the album title, well, I'm afraid I'm responsible for that," says guitarist Robb Weir. "I'd written the track 'Wild Cat' and insisted it became the title of the album . . . '*Wild cats are we, Wild cats, motorbikin' free!*'"

DAVID WOOD, THE HEAD OF OUR RECORD LABEL, NEAT RECORDS, SAID: 'YOU CAN'T DO THAT—IT'S HORRIBLE! BAD TASTE! NOT ON MY WATCH!' ET CETERA. INSTEAD HE TOLD US: 'YOU'VE GOT TWO HOURS—I NEED A COVER IDEA TODAY.' SO I SKETCHED TWO OF THE RAVEN 'FLASHES' INTERLOCKED AND THE NEAT 'GRAPHICS DEPARTMENT' ADDED THE WONDERFUL 'VISTAVISION' EFFECT TO THE ALBUM TITLE. TO BE HONEST, I HATED [IT] AT THE TIME . . . BUT I GUESS IT'S ICONIC AND WE WERE AHEAD OF THE CURVE. IT LOOKS GREAT ON A CD!"—John Gallagher, Raven bassist-vocalist

LEFT Raven's *Wiped Out* (Neat, 1982) is described by John Gallagher as "the most insane album we could come up with at the time. We had the perverse notion of calling it after a song that was not on the album . . . basically as the title summed up the state

TOP LEFT This striking cover graced "Axe Crazy" (Neat, 1982), the second single released by Bristol band Jaguar. Credited to "J Cox," the minimalist pen-and-ink image, with the Jaguar logo following the contours of an aggressive big cat's lower jaw, was likely designed by the band's bass player, Jeff Cox.

BOTTOM LEFT Major record labels were in the grip of NWOBHM fever in the early 1980s, and MCA snapped up Fist on the strength of their "Name, Rank, and Serial Number" single (Neat, 1980). The cover of *Turn the Hell On* (MCA, 1980) was designed by Cream. The distinctive Fist logo originally appeared on the preceding single—albeit without the three blacked-out digits!

TOP RIGHT According to Diamond Head guitarist Brian Tatler, "the cover of *Borrowed Time* (MCA, 1982) was our singer Sean Harris's idea. He had seen a painting he liked in a library book and wanted something similar. It may have been our A&R man, Charlie Ayre, who suggested we use the famous artist Rodney Matthews to bring Sean's vision to life."

BOTTOM RIGHT Def Leppard's *High 'n' Dry* (Vertigo, 1981) featured a man diving into an empty swimming pool. Apparently the image was originally intended for Pink Floyd's 1970 album *Atom Heart Mother* (Harvest) but was rejected—leaving its designer, Hipgnosis, free to use it later.

TOP LEFT Sporting one of the most unsubtle band names in rock, Split Beaver's sole album was released in 1982 on the Heavy Metal label. The cover of *When Hell Won't Have You* depicts a devil-like, stiletto-heeled, Flying V-wielding, winged beauty, presumably ascending into heaven after an unknown time spent in purgatory.

BOTTOM LEFT "We were looking for an artist to do the cover of *Time Tells No Lies* (Arista, 1981), and our management company, Fireball, suggested Rodney Matthews," says Praying Mantis guitarist Tino Troy. "They said he was Roger Dean-ish and they thought he would suit our music, so we went with it, and we were very pleased with what he did." Matthews made a sly reference to the management company by depicting a fireball being launched from the claw of the praying mantis creature.

BOTTOM MIDDLE Bitches Sin were another band to use the services of Rodney Matthews, for their album *Predator* (Heavy Metal, 1982). The cover, unsurprisingly, features a menacing, pterodactyl-like predator swooping from the skies, firing lasers from its eyes. Perhaps surprisingly, Matthews cites Walt Disney as his biggest artistic influence.

TOP RIGHT Hard to believe that Nightwing started out in 1978 under the inauspicious title of Gordon and Friends (after bassist Gordon Rowley, formerly of Strife). The cover of their debut album, *Something in the Air* (Ovation, 1981), depicts what an eagle would look like if it, like the Incredible Hulk, had been bombarded by gamma rays.

BOTTOM RIGHT Belying their exotic-sounding name, Chateaux came not from France but from Cheltenham, Gloucestershire, England. The cover of their debut album *Chained and Desperate* (Ebony, 1983) was by Garry Sharpe-Young, who went on to launch the MusicMight (formerly Rockdetector) online rock database. Sadly, Sharpe-Young died in March 2012.

"ORIGINALLY *PREDATOR* WAS GOING TO BE CALLED *HOT LICKS*—FOR OBVIOUS REASONS, GIVEN OUR STYLE OF MUSIC AND OUR PREVIOUS TITLES AT THAT TIME. IT ALL CHANGED WHEN WE SIGNED WITH HEAVY METAL RECORDS. PAUL BIRCH [LABEL BOSS] WAS FRIENDLY WITH RODNEY MATTHEWS AND OFFERED RODNEY'S SERVICES FOR THE ARTWORK. WE SAID YES; AFTER ALL, WHO WOULDN'T? I LOVE THE SLEEVE NOW AS MUCH AS I DID BACK THEN—IT IS SO EVOCATIVE AND POWERFUL. IN MY HUMBLE OPINION I BELIEVE IT HAS STOOD THE TEST OF TIME AND WOULD NOT LOOK OUT OF PLACE TODAY. THE ALBUM NAME CAME FROM MARK BIDDISCOMBE, WHO I WAS AT COLLEGE WITH AND WAS DRUMMER IN THE BAND AT THE TIME. TO THE BEST OF MY RECALL, I BELIEVE THE CONCEPT WAS RODNEY'S—CERTAINLY THERE WAS NO CONTRIBUTION FROM ME."—Ian Toomey, Bitches Sin guitarist

RIGHT Newcastle's Satan have one of the most underrated mascots in metal: a gnarled skeleton decked out in a judge's robes, complete with curly wig and everything. The cover to debut album *Court in the Act* (Neat, 1983) was inspired by the lyrics to the closing track "Alone in the Dock": "The judge's eyes ablaze with fury/You stand alone now/ Feel the flames begin to burn/ You're gonna stand alone in the dock."

"I FIRST STARTED DABBLING IN ALBUM SLEEVE DESIGN WHEN I SAW A REALLY AWFUL COVER IN *KERRANG!* MAGAZINE. I PHONED THE LABEL [EBONY] AND TOLD THEM THEIR ARTWORK WAS SHIT, AND I COULD DO BETTER. THOSE WERE THE EXACT WORDS I USED! THE GUY DIDN'T SLAM THE PHONE DOWN BUT INSTEAD TOOK UP THE CHALLENGE, SO I HAD TO COME UP WITH SOMETHING QUICK. THE FIRST ARTWORK I SENT IN THEY USED ON THE *METAL WARRIORS* COMPILATION ALBUM [1983]."—Garry Sharpe-Young, designer and journalist

LEFT Grim Reaper's *See You in Hell* (1983) was one of a series of album covers designed by Garry Sharpe-Young for Ebony. "The reaper one I did in one night; it never got finished," said Sharpe-Young. "You can imagine I was quite surprised when it sold 250,000 albums in the US. I was still at school at the time."

THE WARRIOR

TOP LEFT Bronz were, somewhat confusingly, signed to the Bronze label, whose boss was the late Gerry Bron. This is the US version of the cover to their debut album *Taken by Storm* (1983), featuring a voluptuous, Michelangelo-style woman being abducted by a horse-riding skeleton, in the midst of (you guessed it) a lightning storm.

BOTTOM LEFT Blackmayne based their name on a description of Conan the Barbarian by one of his enemies—"the dangerous black mane"—owing to the length and color of his hair. The original sleeve of their self-titled debut album (Criminal Response/Ebony, 1985) was destroyed in a fire. This put the release back several months, which frustrated Blackmayne so much that they split up! Remarkably, the band have recently re-formed, offering the message: "The 'Mayne are back —and they're louder than ever!"

BOTTOM MIDDLE Battleaxe's *Burn This Town* (Music for Nations, 1984) became a cult release due to its (as the band put it) "unusual and unsanctioned album cover." The members were reportedly embarrassed by the cheesy painting of a crudely rendered biker wielding a battle axe. However, the music did the talking, and the album sold well.

TOP RIGHT "The cover of *The Warrior* (Shades, 1984) was by an artist called Liz Bligh," reveals Pete Franklin, Chariot vocalist-rhythm guitarist. "We had written a song called 'Warriors', inspired by the film of the same name. But we didn't want to make it [the cover] about fighting gangs in the USA, so we made it more mythical. The idea was to portray a warrior driving a chariot who would fight to the death and kill anyone who got in their way."

BOTTOM RIGHT Savage's *Loose 'n Lethal* was the second album cover designed by Garry Sharpe-Young for Ebony. "I've always been into the creative aspect of things, designing stage sets, merchandise, T-shirts, et cetera," said Sharpe-Young. "My pinnacle of achievement was making Rob Halford's Painkiller Tour jacket, the one with all the crosses on."

Behind the 'Zines

How the New Wave of British Heavy Metal (NWOBHM) began in monochrome in *Sounds*, then exploded into full-color life in *Kerrang!*

It's no exaggeration to say that weekly music newspapers wielded enormous power in the 1970s. The Big Three—*New Musical Express*, *Melody Maker*, and *Sounds*—racked up issue sales in the hundreds of thousands. In this pre-internet age, the information imparted by the "inkies" was so vital, it was like oxygen to a drowning man.

No bullshit. The weekly music newspapers were that essential.

But fans of hard rock and heavy metal didn't venture within a country mile of the up-your-arse *NME* and *MM*. No, they bought *Sounds*.

Sounds was gritty and down-to-earth. Its writers were irreverent, a bit grumpy, unpretentious, and had a great sense of humor. Its grimy, monochromatic pages were imbued with an indefinable rock 'n' roll spirit. To purloin the punk-rock phrase of the age, *Sounds* meant it, m-a-a-a-n.

The NWOBHM started as a late '70s *Sounds* invention and then grew exponentially, taking on a hydra-like life of its own. Certainly, this writer's May 19, 1979 *Sounds* review of the iconic Angel Witch/Iron Maiden/Samson show in the Music Machine club marked the first use of the "New Wave of British Heavy Metal" epithet. The headline, "If you want blood (and flashbombs and dry ice and confetti) you've got it," was followed by the subhead: "The New Wave of British Heavy Metal: first in an occasional series by 'Deaf' Barton."

All of which carried the unmistakably daft—sorry, *deft*—creative-writing touch of the rag's editorial boss, "Big" Al Lewis.

Sounds was on to a good thing. A new British rock scene began to erupt, and I was dispatched all over Britain to cover a dizzying array of exciting new bands. Meanwhile, the acronym "NWOBHM" was spawning a whole host of look-alikes.

Just under twelve months after the genre-defining Music Machine show, the NENWOBHM (North East New Wave of British Heavy Metal) was born in Wallsend,

> ## "THE NWOBHM STARTED AS A LATE 70s *SOUNDS* INVENTION AND THEN GREW EXPONENTIALLY, TAKING ON A HYDRA-LIKE LIFE OF ITS OWN." —Geoff Barton

near the city of Newcastle-upon-Tyne. The NENWOBHM saw bands such as Venom, Fist, Raven, White Spirit, and the Tygers of Pan Tang creating a matrix of metal mayhem, thriving on the tiny Neat Records label.

Sounds closed 1979 with a lengthy state-of-the-nation NWOBHM update. Iron Maiden, Def Leppard, the Tygers, Praying Mantis, Witchfynde, Diamond Head, Angel Witch, and Sledgehammer all featured prominently, with honorable mentions for the likes of Nuthin' Fancy, Vardis, Ethel the Frog, Toad the Wet Sprocket, Race Against Time, Zorro, Killdozer, Dragonfly, Bastille, Hellenbach . . . the list went on and on.

As a tennis-playing teenager in Denmark, future Metallica drummer Lars Ulrich was enormously influenced by the NWOBHM scribblings in *Sounds*, so much so that he made pilgrimages over to the United Kingdom to check out many of the fledgling bands. If the NWOBHM hadn't impinged on young Lars' impressionable senses, there would likely have been no Metallica. Certainly Metallica's music is firmly grounded in the NWOBHM, as their love for bands such as Diamond Head demonstrates.

In 1981 the NWOBHM went full-color with the launch of *Kerrang!*—a glossy magazine devoted exclusively to metal music. The first issue sold like hot rock cakes, and there was no looking back. Without *Sounds* and *Kerrang!* the NWOBHM would never have existed. Forget Rupert Murdoch's global dominance . . . that's a testament to the true power of the press.

SOUNDS DECEMBER 1 1979 20p

TOM PETTY · THE JAM

THE NEW FACE OF HEAVY METAL
13-PAGE GROSS-OUT, PAGE 21

NOVEMBER 29, 1980 25p

BOW WOW WOW (AGAIN) · GARY GLITTER · NOT THE NINE O'CLOCK NEWS · VISITORS · LAMBRETTAS

OCCULT HEROES
Angel Witch page 22

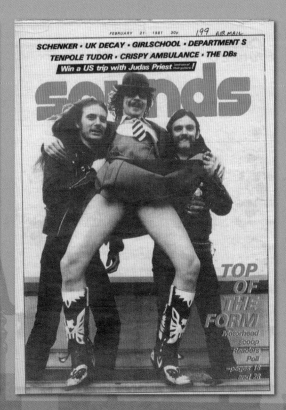

FEBRUARY 21 1981 30p   199 AIR MAIL

SCHENKER · UK DECAY · GIRLSCHOOL · DEPARTMENT S
TENPOLE TUDOR · CRISPY AMBULANCE · THE DBs

Win a US trip with Judas Priest

TOP OF THE FORM
Motörhead scoop
Readers Poll
pages 18 and 28

OPPOSITE *Sounds* was one of the Big Three British music weekly newspapers, the others being *Melody Maker* and *NME* (*New Musical Express*). Launched in 1970 by ex—*Melody Maker* execs, *Sounds* really hit its stride in the mid-'70s under the stewardship of editor Alan "Big" Al Lewis. Always the most down-to-earth and streetwise of the trio of weeklies, *Sounds* spearheaded and popularized the New Wave of British Heavy Metal via a series of groundbreaking articles by writer Geoff Barton. These three classic covers depict (from left) masked Samson drummer Thunderstick; Angel Witch posing beneath a symbolic "Metal Merchants" sign; and the legendary Motörhead trio of "Fast" Eddie Clarke, Phil "Philthy Animal" Taylor, and Lemmy. Sadly, *Sounds* ceased publication in 1991.

ABOVE *Kerrang!* magazine launched from the pages of *Sounds* in 1981 under editor Geoff Barton, with the purpose of capitalizing on the popularity of the NWOBHM and all things heavy metal, and doing so in glossy full color—something that *Sounds*, a so-called "inkie," couldn't match. Initially a one-time publication, *Kerrang!*'s popularity was such that the publishers quickly increased its frequency to monthly, biweekly, and then weekly in 1987. *Kerrang!* also outgrew its UK rock roots and began to embrace American supergroups such as Megadeth, Bon Jovi, Mötley Crüe, Guns N' Roses, and Metallica. But major UK bands, including Iron Maiden, were also mainstays, and remain so today, as *Kerrang!* continues to thrive.

"ALAN CAMPION [RONDELET RECORDS COFOUNDER] AND EXPULSION ARRANGED THE ARTWORK AND COVER DESIGN FOR *CLOAK AND DAGGER*, AFTER WE PROVIDED THEM WITH THE SONG TITLES WHICH WE WOULD BE USING. WE NEVER MET THE ARTIST RESPONSIBLE."—Montalo, Witchfynde guitarist

ABOVE When you're called Tank, there's only one image you should have on your covers. But remarkably, it took the band until its fourth album *Honour & Blood* (Music for Nations, 1984) to wake up to this fact. Previously there had been rabid dogs on *Filth Hounds of Hades*, a bog standard band lineup shot on *Power of the Hunter*, and a trio of gargoyles on *This Means War*. What on earth were they thinking? Tank means TANK!

Witchfynde CLOAK & DAGGER

BLADE RUNNER 'Hunted'

TOP LEFT As you can imagine, a multitude of heavy metal bands have adopted the name Crucifixion—but this lot, who formed in Essex in 1979, were likely the first. Their "Green Eyes" EP, issued on the Neat label in 1984, is one of the NWOBHM's most collectible releases—and its cover, resembling a primitive graveyard etching, is startlingly effective.

BOTTOM LEFT If you know your religion, you'll remember that as a last act of humiliation inflicted on Jesus, Roman officers twisted a crown of thorns and placed it on his head. The cover art of Force's *Set Me Free* (Heavy Metal, 1985) takes this biblical concept and gives it a technological edge, the "thorns" in a metal headband sparking with high-voltage electricity—and causing excruciating results.

BOTTOM MIDDLE With artwork by Garry Sharpe-Young (credited as simply "Gary Sharpe" on the cover), Blade Runner's *Hunted* (Ebony, 1984) features a hammer-wielding barbarian doing his best to repel the advances of a horde of strange-helmeted, intergalactic policemen. Clearly, the artwork takes its cue from Frank Frazetta's famous *Conan the Destroyer* painting.

TOP RIGHT Third album *Cloak & Dagger* (Expulsion, 1983) should have been the one to catapult Witchfynde to the very forefront of the NWOBHM. But record label Expulsion's finances were shaky, and by early 1984 the band were walking away from their second bankrupt label. (Rondelet had released their previous two albums.) Still, at least the stylish, symbol-laden, sacrificial cover art was a step up from previous releases.

BOTTOM RIGHT *Hell Hath No Fury* (A&M, 1983) was released with two different covers: the US had to make do with a plain band lineup photo rather than the stunning Medusa image here. Inspired by seminal gal rockers the Runaways, Rock Goddess first got together as South London schoolgirls in 1977; they had to cancel a tour with UFO around the release of their debut single, because drummer Julie Turner still had to go to school!

TOP LEFT Cloven Hoof's *Dominator*, a sci-fi concept album, was released in 1988 on the FM Revolver label. Jon Blanche of *White Dwarf* magazine painted the cover and depicted the Warrior of the Wasteland character [also the title of one of the album's songs] as an Amazonian warrior. "I saw Jon's work, met with Paul Birch [FM Revolver boss], and insisted on Jon being the artist for the album sleeve," says bassist Lee Payne.

BOTTOM LEFT "I guess you can say that *The Son of Odin* cover is all my fault," says vocalist Paul Taylor of Elixir's 1986 debut album, which was self-released on the band's own label. Taylor blended photos, the band logo and handwritten text to make a black-and-white photocopy of the album cover. "As Phil [Denton, Elixir guitarist] worked for a bank then, he brought some of the colored plastic money bags home, which we cut open and spread over the black and white cover to see which looked best— red, yellow, or blue. I think blue won out, three to two."

TOP RIGHT After the classy sleeve that adorned their self-titled debut album (see page 45), Angel Witch opted for shock tactics for follow-up *Screamin' n' Bleedin'* (Killerwatt, 1985). The central figure is a bizarre amalgam of bare-breasted Medusa and axe-wielding eagle, and the overall effect is undeniably sleazy. (It's no wonder that when it was reissued the cover was changed to the image of a Christopher Lee-style vampire.)

BOTTOM RIGHT Taking their unusual name from James Joyce's *A Portrait of the Artist as a Young Man*, Bradford, England–based Baby Tuckoo released *Force Majeure* on Music for Nations in 1985. The cover is credited to Chris Wade and appears to be his sole published artwork. (Throughout his life Wade has also worked as a songwriter, A&R man, and recording engineer.)

Rough Justice

ABOVE From the ashes of NWOBHM behemoth Angel Witch rose Tytan. Originally scheduled for release in 1983 on the Kamaflage label, *Rough Justice* finally emerged two years later on Metal Masters—after the band had split. (Tytan re-formed in 2010.) At first glance this is a typical war-mongering NWOBHM album cover. But then you begin to notice the black knight's decidedly skimpy armor, studded codpiece, and exposed belly button . . .

"I GREW UP ON A STEADY DIET OF GREEK AND NORSE MYTHOLOGY, OLD HORROR AND SCI-FICTION FILMS, AND MARVEL COMIC BOOKS. THIS AMALGAMATION OF THINGS FUELLED MY IMAGINATION, SYNTHESIZED INTO THE BAND'S SONGS, AND ALSO INFLUENCED OUR CHOICE OF ALBUM COVER ART. THE OVERALL CONCEPT OF THE *DOMINATOR* ALBUM WAS A WARNING ABOUT THE DANGERS OF GENETIC ENGINEERING."—Lee Payne, Cloven Hoof bassist

CHAPTER 3

Hair Metal

"WHEN IT COMES TO ICONIC ALBUM COVERS IN AMERICAN METAL, WHERE WE HAVE TO LOOK FIRST IS POISON'S *LOOK WHAT THE CAT DRAGGED IN*. THAT'S JUST THE NO-BRAINER. THERE YOU HAVE FOUR MEN WHO LOOK LIKE WOMEN WHO KIND OF LOOK LIKE MEN WHO LOOK LIKE HOT WOMEN. YOU KIND OF WANT TO BONE 'EM. 'OH MY GOD, WHO IS THIS GROUP OF FOUR SWEET-LOOKING CHICKS?' THEN YOU REALIZE IT'S A BUNCH OF DUDES FROM PENNSYLVANIA, WHICH KIND OF MAKES YOU FEEL WEIRD, BUT AT THE SAME TIME, WHO CARES? THEY'RE HOT."

—Stix Zadinia, Steel Panther drummer

Pop Goes the Metal

BRYAN REESMAN

The 1980s in America were ripe with outrageousness and excess. Hard-rocking bands led the charge of decadence, spreading from LA's Sunset Strip to the eastern seaboard. Band members donned leather and spandex, raided their girlfriends' closets, teased their hair out and shellacked it with Aquanet, then cranked out raunchy anthems about sex and rebelliousness and sensitive ballads about swelling love and broken hearts.

The term "hair band" still makes artists bristle, but can you blame them? Bands from Ratt to W.A.S.P. to Twisted Sister to Guns N' Roses were lumped together, despite their differences. Fashion statements begat musical stereotypes.

"[Hair band] was a derogatory term that dismissed the bands and music—all of us who spent time working on our music and playing were basically told that it was worth nothing," said bassist Billy Sheehan, who has played with Mr. Big, David Lee Roth, and Talas. "I never thought that there would be a wall put up between musical acts. I came from a time when there wasn't a wall."

Critics be damned, heavy metal was bubbling up in America in the early '80s. Van Halen had been electrifying audiences since the mid-'70s and had sold multimillions, and newcomers Mötley Crüe, Ratt, and Dokken were gestating. Once Judas Priest's *Screaming for Vengeance* (1982) became a smash hit and gained the heavier bands more acceptance on MTV, Quiet Riot's anthemic *Metal Health* (the first metal album to hit No. 1 on the charts) and Def Leppard's hit-laden *Pyromania* fully blew the doors open in summer 1983, followed by Mötley Crüe's raunchy *Shout at the Devil*.

Metal rocked MTV in 1984, and the commercialization began. Hair got bigger (Finnish glam rockers Hanoi Rocks majorly influenced Mötley Crüe and later Guns N' Roses), sales soared, and concerts grew to arena size and beyond. Van Halen's massive *1984* brought in synths. Ratt's melodic *Out of the Cellar* exploded.

"BANDS LIKE QUEENSRŸCHE AND IRON MAIDEN HAD GREAT LOGOS, MERCHANDISE AND IMAGERY THAT WAS ALL WORKING PROPERLY IN PUTTING ACROSS WHAT THEY WERE IN THE RIGHT LIGHT. FROM LA, I WAS LOOKING AT BANDS LIKE MÖTLEY CRÜE AND DOKKEN, AND IT WAS JUST GENIUS. BON JOVI EVEN, FOR WHAT THEY WERE, IT WAS ALL CORRECT."

—Tony Harnell, solo artist, ex-TNT front man

Twisted Sister's dark *Stay Hungry* scored huge with two upbeat anthems. Dokken's power ballad "Alone Again" from *Tooth and Nail* (1985) became a hit, inspiring more hard rockers to showcase their sensitive sides. By 1986, keyboards saturated many heavy rock albums. Bands sought daytime airplay on MTV, which began banishing controversial metal clips to nighttime rotation in 1985.

The game changer was Bon Jovi's über-slick *Slippery When Wet* (1986), a multiplatinum smash with a potent combination of looks and licks that opened up more hard rock airplay on the radio. That same year also saw popular releases by David Lee Roth, Cinderella, Stryper, Poison, Europe, and Van Halen. On the West Coast, the gritty bombast of Guns N' Roses exploded with the release of *Appetite for Destruction* (1987) and boosted fellow sleaze rock bands like Faster Pussycat and L.A. Guns, and metalheads Skid Row.

Big hair, big hooks, and power ballads ruled. A major makeover for bluesy Brits Whitesnake on their self-titled album (1987) turned David Coverdale and company into superstars. The superglam group Poison's *Open Up and Say . . . Ahh!* (1988) became another megaplatinum success, partly due to the No. 1 single "Every Rose Has Its Thorn," and Def Leppard's *Hysteria* (1987), initially a flop, skyrocketed after "Pour Some Sugar on Me" became a strip club hit in 1988. The key to all of these big albums? Women.

"By the time Whitesnake hit with the video for 'Is This Love' in '88, it was ladies' night," revealed bassist Rudy Sarzo, who previously played with Quiet Riot, Ozzy Osbourne, and Whitesnake. "It was 75 percent women in the audience. We knew the significance of having females."

Ex-Runaways member Lita Ford, a female performer in the midst of all this testosterone, became a platinum artist by 1988, but she admitted her label was often clueless about how to market her. "They couldn't sell me as a musician because I was a girl," said Ford. "Then they would try to sell me as a sex symbol, but that wasn't really true either because I was a musician. Sometimes people would say, 'Lita, we don't know what to do with you.' I would say, 'What do you mean? I'm a guitar player. Rock 'n' roll is sexy. I'm not the only one who wears my shirt unbuttoned.'"

Album art throughout the '80s was vibrant and colorful, especially when practiced by art designer Bob Defrin, who worked on iconic covers for AC/DC, Mötley Crüe, Ratt, Dokken, and Twisted Sister, among others. Hugh Syme brought in surrealist art influences. Leading American rock photographers Neil Zlozower and Mark Weiss created dramatic studio shots and dynamic live photos with a larger-than-life quality essential in selling their subjects as rock gods.

Def Leppard guitarist Phil Collen believes that many '80s metal album covers were great for their day. "*Metal Health* was so perfect for Quiet Riot right then," he stated. "If you take it out of context then it probably looks silly, but in context it was a great album sleeve that represented them well."

Many '80s album covers embraced outrageousness. Van Halen's *1984* featured a cherub stealing a cigarette. Twisted Sister's *Stay Hungry* showed Dee Snider about to chomp on a giant bone. Mötley Crüe's *Too Fast for Love* (1981) displayed a leather crotch shot. But then the Parents' Music Resource Center (PMRC) made a stink about album lyrics and imagery in 1985. Some covers' sexual suggestiveness pushed retail buttons and were censored or altered: the original *Slippery When Wet* was a busty T-shirt tease; *Open Up and Say . . . Ahh!* featured a demonic woman with a giant tongue lasciviously protruding from her mouth; *Appetite for Destruction* portrayed a robot rapist about to be attacked by an alien. Controversy generated buzz.

Beyond retail marketing, MTV's influence was staggering. "Once we started making the transition into video, we wondered if an album cover was going to pop up on a [store] endcap," noted bassist Sarzo. "It became more marketing than anything else rather than making a statement of what was inside."

T-shirts and posters became important marketing tools. "Merchandise was huge," said Ford, the subject of many sexy photos. "You would get massive advances from the merchandising companies. They would put out all these T-shirts and posters and supply you with merch for the tour." Groups like Ratt, Mötley Crüe, and W.A.S.P. presented provocative imagery.

Sometimes unofficial band shirts were cooler than the legit products. "We were always more impressed by the bootleggers and the shirts that they came up with," admitted Sarzo. "The ink might have been toxic, because it was definitely more vibrant and more colorful. They were just forced to be more eye-popping because of the competition." He recalled how many bands used bright colors for flashy shirts that young fans craved. "It was like Technicolor dog vomit on the shirt."

"I WAS GOING TO START A BAND WITH A PRETTY FAMOUS GUITAR PLAYER AROUND '87/'88, AND HIS POINT TO ME WAS, LET'S GO TO THE RAINBOW AND FIND SOMEBODY WHO LOOKS LIKE A SINGER, THEN WE'LL SEE IF HE CAN SING AND MAYBE GET HIM VOICE LESSONS. I SWEAR TO GOD." —Billy Sheehan, Mr. Big bassist

"The further along the '80s got, they started getting more crazy with the artwork," noted Patrick Klima, owner of the WyCo Vintage eBay store. "They went from shirts with just the band's name to pushing their image or using expletives or nudity to shock, because they were all competing against each other."

The glam approach of multiplatinum Sunset Strip bands like Mötley Crüe filtered to established artists like Ozzy Osbourne, Scorpions, Aerosmith, and Judas Priest, to varying degrees—much to the chagrin of diehard fans. Hair styles got poofier and clothes more colorful.

"In the '80s, it almost became like Wall Street," stated former TNT front man Tony Harnell. "Like somebody saw the potential of this incredible, billion-dollar money-making industry, and they started turning music into shoes or Kellogg's. It got away from what it was originally supposed to be. The long hair, which started in the late '60s, was embraced by musicians but what started as a movement against society and the [Vietnam] war suddenly turned into an image thing."

"After *Slippery When Wet* exploded, every time a hair metal band would get big, a label would have to sign five of them," recalled veteran rock/radio journalist Gail Flug. "They would throw them at the wall and see what stuck. Everyone was sounding and looking alike, and that's why people got sick of it in the early '90s."

The next wave of '80s hard rock bands—including Warrant, Winger, Danger Danger, Extreme, Mr. Big, and Slaughter—

was the last. Excess had become passé, and a flood of bands started to overwhelm the fans. Grunge and alternative swept the States by 1992. "It wasn't cool to be a rock star anymore, and nobody wanted to pose," explained Zlozower. "That's when all the magazines folded. There were forty American rock mags up until that point."

Although the '90s were a bad time for '80s hard rock and metal acts—many attempting unsuccessfully to adjust to trendy musical styles—a resurgence began in 1999 that lead to a '80s revival in the 2000s, minus the crazy hair and overindulgent lifestyles. Modern revamps also emerged: The Darkness, Steel Panther, Hinder, Buckcherry, Black Veil Brides, and Scandinavian sleaze rockers Vains of Jenna.

Hinder front man Austin Winkler grew up watching videos on MTV that got him stoked to grow up and join a party that would end before he arrived. "We tried our damnedest to bring it back, and we had a lot of fun," said Winkler, who was awed by '80s stadium shows. "The fact that it was so huge still baffles me, and the fact that it's not anymore crushes me."

Old school fans have now embraced the term "hair band" in a positive way. "Like anything, the decade previous to whatever decade you're in is really uncool," noted Phil Collen, "but the one before that comes around again. It becomes passé, but if you give it a decade, people dig it for the same reasons they dug it in the first place."

"EIGHTIES ALBUM COVERS OFTEN EMBRACED OUTRAGEOUSNESS. SOME COVERS' SEXUAL SUGGESTIVENESS PUSHED RETAIL BUTTONS AND WERE CENSORED OR ALTERED. CONTROVERSY GENERATED BUZZ." —Bryan Reesman

ABOVE For KISS's *Asylum* (Vertigo, 1985), "Paul Stanley wanted to do something like the Motels cover [*All Four One*, Capitol, 1982]," said art director–cover artist Dennis Woloch, who turned black-and-white portraits of each band member into toneless, high-contrast photostats. He then combined them into one photostat and painted over them on clear acetate film overlays. The lip color of each band member mirrored the backlighting of their earlier solo albums.

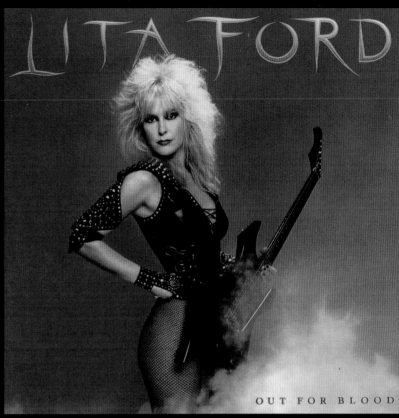

TOP LEFT Hiro Ito's cover image of influential Finnish band Hanoi Rocks for *Two Steps from the Move* (CBS, 1983) is certainly '80s iconic. "Mötley Crüe brought in that shag look, and I think they got it from Hanoi Rocks, who brought in the tattoos and that upside-down hair," said Lita Ford. "I asked Nikki, 'How do you get your hair to stay like that?' He would say, 'Oh, I just flip upside down in the closet.' Like a bat."

BOTTOM LEFT For the cover of *Dangerous Curves* (RCA/BMG, 1991), Lita Ford wanted photographer Jeff Katz to reproduce the pose of a Prince protégée that he had shot for a test shoot. "She went crazy over that picture," recalled Katz. "That made this unusual. It was exactly the same pose, lighting and everything." He shot black-and-white photos at his Hollywood studio, then applied a little diffusion and blue dye by hand to get the distinct look.

TOP RIGHT This is the alternate cover for Lita Ford's *Out for Blood* (Mercury, 1983) photographed by Herbert Worthington III. The original featured Ford holding two halves of a Mockingbird BC Rich guitar ripped in half, blood and guts oozing out of the injured axe. "So they banned the cover and replaced it with another shot where I'm not wearing any pants," said Ford. "The guitar I'm holding is covering my crotch, but you can see my ass sticking out."

BOTTOM RIGHT The image of fan hands reaching up to touch their rock gods was very apropos for the '80s for the KISS greatest hits collection *Smashes, Thrashes & Hits* (Vertigo, 1988). The previous year, Judas Priest's *Priest . . . Live!* used the same concept. KISS had a history of portraying themselves as larger than life, so this image fits naturally within their visual repertoire.

TOP LEFT Canadian rockers Kick Axe had seen the artwork of Italian painter Dario Campanile and got to meet him while recording *Vices* (Pasha, 1984). "He offered to do a painting for us, and we thought it was great," said Kick Axe guitarist Larry Gillstrom. "That's still the logo that we use today. That was probably the most marketable cover that we had." Campanile brought his classical and surrealist influences to the cover's surreal "vice monster" imagery.

BOTTOM LEFT "A lot of people think of 'The Final Countdown' as what Europe is all about," said veteran rock journalist Gail Flug. "But if you listen to *Wings of Tomorrow* (Hot, 1984) and other albums, you hear much more influence from the New Wave of British Heavy Metal and Deep Purple. A lot of people don't give them enough credit. John Norum is an amazing guitar player." Peter Engberg's fierce cover art reinforced the album's heaviness.

TOP RIGHT While many early '80s hard rock covers featured the expected imagery, Night Ranger's *Dawn Patrol* (Epic, 1982) took a more moody approach. Shorty Wilcox's cover image of massive antennae in New Mexico receiving (or emitting?) red beams of light implied contact with alien intelligence; Val Gelineau's back cover featured band members standing in a forest being touched by the same red beams (are they aliens?), giving the packaging a subtle sci-fi twist.

BOTTOM RIGHT "The idea for the devil sitting on the bed getting ready for work was mine; the execution of the idea [was] totally [art director's] Heather Brown," said Helix front man Brian Vollmer of *No Rest for the Wicked* (Capitol, 1983). "The odd thing about the cover is that the Helix 'spiral' is seen hidden on it. This would start a tradition of having it on all album covers, although I haven't bothered on the last few."

QUIET RIOT

AL HEALTH

ABOVE Former QR bassist Rudy Sarzo said that he contributed the idea of the mask to the cover of *Metal Health* (Epic, 1983). "It was the universal headbanger, and, of course, the mask was going to be protecting you from bashing your face," explained Sarzo. "The artist that we commissioned [Grammy-nominated illustrator Stan Watts] took a photo of himself, and Frankie gave the motorcycle jacket that he wore backwards.

There's a photo button of each guy in the band, because he was supposed to be a Quiet Riot fan."

"WITH ALL OF THE SUNSET STRIP BANDS, THE LOOK THAT WE HAD ON STAGE CAME FROM BEING STARVING MUSICIANS LIVING OFF THE GENEROSITY OF THE GIRLFRIENDS THAT WE HAD. THEY WOULD TAKE CARE OF US, AND WE WOULD RAID THEIR CLOSETS. WE WERE ALL SKINNY BECAUSE WE WERE STARVING, AND WE LOOKED THE WAY WE DID BECAUSE THAT'S HOW OUR GIRLFRIENDS DRESSED."

'WE SPENT ALL THIS TIME AND MONEY MAKING THESE RECORDS, AND THANK GOD WE HAD [PRODUCER] MUTT LANGE AROUND. HE SAID, 'YOU GUYS COULD BE A REALLY GOOD ROCK BAND OR A GREAT ARTIST THAT IS AROUND FOR YEARS.' SO WE OPTED FOR SCENARIO TWO. BUT EVERYONE ELSE DIDN'T NECESSARILY DO THAT. IT WAS A LOT CHEAPER. THE MOTIVATION WAS CHEAPER. IT WAS THE DIFFERENCE BETWEEN BEING A BAND AND BEING AN ARTIST, THAT'S THE WAY I LOOK AT IT." —Phil Collen, Def Leppard guitarist

LEFT Graphic designer Andie Airfix brought

WARNING THE LYRICAL CONTENT OF THIS RECORD MAY BE CONSIDERED OFFENSIVE.

W. A. S. P.

ANIMAL (F**K LIKE A BEAST)

W.A.S.P.

LIVE ANIMAL

F**K LIKE A BEAST

W.A.S.P

PKUT 109

1. FRONT SIDE: Animal (F**K Like A Beast)
2. BACK SIDE: Show no Mercy

TOP LEFT The concept for the codpiece cover of W.A.S.P.'s infamous "Animal (F**k Like a Beast)" single (Music for Nations, 1984) came from band manager Rod Smallwood. "He wanted to do something outrageous, and it did work because it made Blackie seem dangerous," said photographer Ross Halfin, who quickly shot this cover as part of a longer magazine session. "It's so badly lit and composed that I suppose it looks good. In a sense, it sums up the '80s, so I don't mind it. I quite like the fact that it looks really cheesy."

BOTTOM LEFT Rock journalist Gail Flug noted that W.A.S.P. manager Rod Smallwood also handled Iron Maiden. "He was really into putting out picture discs and collectibles," she said. "Back then, a lot of bands put out picture discs. That was a big thing in England. For instance, when Iron Maiden would put out a single, they would put seven-inch, a twelve-inch, and a picture disc. And sometimes a shaped disc." Like this pig from W.A.S.P.

TOP RIGHT Although W.A.S.P. front man Blackie Lawless relished offending people back in the day—such as with this bestiality-themed picture disc for "Animal (F**k Like a Beast)"—he has since become a born-again Christian and forsworn his old ways. "I renounce, denounce, and pronounce that I will never play that song live again," Lawless declared in 2010. "Actually, I've not played it live for several years."

BOTTOM RIGHT "Animal (F**k Like a Beast)" ended up on the "Filthy Fifteen" list of songs from the Parents' Music Resource Center (PMRC), a watchdog group formed in 1985 by US senators' wives (including Tipper Gore) that sought to censor rock albums. Out of the subsequent senate hearings emerged the "Parental Advisory" warning stickers that still exist today.

Syme of the Times

There were numerous artists who toiled tirelessly on "big hair" metal covers throughout the 1980s and early 1990s; among these was Hugh Syme, a talented, Juno Award—winning artist from Canada who built up a strong portfolio while working against the grain. He has designed every Rush cover since 1975's *Caress of Steel* and has worked with many iconic hard rock artists, including Whitesnake, Scorpions, Stone Sour, and Def Leppard. But he does not seek to pander, and he continually works outside of the box.

For some, the 1980s may have been the decade of decadence, but for Hugh Syme it was more about elegance. Even as some artists and labels tried to push the boundaries of taste, he encouraged his musical clients to navigate away from obvious trends. By the late '80s, he had the credentials to do what he felt was warranted, balanced with shelf appeal.

"I was generally engaged for my conceptual work," recalled Syme, who has been influenced by painters as diverse as Salvador Dali, Johannes Vermeer, and M. C. Escher. "I even tried to make a conscious effort to be responsive to the title of each project, almost without regard to the band's styling—hair, spandex, leathers. There were exceptions, like Great White's *Hooked*, where I was serving the title with a nod to the alpha male sexual aggression so prevalent in the '80s."

Many of his colorfully designed covers featured surreal landscapes or collages displaying Syme's signature "improbable reality." He occasionally veered into areas that were suggestive (Slaughter's *Stick It to Ya*), sinister (Iron Maiden's *The X Factor*), quirky (the female "fan club" of Kick Axe's *Welcome to the Club*), and even kinky (Hurricane's *Slave to the Thrill*).

Syme occasionally created cover art entirely himself; two of his most famous covers were for the multiplatinum albums *Whitesnake* and *Slip of the Tongue*.

Despite the penchant of Whitesnake front man David Coverdale for naughty lyrics, the images were stripped of sex. "*Whitesnake* came after meeting Lord David," said Syme. "There was something about his über British demeanor and how meetings with him were like holding court. A heraldic crest just seemed right."

Bassist Rudy Sarzo recalled, "I would say that the only mainstream band that I played with as far as having something of a dignified artwork or graphic was actually Whitesnake. They went more for that classy look, almost a throwback to the '70s."

For Def Leppard's *Retro Active* rarities package, Syme riffed on the classic *All Is Vanity* image by illustrator Charles Allan Gilbert from 1892, which transforms a woman and her reflection into the shape of a skull. "The concept of 'looking back' or 'retroactive' and the reflectivity of the mirror as a metaphor just seemed to work," said Syme. "I have always been a huge fan of trompe l'oeil and optical illusions and decided to tackle, and pay homage to, the great Victorian image by Gilbert."

Def Leppard guitarist Phil Collen really liked Syme's cover for *Retro Active*. "The Andy Airfax stuff was very synonymous with what we were about in the '80s," noted Collen, "but coming into the '90s post-grunge and in retrospect looking back on yourself, this was perfect for the time."

Nearly forty years into his prolific career, Syme continues to stay busy with artists like Dream Theater and Carrie Newcomer as well as his permanent gig with Rush. "As Neil [Peart] so aptly and kindly put it, I am 'serving my life sentence as their art director' because we have collectively always strived for growth," explained Syme. "I have enjoyed this mutual respect and loyalty that will always inspire me to push the envelope, and keep in step with their ever-changing themes and styles. When I get the call to work on each project for Rush, I generally clear my schedule."

TOP LEFT What is the most valuable thing Hugh Syme has learned during his nearly four decades in the business? "A good—in my case, obsessive—work ethic is key, but to strike a balance between that insular, studio-hermit existence and taking time out to live and play," he replied. "That and the humbling notion that luck is the ally of talent, and perfect is the enemy of good. And to remain ever grateful."

"WHILE I MIGHT HAVE MY SUPPOSEDLY EVOLVED NOTION TO WHAT 'SHELF APPEAL' MEANS, I STILL ENCOURAGED AND WELCOMED COMMENT, CRITIQUES FROM THE CLIENT, THE BUYERS, AND EVEN MY SAVVY DAUGHTERS."—Hugh Syme, artist

OPPOSITE, BOTTOM LEFT While it could be stressed that it was fair-weather fans who turned Whitesnake into a multiplatinum act with this self-titled album (EMI, 1987), singer David Coverdale embraces everyone. "I welcome whoever," he said in 2008. "Who am I to turn around and say these are fair-weather friends or not? The circumstance is, they feathered my nest to the point where I'm still living extraordinarily well."

OPPOSITE, BOTTOM RIGHT "The cover was cool and tried to incorporate ideas from the songs, and I liked that," said Kick Axe guitarist Larry Gillstrom of Hugh Syme's cover design for *Welcome to the Club* (Pasha, 1985). "We weren't sure of exactly what it represented. If you didn't know the band and looked at it, what kind of music would you think the band played? But it was well done."

TOP LEFT This seemingly benign image of a bizarre-looking machine had a more lascivious connotation in its uncensored form (see page 87). In this toned-down variation of Hurricane's *Slave to the Thrill* (Enigma, 1990), John Scarpati's photograph offers a sci-fi vibe that seems a bit incongruous with the title of the album. Yet it is still somewhat eye-catching in its cryptic placement.

BOTTOM LEFT "We sent the album out with the girl completely out of the water [see page 87], and after the first run they were pulled," said Great White keyboardist-guitarist Michael Lardie of the cover for *Hooked* (Capitol, 1991). "They had thought forward enough to take a picture of her immersed in the water, so it was easy to switch over to that. Retail was more conservative, as there was a shift in the moral climate at that point."

ABOVE RIGHT Photographer Nels Israelson's cover image for Def Leppard's *Retro Active* (Bludgeon Riffola, 1993) could be considered *vanitas* art, as the image of a beautiful woman seated before her mirror transforms, when viewed from a wider perspective, into the image of a skull. Although this is a more morbid album cover than one might expect from the usually upbeat Def Leppard, it fit the shift in mainstream rock and metal toward darker sounds at the time.

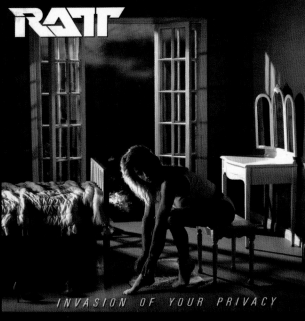

ABOVE LEFT This Ratt concert poster by Dean Tomasek combines a group shot with a hot babe riding a missile, a not-so-subtle sexual metaphor that was highly apropos for the late '80s. A year later, the band's video for "Shame Shame Shame" would feature a beautiful blonde in a small WWII fighter plane engaged in a dogfight with the Ratt boys in a WWII bomber.

TOP RIGHT The cover of Ratt's second album *Invasion of Your Privacy* (Atlantic, 1985) spotlighted Playboy cover model and Playmate of the Year Marianne Gravatte, who also appeared in the band's video for the album's first single, "Lay It Down." "Ratt had cool stuff," recalled Dokken bassist Jeff Pilson. "They made good videos and knew how to market themselves quite well."

BOTTOM RIGHT The concept for the uncensored version of the infamous Neil Zlozower cover for Poison's mega-selling *Open Up and Say . . . Ahh!* (Capitol, 1988) came from the band. "That wasn't Photoshopped, as there wasn't any Photoshop back then," said Zlozower. "They brought in a chick to do special effects, and she brought that tongue, which was supposedly really uncomfortable to keep in the model's mouth. It took a long

time to do the makeup." The background was originally painted fluorescent "Poison green," but the cover photo was tweaked by the art direction team to have a different color scheme and to give Bambi (the model) glowing green eyes.

"LET'S FACE IT: AS MUCH FUN AS WE WANT TO MAKE OF IT, THERE WAS A LOT OF GREAT MUSICIANSHIP AND SINGING AND VERY GOOD SONGWRITING THAT WAS GOING ON. DID THINGS GET SILLY? YEAH. DID THINGS GET GENERIC AND PREFAB? ABSOLUTELY. BUT THERE WAS A LOT OF GOOD MUSIC THAT CAME OUT OF THAT, AND YOU CAN'T THROW AWAY A WHOLE GENRE. A LOT OF IT STANDS THE TEST OF TIME."—Jeff Pilson, Foreigner bassist

TOP LEFT A group shot in makeup was the plan for Twisted Sister's *Stay Hungry* (Atlantic, 1984), but as front man Dee Snider recalled, in each of those shots, "there was a light bulb hanging down in front of the band members' faces when they were standing up. So we couldn't use the pictures." As fate would have it, the last shots taken by Mark Weiss during the day-long shoot were of Dee fooling around with a large bone that had been left unrefrigerated for a week. "That

BOTTOM LEFT For Twisted Sister's *Come Out and Play* (Atlantic, 1985), art director-photographer Mark Weiss used a specially constructed manhole, in a street set in which Dee Snider emerged from below. The cover image was an overhead shot featuring the singer's hands creeping out from under the manhole. The nice twist for the original vinyl version was that the manhole popped up to reveal the snarling front man in all his glam glory.

ABOVE RIGHT The original cover for Twisted Sister's *Under the Blade* (Secret, 1982) features a more aggressive stance from Dee Snider as photographed by Fin Costello, who also shot the cover for KISS's *Alive!* "The front cover shot was taken in my London studio in Islington and the back cover shot in the local Chapel Street market afterwards in July 1982," said Costello. "When they arrived at the studio,

Dee insisted that neither my crew nor myself were allowed to see them until they were fully made up and dressed. He was looking for a 'shock effect,' and he got it."

"MUSICIANS CHOOSE ME FOR MY PHOTOGRAPHIC STYLE. WHAT DATES THE IMAGES AND DEFINES THE MUSICIANS' CHRONOLOGICAL GENRE ARE THE WARDROBE, HAIR, AND MAKEUP. I STILL SHOOT MY CURRENT MUSIC PROJECTS WITH MUCH OF THE SAME PERSONAL VISION, WHEREAS IN MOST OF MY PURE ADVERTISING ASSIGNMENTS THERE ARE VERY SPECIFIC STANDARDS REQUESTED ON HOW I SHOOT EACH SPECIFIC PERSON, PLACE, OR THING."—Jeff Katz, photographer

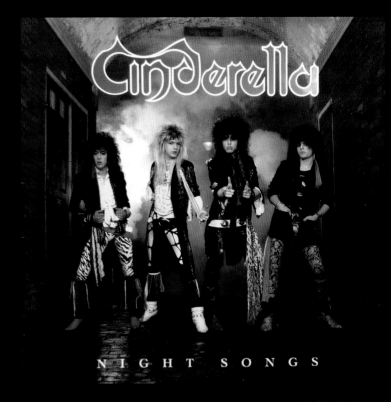

ABOVE LEFT For his tour posters, the artist Scrojo will do "a pencil draft of the image, scan it, then do the 'ink,' color, and layout in Adobe Illustrator," he explained. The original concept for this 2011 Cinderella poster "came from the Debbie Harry album *Koo Koo*, designed by H. R. Giger, with the plan to do a glam version. As I got into designing it, my own personal tastes crept in and things took a darker turn."

TOP RIGHT Then-Polygram A&R executive Derek Shulman recalled that this Mark Weiss–photographed cover for Cinderella's *Night Songs* (Mercury, 1986) was initiated by the band and their management, and he believed at the time that, given MTV's ascension, their image was important. "This may or may not have hurt the band ultimately, because Cinderella was labeled a 'hair band,' and Tom and the band [were and are] *much* more than this," said Shulman. "But the imagery at the time was a quick route to marketing their music."

BOTTOM RIGHT Dave Williams, a good friend of Dokken who created their logo, came onboard for the cover of *Back for the Attack* (Elektra, 1988). "He was very involved with the creation of the eagle or whatever that bird is," noted former Dokken bassist Jeff Pilson. "Frankly, I trusted Dave. He was great. We knew it would be a cool thing, and I still see jackets and shirts with that design on it."

BON JOVI

The original cover to one of the biggest rock albums of the '80s, Bon Jovi's *Slippery When Wet* (Mercury, 1986), was pulled at the last minute. The original concept by Jon Bon Jovi and the art department was meant to be "titillating and tantalizing" but came off looking pornographic. However, this original cover graced the Japanese release, as they were too late to pull it there.

"IT WAS FINALLY JON WHO GRABBED A GARBAGE BAG AND SPRAYED IT WITH WATER AND WROTE 'SLIPPERY WHEN WET' ON IT. ALL MARK WEISS HAD TO DO WAS PHOTOGRAPH THIS IMAGE ON THE TABLE, WHICH TOOK ALL OF TWO MINUTES." —Derek Shulman, then-Polygram A&R executive

POSTERS CAN BE DESIGNED EITHER THROUGH THE BAND OR THE VENUE/PROMOTER. IT'S PRETTY DIFFICULT GETTING A CONSENSUS OPINION ON ANYTHING FROM A MULTIMEMBER BAND ON THE ROAD, SO THE MAJORITY OF THE GIG POSTERS I DO ARE THROUGH THE VENUE. TOUR POSTERS WILL HAVE BAND INVOLVEMENT. OCCASIONALLY THERE WILL BE SPECIFIC REQUIREMENTS IN A BAND'S RIDER CONCERNING POSTER/PROMOTIONAL DESIGN. THESE ARE USUALLY ALONG THE LINES OF WHAT NOT TO USE—LITERAL TRANSLATION OR PARODY OF BAND NAME, MENTION OF A CELEBRITY MEMBER OR RELATION TO CELEBRITY, REFERENCE TO SOME SCANDAL INVOLVING A BAND MEMBER—MORE THAN ANY ART DIRECTION ON WHAT TO DESIGN."—Scrojo, artist

GUNS N' ROSES USE YOUR ILLUSION II

TOP LEFT Painter and composer Mark Kostabi —whose influences include Caravaggio, Hopper, and Picasso—brought his surrealist touches to this Guns N' Roses cover. Instead of going gritty, the controversial LA band chose two covers (the same image with different color schemes), to differentiate between the two *Use Your Illusion* releases (Geffen, 1992), which offered a more classical feeling. It was a wise move, as they certainly stood out at retail stores.

BOTTOM LEFT Though the title and Ioannis' edgy cover art indicate that Extreme's *Extreme II: Pornograffitti* (A&M, 1990) was a hard-rocking album, not everyone got the message. "Extreme was a band that got tagged by their hit [ballad] 'More Than Words,'" explained rock journalist Gail Flug. "I remember many times people would buy the record thinking that the whole album would sound like that song, then take it home and discover that the rest of the record didn't."

TOP RIGHT *Permanent Vacation* (Geffen, 1987), Aerosmith's most successful release in a decade, featured a striking cover illustration by Andy Engel, blending Vegas, Hawaii, and rock imagery into a lively red and black milieu, with the band's logo boldly popping out in yellow. The tone may be upbeat, but the insects, snakes, and knife add an element of danger.

BOTTOM RIGHT LA band Love/Hate imbued the party-hearty Sunset Strip aesthetic with a more aggressive approach, and Skippo Von Rauschenburg's trippy cover design for *Blackout in the Red Room* (CBS, 1990), which looks like it would fit comfortably within the grunge arena, reflects the group's deviation from their peers.

"SOME FANS WANT THAT SAME THING OVER AND OVER AGAIN. I GET COMPLAINING E-MAILS FROM YOUNG LADIES THAT I DON'T HAVE LONG HAIR ANYMORE. I'VE SAID THAT I'M NOT GOING TO HAVE THE SAME HAIRSTYLE FOR MORE THAN TEN YEARS. I'M NOT GOING TO WEAR THE SAME SHOES FOR MORE THAN TWO. THAT'S THE WAY THAT THE WORLD GOES. I DON'T DRESS THE SAME AS I DID FIVE OR TEN OR FIFTEEN YEARS AGO. IT'S EVOLUTION. THAT DOESN'T MEAN HOW I WAS DRESSED WAS WRONG. IT'S FUNNY."—Billy Sheehan, Mr. Big bassist

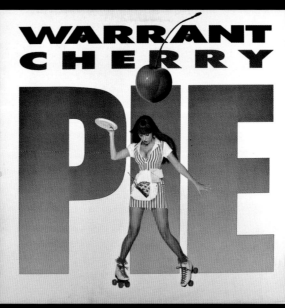

TOP LEFT "The art department came up with an idea of a girl in provocative high heels pushing down a dynamite plunger," revealed Mr. Big bassist Billy Sheehan of their sophomore album *Lean Into It* (Atlantic, 1991). "We all went out to dinner with the label and thought it was horrible, clichéd, and rotten. On the wall was this famous photo of a train crashing through a station in France. I said that would be a better cover, and sure enough, they listened."

BOTTOM LEFT The intense image for Skid Row's hard 'n' heavy sophomore album *Slave to the Grind* (Atlantic, 1991) comes from a sixteen-foot mural painted by Sebastian Bach's late father David Bierk, whose art also appeared in Skid Row's *Subhuman Race* and Bach's *Angel Down* and *Bring 'Em Bach Alive!* Bach's father had works commissioned by a diverse range of clients, from the US State Department to the Canada Post Corporation.

TOP MIDDLE Painter Mark Ryden is considered to be a part of the pop surrealism movement. Warrant's *Dirty Rotten Filthy Stinking Rich* (Columbia, 1989) was his first album cover; it depicted a corporate sociopath named Fugazi (which was Vietnam-era military slang for "fucked up") adorned with and smoking money. There's an irony in depicting a rich fat cat as devilish when Warrant wanted to be filthy stinking rich themselves.

BOTTOM MIDDLE It was hard to miss the Hugh Syme–designed cover for Warrant's *Cherry Pie* (CBS, 1990) back in the day. That and the racy video starring model Bobbie Brown raised charges of sexism, and the controversy probably fueled sales. "If you say iconic, I totally agree," quipped Steel Panther drummer Stix Zadinia. "That's just a bitchin' look. You know what record it is. The printing doesn't even have to be on it, just the visual."

ABOVE RIGHT Scrojo's inspiration for this raunchy, nipple-baring Warrant poster from 2011 was the PMRC, the group of US senators' wives that wanted to ban certain albums. "The date and venue info is made to look like the old PMRC warning sticker," explained Scrojo. "Warrant added a little 'fuck you' to Tipper Gore, head of the PMRC, on the *Cherry Pie* album, so I was just following the lead of inappropriate material."

L.A. GUNS

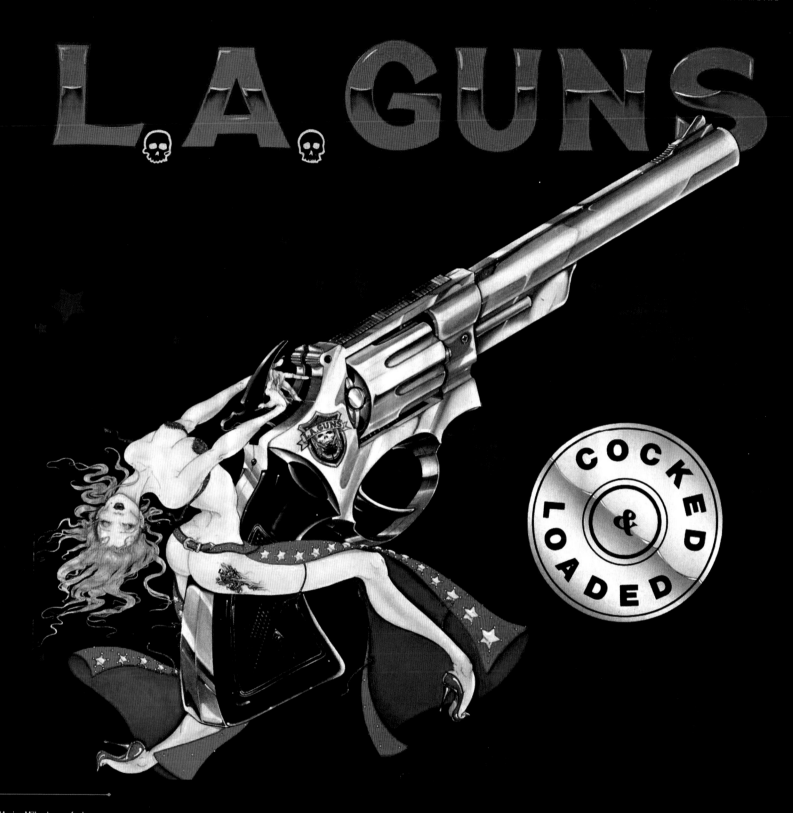

COCKED & LOADED

ABOVE Artist Maxine Miller, known for her ancient Celtic and Wiccan-inspired paintings, statues, jewelry, and other items, has also done some rock 'n' roll work over the years, including illustrating the second L.A. Guns album, *Cocked & Loaded* (Vertigo, 1989). The highly provocative image of a scantily clad, sexually charged woman riding and cocking a gigantic pistol just screams sex. It epitomized the thoroughly decadent vibe of its day.

"FOR ME IT'S ALWAYS BEEN ABOUT THE IDEA AND CAPTURING THE ESSENCE OF THE IMAGE WITH PHOTOGRAPHY. THAT HASN'T CHANGED SINCE MY ART SCHOOL DAYS, WHEN I STARTED DOWN THIS PATH AND WAS GETTING MY FIRST ALBUM COVER GIGS. NOW THE TECHNOLOGY MAKES THE PROCESS OF SEAMING THE ELEMENTS TOGETHER MUCH FASTER. THE OTHER MAIN CHANGE IN RECENT YEARS IS THAT I USE MORE CGI MODELS VERSUS PRACTICAL MODELS."—Glen Wexler, photographer-art director

Larger Than Life

Big hair ruled the pop and rock music scene of the '80s, from the glossy world of dance music to the raucous realm of glam metal. It especially became a huge selling point for the post-Bon Jovi wave of pop metal acts that capitalized on the demand for weepy ballads, sex appeal, and poofy manes. But other elements also came into play throughout the decade of decadence, when image was king and concert T-shirts and posters helped build the mystique of the rock god.

Concert T-shirts in particular were an extension of the larger-than-life artwork that adorned albums and, by the mid-'80s, the videos, which had to be tamed to receive daytime MTV airplay. Merchandising also allowed groups to get a little wilder without record label scrutiny. "Labels didn't really have input on the merchandise," recalled bassist Rudy Sarzo. "If you had a proper record deal—not a 360 deal, which is the standard of the industry nowadays—the only input that they would have is if you had a record deal where the album cover could not be reproduced on merchandising. Basically, they owned the artwork or the album cover, so you had to get creative."

Some provocative shirts from the first half of the decade included a head-banging man gushing blood (Quiet Riot); a giant rodent attacking an arena (Ratt); the angry, big-maned Allister Fiend brandishing a gun (Mötley Crüe); and band members' animated, severed heads impaled on stakes (W.A.S.P.). By the latter half of the decade, things got more sexed up, such as with Paul Stanley flanked by two nude women (KISS); and scantily clad women (or often just their lower halves) emerging on shirts by Mötley Crüe, Bon Jovi, AC/DC, Ratt, Poison, and others. Profanity crept into a few designs, and outlaw imagery became popular. A few lighter bands, like Poison, Bon Jovi, and Cinderella, brought in some skull or skeleton imagery; these seemed more appropriate for bands like Guns N' Roses, who used it to greater effect.

"You couldn't go wrong with skulls, cigarettes, sex, and curse words in terms of the '80s," quipped Patrick Klima, owner of the WyCo Vintage e-Bay store. "People eat that stuff up. They love it."

He also noted a comic book slant with some T-shirts, including "a bad ass" Def Leppard item titled *Women of Doom*, with a *Silver Surfer*-inspired illustration. "Bon Jovi did the same thing. He had the *Captain Kid* shirts, and Anthrax had [British character] *Judge Dredd*. Towards the end of the decade, a lot of bands made shirts with comic book themes."

Many American headbangers who loved classic metal disdainfully called the pop wave the "glam fags," perhaps inspiring grittier T-shirt images from a few of those bands to appeal more to their male demographic. While many thrash acts explored serious issues like politics, war, and social disharmony, the pop acts mainly focused on hedonism, with a socially conscious song occasionally tossed in for good measure. From a mainstream and sales perspective, however, glam was king. Band shots showcasing their large manes and tight leather and spandex attire were common, because appealing to the female portion of the audience was important. Studio and concert posters exploited such imagery, often in a montage of photos meant to be plastered across bedroom walls.

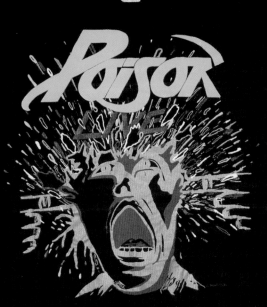

PLAY IT LOUD, MUTHA!

WyCo Vintage owner Patrick Klima offers his thoughts on vintage '80s concert T-shirts.

OPPOSITE, BOTTOM LEFT Van Halen 1984 world tour shirt. "This shirt is by far one of the most iconic '80s metal tees. The artwork is amazing, and it really stands out compared to some of the more elaborate artwork that bands were using at the time. No cheese, all meat."

OPPOSITE, BOTTOM MIDDLE KISS fantasy shirt. "This was one of the first KISS shirts to have an image other than just the word KISS or the band themselves. Mid- to late-'80s, KISS imagery leaned on the 'sex sells' school of economics. There were several shirts from the Crazy Nights Tour that were over the top. The 'Life Is Like Sex' shirt, along with the women's legs shirt, equal hot in the shade!"

OPPOSITE, BOTTOM RIGHT Whitesnake *Slide It In.* "This shirt has a lot of variants because of the graphic nature. I have seen bootlegs go all out on the imagery with *Slide It In.* The best official tour shirt in my opinion has Whitesnake with the woman's body inside. There were other versions printed without the woman inside, and that really takes away from the shirt. The best shirts include women—imagine that."

BOTTOM LEFT Poison Live. "Not a lot of shirts dropped F-Bombs, but this one did it loud and proud. In later versions [such as the one pictured here], the obscenity was removed, so it instantly became a sought-after item. The actual artwork leaves more to be desired, but because it says BLOW YOUR FUCKIN' MIND, it helps pull it altogether."

BOTTOM MIDDLE Twisted Sister—Play It Loud, Mutha! "Quite possibly the most obnoxious graphic ever to be printed on a shirt. Dee's giant life-size mug is extremely bright and really catches your attention. The front is so mild in comparison. This is one of my favorite shirts, and unfortunately I have yet to find one in my size."

"BEING A GIRL, ONE THING MOST WOMEN LOVE IS TO DRESS UP. I NEVER REALLY DID WHEN I WAS A LITTLE GIRL, BUT WHEN I GOT OLDER AND GOT A FEW DOLLARS IN MY POCKET AND WAS ABLE TO GO OUT AND WEAR OUTRAGEOUS CLOTHING AND GET AWAY WITH IT, IT WAS SOMETHING THAT I LOVED. I LOVED TO GO SHOPPING, SPEND $2,000 ON A LEATHER JACKET, BRING IT HOME AND HAVE IT TAILORED [TO ME] OR HAVE SOMEBODY PAINT OR WRITE SOMETHING ACROSS THE BACK OF IT. AND SAY, 'THIS FUCKING THING IS GOING TO LAST UNTIL THE DAY I DIE.'"—Lita Ford, solo vocalist-guitarist

LEFT "The [Great White] record *Once Bitten* . . . (Capitol, 1987) had a picture of a young ingénue with a shark-tooth necklace," said keyboardist-guitarist Michael Lardie. "Moving into . . . *Twice Shy* (Capitol, 1989), it was the original ingénue grown up wearing a diamond anklet. The new ingénue coming up is now wearing the shark piece." A shark fin slices through the dividing line between innocence and experience.

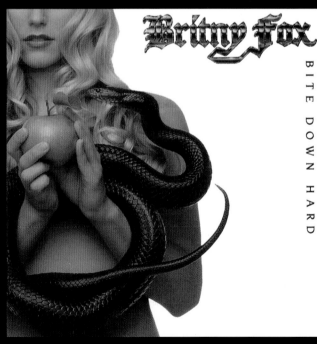

TOP LEFT Photographer John Scarpati shot Great White's *Hooked* (Capitol, 1991) in just twelve frames using a reflecting pool. Metal sculptor Fred Sutherland created the giant hook, and a bicycle seat was added for the model. As the record label did not want her nude, the model was draped with kelp, but evidently not enough of it, so for the second pressing she was partially submerged in the water (see page 75). The first pressing of 180,000 copies still made it to retail stores,

BOTTOM LEFT Art director-photographer Glen Wexler said that Slaughter's manager was dubious about his cover concept for *Stick It to Ya* (Chrysalis, 1990), but "when I asked the model [Playboy Playmate Laurie Carr] to arch her back, his eyes lit up when he saw the 'magic' happen. Her expression and body language fell perfectly into place." Behind the target wheel, the carnival set was suspended in perspective in front of

a painted cloud backdrop. "I shot about forty sheets of film with a 4x5 view camera. The following day I set up the foreground miniature with miniature debris and newspaper. I then double-exposed the two sheets of film in my darkroom onto 8x10 film. That was sent out for a bit of beauty retouching to finish the image."

TOP RIGHT The uncensored version of Hurricane's *Slave to the Thrill* (Enigma, 1990), shot by John Scarpati, includes a restrained woman who looks like she is about to have sex with this bizarre mechanical contraption. It's a torturous concept that could have come from the mind of H. R. Giger. Though the uncensored cover was reportedly unavailable for years, it was reissued on CD in 2008.

BOTTOM RIGHT While the first couple of Britny Fox album covers amped up either male glam sex appeal or exaggerated violence, the third one, *Bite Down Hard* (EastWest, 1991), was surprisingly sensual. The evocation of Eve and the fall of man, photographed by John Scarpati, certainly delivers the appropriate "loss of innocence" connotation that was common in many '80s hair metal sex anthems.

'THAT WAS THE QUANDARY—THE LABELS WANTED HITS. I LIKED HITS, BUT ON THE OTHER HAND I REALLY LIKED METAL. THE BANDS THAT REALLY KNEW THAT THEY WANTED TO BE COOLER, DARKER, DEEPER, AND MORE METAL STUCK TO THEIR GUNS AND WON. BUT THE ONES THAT TEETERED ON THE EDGE WERE MORE OF A METAL BAND THAT WAS CONVINCED TO GO OVER TO THE OTHER SIDE, IF THEY DIDN'T REALLY HIT ONE OUT OF THE PARK AND FAILED." —Tony Harnell, solo artist, ex-TNT front man

TOP LEFT Artist Mark Wilkinson had eight days to design and create this cover for the Darkness' *One Way Ticket to Hell . . . and Back* (Atlantic, 2005). "The brief was to design this runaway train hurtling down the tracks from heaven through a traditional English countryside and end up in Hell!" said Wilkinson. Front man Justin Hāwkins supplied him with a rough conceptual sketch plus newspaper pics of the "face of Satan" seen in tabloid photos of the Twin Towers explosions on 9/11. "I did the basic drawing of the train and colored that in digitally. The rest was a mixture of photos and digital FX."

BOTTOM LEFT The biggest all-female hard rock band of the '80s, Vixen made a splash with their self-titled debut (EMI/Manhattan, 1988), which included the Richard Marx-penned single "Edge of a Broken Heart." The group lasted for two albums; they re-formed in the mid-'90s and have toured on and off in different configurations since. This cover features standard metal imagery, specifically a leather-clad rider on a motorcycle, but the boot heel indicates that this is a female band.

ABOVE RIGHT "I was taught that a poster's main aim is to attract the *potential* fan," said Scrojo, the artist who created this lounge-inspired tour poster in 2008, connected to Bret Michaels' *Rock of Love* reality show. "'Band X' with the date and venue in Helvetica will attract all the hardcore fans, but if you want to keep a venue open you've got to have something that catches the eye of those that don't religiously follow. Because of that, I have a bit of leeway with the imagery, and sometimes I abuse the fuck out of that wiggle room."

ABOVE "Somebody had the idea of naked chicks bodypainted as different sports balls," recalled Steel Panther drummer Stix Zadinia of the conception of the cover for *Balls Out* (Universal Republic, 2011). "But that's kind of Huey Lewis and the News. I think this was my idea—what if there was a hot chick standing there holding these steel balls right between her legs? We scheduled the photo shoot, got the model, and proceeded to

"I'M NOT AN ART DIRECTOR, I'M A PHOTOGRAPHER. MY JOB IS TO GIVE THE ART DIRECTOR THE BEST PHOTOS TO WORK WITH. NOW, IF HE WANTS TO CHANGE THE BACKGROUND OR NEEDS TO CUT THE HEAD FROM ONE GUY'S SHOULDER AND PUT IT ON ANOTHER, THAT'S UP TO HIM. I JUST TRY TO MAKE HIS LIFE EASIER AND START WITH THE BEST IMAGE POSSIBLE."—Neil Zlozower, photographer

CHAPTER 4

DOOM & STONER METAL

"DOOM AND STONER ROCK HAVE CO-OPTED A CONSIDERABLE AMOUNT OF VISUAL IDEAS FROM THE TAIL END OF THE PSYCHEDELIC ROCK MOVEMENT, PARTICULARLY ELEMENTS INSPIRED BY RECREATIONAL DRUG USE AND THE EMERGENT DARK SIDE OF THE HIPPIE MOVEMENT. THROW IN THE MISCHIEVOUS INPUT OF CARTOONISTS LIKE ROBERT CRUMB AND GILBERT SHELTON, THE HALLUCINATORY FLIGHTS OF FANCY CREATED BY PROG ROCK ARTIST EXTRAORDINAIRE ROGER DEAN, AND THE UNAVOIDABLE LEGACIES OF SUBVERSIVE LEGENDS LIKE WILLIAM BLAKE AND SALVADOR DALI, AND YOU WILL END UP WITH A POTENT AND VERSATILE BREW OF EYE-POPPING IDEAS."

—Dom Lawson

STONED, DOOMED & DESERTED:

Squinting Through Metal's Twitching Third Eye

DOM LAWSON

As with every one of the countless mutant strains of heavy metal that have made the scene such a vibrant and diverse musical spectacle over the past four decades, the sound of stoner rock and doom—and, indeed, its attendant imagery—can be traced directly back to the opening notes of Black Sabbath's self-titled theme song: the opening track from their legendary 1970 debut album. But unlike the vast majority of other post-Sabbath substrains, the doom metal phenomenon adheres rigidly to an atavistic and timeless code that is wholly indebted to the menacing distorted riffs and otherworldly allure propagated by Tony Iommi and his pioneering comrades. Like all metal music, these are subgenres driven by a never-ending quest for the perfect riff, but rather than embracing evolution and allowing other influences to infiltrate that original idea, both doom and stoner rock belong spiritually to the early '70s and seldom make any attempt to deviate from an ethos of riffs, riffs, and more riffs. The same can also be said of the artwork and lyrical preoccupations that give this resolutely underground movement its aesthetic focus. Look back to that iconic Black Sabbath album cover, and the essential ingredients found in nearly all subsequent doom art can be seen: a hint of the supernatural, a big dose of religious iconography, and an overwhelming sense of time being halted in its tracks as the specter of death casts its terrifying shadow over everyone and everything.

In musical terms, of course, Black Sabbath was by no means the only band to play a significant role in the birth, growth, and ageless power of doom. In broad terms, rock giants such as Led Zeppelin, Deep Purple, and Uriah Heep are all often cited as influences, particularly by those contemporary bands who go to great lengths to recapture the analogue warmth and technology-shunning grit of the proto-metal era. More obscure bands—

> **"LOOK BACK TO THAT ICONIC BLACK SABBATH ALBUM COVER, AND THE ESSENTIAL INGREDIENTS FOUND IN NEARLY ALL SUBSEQUENT DOOM ART CAN BE SEEN: A HINT OF THE SUPERNATURAL, A BIG DOSE OF RELIGIOUS ICONOGRAPHY, AND AN OVERWHELMING SENSE OF TIME BEING HALTED IN ITS TRACKS AS THE SPECTER OF DEATH CASTS ITS TERRIFYING SHADOW OVER EVERYONE AND EVERYTHING."**—Dom Lawson

like Sir Lord Baltimore, Leafhound, Atomic Rooster, Captain Beyond, and, most notably, Bobby Liebling's Pentagram—are all regarded as primary sources for the doom generation, and although few of them can be said to have contributed as much as Sabbath to the artistic traditions running in parallel with their musical counterparts, all are essential to the same legacy. In truth, the visual obsessions that have been sustained over four decades owe plenty to nonmusical realms too. Appropriately enough—given that Black Sabbath named themselves after a low-budget horror movie—imagery widely used by cinema's macabre contingent has had a huge impact, including everything from the melodramatic schlock portraits beloved of the notorious Hammer franchise and directors like Lucio Fulci and George A. Romero down to the corrupted psychedelic fonts that adorned many promotional movie posters of the late '60s and early '70s. It is also undeniably true that doom and stoner rock have co-opted a considerable amount of visual ideas from the tail end of the psychedelic rock movement, particularly elements inspired by recreational drug use and the emergent dark side of the hippie movement that obliterated notions of a peaceful revolution during the Vietnam War and beyond. Throw in the mischievous input of cartoonists like Robert Crumb and Gilbert Shelton (creator of the *Fabulous Furry Freak Brothers*, surely the ultimate stoner rock icons), the hallucinatory flights of

fancy created by prog rock artist extraordinaire Roger Dean, and the unavoidable legacies of such subversive legends as William Blake and Salvador Dali, and you end up with a potent and versatile brew of eye-popping ideas that has been employed and exploited in all manner of wild and wonderful ways by bands in thrall to that original Sabbath blueprint.

Although purists may argue that doom came to life when Tony Iommi struck those all-conquering initial foreboding notes, it was the wave of bands that appeared at the end of the '70s and the beginning of the '80s that truly define doom metal as it is widely recognized today. Albums by Witchfinder General, the "white metal" riff lords Trouble's *Psalm 9* and fuzzed-up nihilists Saint Vitus' self-titled debut (both released in 1984) and *Epicus Doomicus Metallicus* (1986), the debut album by Swedish sons of Sabbath Candlemass clearly paved the way for the proliferation of like-minded acts in the years that followed. All three of those albums bore cover art that has been endlessly imitated and saluted by admiring acolytes of the bands' genre-defining music: artist Gary Docken's sinister and bleak *Psalm 9* cover is the only one of the three to exhibit any color whatsoever, but its depiction of a dead tree and a ghostly skull lurking amid the lifeless debris below offers nothing in the way of hope. The *Epicus Doomicus Metallicus* sleeve also makes no bones (pun intended!) about its subject matter:

doom metal is almost exclusively concerned with mortality and the futility of human existence, and that monochrome image of a skull and Christian cross locked in macabre harmony remains one of the genre's most unforgettable and iconic images as a result.

But the Candlemass cover art is significant on another level too: at this stage in the evolution of heavy metal, the bands playing this kind of slow, crushingly heavy and relentlessly despairing music were as far removed from mainstream notions of metal as it was possible to be. This was—and still is—ferociously and proudly underground music, and in many ways doom was more closely related to the DIY ethics and primitive aesthetic of the hardcore and punk scenes than it was to anything that Judas Priest or Iron Maiden were doing at the same time. Of course, the lines are blurred between doom and hardcore anyway: US punk legend Black Flag's 1985 masterpiece *In My Head* was a doom album by any other name, and its homemade cut 'n' glue artwork had a profound effect on the inelegant and deeply hostile substrain of doom that burst into hideous life toward the end of the '80s. Bands like Grief, Eyehategod, and Buzzov•en were using the same musical tools as their more traditional forebears, but sludge metal—as it is usually known—was a far grubbier and more vicious beast; the bands' slow and heavy riffs colliding with anguished howls and screams and a remorseless fascination with the grimmest and most squalid aspects of drug culture, as showcased on albums like Eyehategod's *In the Name of Suffering* (1992) and *Take as Needed for Pain* (1993).

Perhaps the key defining characteristic of the art that accompanied the marginally more high-profile explosion of doom metal and stoner rock bands during the '90s—instigated primarily by Cathedral in the United Kingdom and Kyuss in the United States—was that while many other metal subgenres were embracing technology and the ability to create futuristic imagery,

"BANDS WERE EITHER ALIGNING THEMSELVES WITH THOSE EVER-REVERED ARCANE IMAGES THAT SPROUTED FROM SABBATHIAN ROOTS . . . OR THEY WERE FIRING UP THEIR BONGS AND EMBRACING A MUCH MORE COLORFUL AND EVEN LIGHT-HEARTED APPROACH THAT CELEBRATED MIND-EXPANDING STIMULANTS, SURREALIST SCI-FI, AND THE HAZY ALLURE OF MUSCLE CARS DRIVEN AT DANGEROUS SPEEDS THROUGH ENDLESS DESERTS." —Dom Lawson

this scene remained firmly entrenched in notions of painting, collage, and cartoons. Cathedral's album covers certainly stood apart: their loyal artist Dave Patchett's insanely inventive and colorful psycho-delic nightmare visions are far too idiosyncratic to be effectively imitated by anyone else. But elsewhere, bands were either aligning themselves with those ever-revered arcane images that sprouted from Sabbathian roots—for details, see the permanently despondent Electric Wizard and their fondness for low-budget horror, satanic rituals, and blank-eyed urban disquiet!—or they were firing up their bongs and embracing a much more colorful and even light-hearted approach that celebrated mind-expanding stimulants, surrealist sci-fi, and the hazy allure of muscle cars driven at dangerous speeds through endless deserts. Many of the bands on British imprint Rise Above Records released albums during the '90s that boasted vibrant colors and cartoon imagery that perfectly suited the red-eyed exuberance of the music itself, as did several acts signed to the California label Man's Ruin. These included the Hellacopters, Zeke, the Melvins, Alabama Thunderpussy, and Josh Homme's Desert Sessions project—which was owned and founded by godlike poster artist and designer Frank Kozik. All of this art gave much of the global stoner rock scene its distinct aesthetic flavor. The gloriously myopic and unpretentious Fu Manchu, on the other hand, preferred

brightly hued photos of cars to represent their numerous songs about flooring the accelerator and tearing up the asphalt. Whether being endearingly matter-of-fact about their reasons for getting up in the morning—see Bongzilla's self-explanatory *Amerijuanican* (2005)—or simply surrendering to unabashed weirdness— such as the grotesque eccentricity of Clutch's *Blast Tyrant* (2004)—the wired and wild world of stoner rock stubbornly refused to buy a copy of Photoshop; a reflection, it seems fair to say, of its participants' similarly retrogressive approach to making music. As much as the scene has diversified over the years, expanding to incorporate everything from the commercially potent slacker rock of Queens of the Stone Age to the devastating avant-garde drones of Sunn O))), its treasured indifference to outside trends and reverence for a noble past have ensured a degree of continuity and coherence that has the additional effect of strengthening a sense of community. Artists like Arik Roper, Stephen O'Malley, and John Baizley all have their own idiosyncratic styles, and all have provided artwork for bands not necessarily connected to the stoner rock or doom scenes. But just as the mighty riff continues to drive this section of the metal world forward, so too the natural talent and organic modus operandi of these creative dynamos continue to reflect heavy music's immortal heart with insouciant panache and lungs full of nature's finest.

"THE PSYCHEDELIC ERA WAS A GREAT TIME FOR ALBUM COVERS. WE HAD BARNEY BUBBLES DOING A LOT OF WORK FOR US, AND HE WAS GREAT AT BRINGING OUR IDEAS TO LIFE. THERE WAS SO MUCH MORE POTENTIAL IN THE DAYS OF VINYL. YOU CAN'T REALLY FIT ALL THOSE IDEAS ONTO A CD COVER, CAN YOU? I'M SURE THAT A LOT OF OUR FANS SPENT HOURS LOOKING AT THE COVERS WHILE IN VARIOUS STATES OF RELAXATION! HA HA HA!"—Dave Brock, Hawkwind guitarist

TOP LEFT In stark contrast to the eerie image on their self-titled debut, Black Sabbath's 1970 follow-up, *Paranoid* (Vertigo), bore artwork that made sense only with chemical assistance. Photographer Marcus Keef's surreal but oddly compelling and iconic portrayal of a sword-wielding warrior fits much better with the album's original title *War Pigs*.

BOTTOM LEFT Much as prescient power trio Sir Lord Baltimore helped to pioneer what would later be known as heavy metal, so artist Doug Taylor's artwork for the Americans' *Kingdom Come* debut (Mercury, 1970) helped to establish the macabre but mesmerizing tone that has since dominated doom metal artwork.

ABOVE RIGHT Artist Rick Breach's artwork for Black Widow's 1970 opus *Sacrifice* (CBS) deserves to be regarded as one of the more ingenious cover designs of the '70s, not least due to its deft blurring of the lines between heavy metal's grim preoccupations and the more colorful instincts of the flourishing prog rock movement.

TOP LEFT Hawkwind's Dave Brock recalls: "We all loved psychedelic art, and Barney Bubbles came up with some great stuff for us. *Space Ritual* [United Artists, 1973] came in a really elaborate sleeve with lots of different pull-outs and panels. It was all part of the trip at the time, wasn't it?"

TOP RIGHT Dave Brock: "*In Search of Space* [United Artists, 1971] is my favorite sleeve from that time. It was very clever, the way Barney Bubbles put it all together. He really understood what we were getting at. It's psychedelic with a difference, I think. He won awards for that cover, I believe!"

BOTTOM LEFT & RIGHT Dave Brock comments on artist Pierre Tubbs' work for Hawkwind: "The *Warrior on the Edge of Time* [United Artists, 1975] sleeve was really strong visually. When you opened it out, it turned into a big penis. Ha ha! With those big gatefold sleeves, if you were stoned you could really see everything in 3-D and get sucked right in."

TOP LEFT Candlemass bassist Leif Edling's doom metal vision was always intensely focused and never more directly expressed than on the band's classic debut album *Epicus Doomicus Metallicus* (Black Dragon, 1986), with its primitive but powerful cover image of a crucifix and human skull in warped harmony. A heavy-handed metaphor, perhaps, but an unforgettable one too.

BOTTOM LEFT As they were one of the first bands to propagate true doom metal, Trouble's artwork could hardly fail to be influential. Their second album, *The Skull* (Metal Blade, 1985), was adorned with artist Gary Docken's unsettling and gently hallucinatory painting, which perfectly matched the supposedly Christian band's riff-driven cautionary tales.

TOP RIGHT Taken from nineteenth-century artist Thomas Cole's series of contemplative paintings *The Voyage of Life*, the art used for Candlemass' second album, *Nightfall* (Axis, 1987), represents old age, a theme very much in keeping with doom metal's obsession with mortality and the inexorable dying of the light.

BOTTOM RIGHT Graveyards and the looming presence of death have long been recurring themes in doom metal, thanks largely to Black Sabbath's iconic debut album, but Witchfinder General controversially added nudity to the grim vista on their *Death Penalty* debut (Heavy Metal, 1982), which starred topless model Joanna Latham.

Day of Reckoning

TOP LEFT Keeping things simple with a stark black background adorned with only their own logo in white, the first Saint Vitus album (SST, 1984) was a focused and purposefully narrow statement of intent from these doom metal pioneers. Note the omnipresent cross within the logo, a perennial quasi-religious icon in doom circles.

BOTTOM LEFT To commemorate Pentagram's final tour with guitarist Victor Griffin in 2012 and the performing of the band's *Relentless* album (Pentagram, 1985) in its revered entirety, Dutch artist Richard Schouten created this pointedly epic and ominous poster that mirrors the US band's mysterious, dramatic, and near-mythical reputation.

TOP RIGHT Brooklyn-based illustrator Dilek Baykara wrings fresh inspiration from the ageless riffing of Saint Vitus with this powerful concert poster, in which wild horses stampede amid a blizzard of sperm-like shooting stars. The hand-drawn simplicity harmonizes perfectly with the band's own primitive approach. Doubtless the gig itself was every bit as tumultuous.

BOTTOM RIGHT As with Saint Vitus' debut album, protometal gods Pentagram understood the power of a simple image. This startling combination of stark logo on black background and classic Baphomet design provided the band's 1993 Collectors Club 7″ single "Relentless"/"Day of Reckoning" with a suitably definitive facade.

"DAVE WYNDORF WANTED THE BULLGOD WITH LONG HORNS AND TUSKS EXTENDED
TO FORM AN X-SHAPE. THE SPINE GOING THROUGH THE BULLGOD'S HEAD IS
THERE TO TIE IN WITH THE ALBUM TITLE. TO GIVE A BULL'S-EYE EFFECT TO THE
COMPOSITION, WE AGREED UPON ADDING THE ZODIAC RING AROUND THE
BULLGOD'S HEAD. INSTEAD OF ACTUAL ZODIAC SYMBOLS, I MADE UP SOME
HIEROGLYPHS THAT REPRESENTED DIFFERENT DRUGS."—Rob Leecock, artist

ABOVE Thanks to the vivid imagery conjured
by their frequently ferocious reinvention of
the space and fuzz rock blueprints, Monster
Magnet's bullgod mascot became something
of an icon during the birth and upward surge
of the first wave of stoner rock. On the cover
of *Spine of God* (Caroline, 1991), artist Rob
Leecock brought front man Dave Wyndorf's
vision brutishly to life.

Lunar Womb

TOP LEFT Building on the psychedelic bravado of the *Spine of God* album cover, artist Rob Leecock embraced more hallucinatory hues and made Monster Magnet's bullgod mascot a more menacing and dominant presence on the painting he created for the cover of *Superjudge* (A&M, 1993): the band's bad trip ethos writ large.

BOTTOM LEFT Pieced together by the band themselves, the collage-style artwork beloved of underground punk and hardcore bands perfectly suited the nihilistic, drug-ravaged gutter metal that Eyehategod sought to define on their second album, *Take as Needed for Pain* (Century Media, 1993). Drugs, death, decay, torment: it's all here.

TOP RIGHT Arguably the most important album in the evolution of stoner rock, Kyuss' *Blues for the Red Sun* (Dali, 1992) did not conform to any of the usual psychedelic clichés or DIY primitivism that later dominated the genre's artistic perspective. Instead, designer Skiles focused on hazy atmosphere, evoking the shimmering, red-hot glare of the desert sun.

BOTTOM RIGHT Continuing a tradition of borrowing from macabre nineteenth-century art that has contributed greatly to doom metal's unearthly aesthetic, The Obsessed's second album, *Lunar Womb* (Hellhound, 1991), featured Spanish artist Francisco de Goya's *Saturn Devouring His Son*, a gruesome depiction of the Greek myth of the Titan Cronus.

FROM OBLIVION TO DESPAIR...
The Amorphous World of Doom & Stoner Metal

Eschewing the aesthetic doom metal status quo in favor of a gloriously surreal and idiosyncratic visual world that has become an essential companion to one of the genre's most significant bands, Dave Patchett's artwork has added a depth of color and conception to an often visually conservative musical realm. The Brighton-based painter has been responsible for some of the most extravagant and adventurous art in heavy metal history.

Despite being the single most important doom metal band of the last two decades—due in no small part to front man and founder Lee Dorrian's stewardship of Rise Above Records—Cathedral have consistently asserted their uniqueness and refusal to rely solely on the same musical or visual elements used by many of their peers. In terms of establishing a distinctive atmosphere, the most powerful weapon in the band's arsenal has long been artist Dave Patchett, whose vivid, disturbing, and wildly surreal paintings have graced the majority of Cathedral releases since their formation in 1989. He became a full-time artist in 1982 and has exhibited his work extensively ever since, forging a relationship with Dorrian and his band along the way.

A stunning tableau comprising a grotesque but compelling array of peculiar beasts and eccentric characters, the cover art for Cathedral's 1990 debut album *Forest of Equilibrium* introduced Patchett's remarkable talents to the metal world. In what could be a macabre reinvention of Lewis Carroll's *Wonderland*, his extraordinary use of color and unerring knack for evoking the atmosphere of a bygone era that exists only in the dark recesses of the doom diehard's imagination contributed hugely to the impact of the British band's music. For *The Ethereal Mirror* (1993) Patchett's conceptual universe expanded much further to include bomb-distributing airborne critters and mutant cherubs in a painting that was far too large to be adequately represented on the small surface area of a CD booklet, thus necessitating the foldout poster art that has since become a regular feature of Cathedral's albums. This was a particularly effective approach for *The Carnival Bizarre* (1995), one of the most powerful Patchett creations and a monumental endeavor that took the artist a full six months to complete.

> "THE CATHEDRAL STUFF IS STUCK IN THE MIDDLE AGES AND IDEAS OF THE APOCALYPSE, AND I DO LIKE TO MOVE AWAY FROM THAT OCCASIONALLY. BUT I DO ENJOY LEE'S IDEAS. WE DO BOTH HATE THE CHURCH, AND WE BOTH THINK THAT IF SOCIETY ISN'T CAREFUL, IT'LL SMASH ITSELF TO PIECES, SO WE THINK ALONG THE SAME LINES."—Dave Patchett, artist

"The main idea behind *The Carnival Bizarre* was that there's a male side and a female side. Lee loves to find contrasts and to synchronize them in a single painting," Patchett explains. "If you look at it in detail, the feminine aspects are all on one side and the male aspects are on the other, and there's Jesus and his mum at the center. It's a really good painting, I think. The main idea from Lee was that he wanted the most detailed picture ever painted, pretty much!"

In a similarly detailed way, the full-size painting for the album *The Garden of Unearthly Delights* (2006) is set in a fantastical but malevolent Eden, in which the Tree of Life hangs heavy with demonic figures surrounding the biblical apple that brought about the fall of humankind.

Not every Cathedral album cover has featured a Patchett painting: *Endtyme* (2001) featured work by Stephen O'Malley. But the close relationship between the artist's disorienting worldview and Lee Dorrian's stridently imaginative lyrical conceits has held fast throughout the band's career, reaching a remarkable high point on their studio album *The Guessing Game* (2010). The sheer level of detail and invention involved in this audacious piece of work takes the breath away, while also demonstrating once again why the cold technicality of computer-generated art will never come close to matching the evocative power of real painting. Patchett's work also belongs to a fine heavy metal tradition of album covers that offer more than a quick fix: these are elaborate and endlessly fascinating works that demand to be pored over at length and leisure, even though Cathedral's somewhat morose philosophy satisfies only one aspect of the artist's own capabilities. Numerous examples of Patchett's work, including several paintings unconnected to his relationship with Cathedral that reveal different layers to his vision, can be viewed at his official website: www.davepatchett.com.

OPPOSITE, BOTTOM LEFT One of several Cathedral album covers that, due to the limitations of CD, presented only one part of Patchett's original painting, *The Ethereal Mirror* (Earache, 1993) provided a tantalizing glimpse into the artist's wildly imaginative visual world, hinting at a breadth of vision that would be explored more fully on later releases.

OPPOSITE, TOP RIGHT As if to mirror Cathedral's unassailable status as both masters of UK doom metal and one of the few bands with a truly unique sound that transcends the genre's standard formulae, Dave Patchett's eccentric, extraordinary, and often thoroughly demented artwork stands proudly apart from the efforts of the acclaimed artist's few comparable peers.

OPPOSITE, BOTTOM RIGHT It is the sheer density of detail in Dave Patchett's work that makes him one of the truly great album cover artists of all time. The cover for Cathedral's 2005 masterwork, *The Garden of Unearthly Delights* (Nuclear Blast), is spiritually connected to the era of vinyl and elaborate gatefold sleeves.

ABOVE Part of Cathedral's charm has always been their shrewd combining of surrealism and fantasy with a fierce intelligence and awareness of human reality. *The Carnival Bizarre* (Earache, 1995) explores the contrast between male and female preoccupations and desires via a bewildering level of detail and subversive complexity.

"MANY BANDS RELEASED ALBUMS DURING THE '90S THAT BOASTED VIBRANT COLORS AND CARTOON IMAGERY THAT PERFECTLY SUITED THE RED-EYED EXUBERANCE OF THE MUSIC ITSELF, AS DID SEVERAL ACTS SIGNED TO CALIFORNIAN LABEL MAN'S RUIN, WHICH WAS OWNED AND FOUNDED BY GODLIKE POSTER ARTIST AND DESIGNER FRANK KOZIK, WHO GAVE MUCH OF THE GLOBAL STONER ROCK SCENE ITS DISTINCT AESTHETIC FLAVOR."—Dom Lawson

TOP LEFT Legendary artist Frank Kozik's subversive approach to album cover art has always made his work stand out, and his willful twisting of superficially innocent images ensured that the cover of Melvins' classic *Houdini* album (Atlantic, 1993), with its two-headed puppy, was as subtly disturbing as the music itself.

BOTTOM LEFT Best known for her work for the X-Files comic book series, New York-based artist Miran Kim's mastery of surrealism and amorphous color schemes is second to none. Back in their doom-death days, Finnish metal crew Amorphis benefited greatly from the warped intensity of her painting on *The Karelian Isthmus* (Relapse, 1992).

ABOVE RIGHT Specializing in graphic design and concert posters and flyers, Israeli-born Emek Golan is also a fine-art painter. You can see the depth of finesse and detail in his work in this poster for sludge gods Melvins' 2007 show in Tel Aviv. A dazzling combination of ancient symbolism and psychedelia.

CATHEDRAL

Statik Majik

TOP LEFT Graphic designer Jennifer Roddie eschewed the usual stoner rock staples to give Clutch a strident visual impact on their self-titled 1995 album (Eastwest). From the band's distinctive logo, rendered in 3-D, to the bleak view of the moon's surface, this

BOTTOM LEFT A far more straightforward and minimalist design compared to most Cathedral sleeve art, the "Statik Majik" EP (Earache, 1994) seemed like a subtle homage to great Hammer Horror films of the '60s and '70s, replete with flames, bones,

ABOVE RIGHT Renowned for his work for numerous doom, stoner, and underground rock acts, Arik Roper came very close to equaling the laudably apposite efforts of Cathedral's loyal associate Dave Patchett on this poster heralding the band's final UK

TOP LEFT Digby Pearson, founder of Earache Records, on Sleep's *Holy Mountain* (Earache, 1993): "This album cover was commissioned by the band themselves. A local artist, Klem, really worked his magic. The Sleep logo wrapped in a pot leaf pretty much came

BOTTOM LEFT Thanks to his extraordinary versatility, Arik Roper has become one of the most sought-after artists in the stoner rock and doom realm. This concert poster for Californian legends Sleep harnesses the dark side of science fiction and filters it

TOP RIGHT Artist Arik Roper states: "This was one of the first record covers I created. The style looks rather primitive compared to my later work. The idea was to represent the Greek myth of Icarus, who flew too close to the sun, which corresponds with a track on

BOTTOM LEFT In contrast to stoner rock's cheery hedonism, the best sludge metal always teetered on the brink of ruinous despair and never more so than on New Orleans' reprobates Buzzov•en's second album, *Sore* (Roadrunner, 1994). Artist Craig Lima's sickening surrealism made for a fittingly grotesque frontispiece to match the album's squalid contents.

TOP RIGHT UK sludge brutes Iron Monkey were well served by notorious artist Mike Diana's twisted artwork for *Our Problem* (Earache, 1998). Diana says, "I did a pencil drawing for the band's approval, but word came back that they were asking 'Where's the giant dick?' "Soon after that I sent them the new dick sketch, and they went nuts for it!"

BOTTOM RIGHT Bassist Eric C. Harrison drew this gleefully repellent cover art—another example of sludge metal's despondent worldview—for his band Grief's second album, *Come to Grief* (Vacuum, 1994). Somewhere between light-hearted comic book illustration and nightmarish surrealism, it neatly encapsulates the Boston crew's misanthropic vision.

KARMA TO BURN

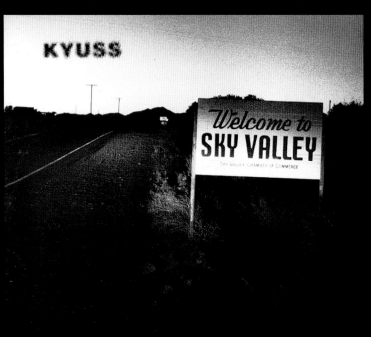

"THE INSPIRATION FOR FU MANCHU'S *IN SEARCH OF . . .* COVER CAME DIRECTLY FROM THE BAND'S LYRICS, ATTITUDE, AND OVERALL WORSHIP OF THE 1970S. AMERICAN HOT RODS, CALIFORNIA LIVIN', HOT CHICKS, AND PSYCHEDELIC HEAD TRIPS OF THE HIGHEST ORDER, KICKING OUT THE INTERSTELLAR JAMS WITH BLISTERING PSYCH MUSCLE RIFFS AND DEVASTATING BONG HITS! THE PHOTOGRAPH MAGICALLY CAME TOGETHER AND REMAINS ONE OF MY FAVORITE ROCK 'N' ROLL IMAGES."

—Alex Obleas, photographer

TOP LEFT Japanese artist Hajime Sorayama is famous for his erotic hand-painted portraits of women and she-robots, but his work for Karma to Burn's explosive second album, *Wild, Wonderful Purgatory* (Roadrunner, 1999), brilliantly taps into the band's sense of urgency and exuberance while poking gentle fun at banal notions of the American Dream.

BOTTOM LEFT "I love driving through the desert, and I think the shot really captures the vibe when the heat goes down and you look at those beautiful sunsets," says photographer Alex Solca. "The guys in Kyuss told me that they wanted something to represent the area where they lived" (*Welcome to Sky Valley*, Elektra, 1994).

ABOVE RIGHT The malevolence and menace of doom metal is almost entirely absent from so-called "desert rock," as demonstrated by bright and colorful photo-based covers like this one from the Atomic Bitchwax. Eschewing the psych-influenced erotica of their first two albums, the band's third full-length album, *3* (Meteor City, 2005), tells a tale of rock 'n' roll and nothing else.

ABOVE "On an October afternoon, way back in 1995, in San Juan Capistrano, California, everything we needed for this photograph fell into place. Even if I'd had nothing to do with it, *In Search of* . . . [Mammoth, 1996] would easily be my favorite Fu Manchu

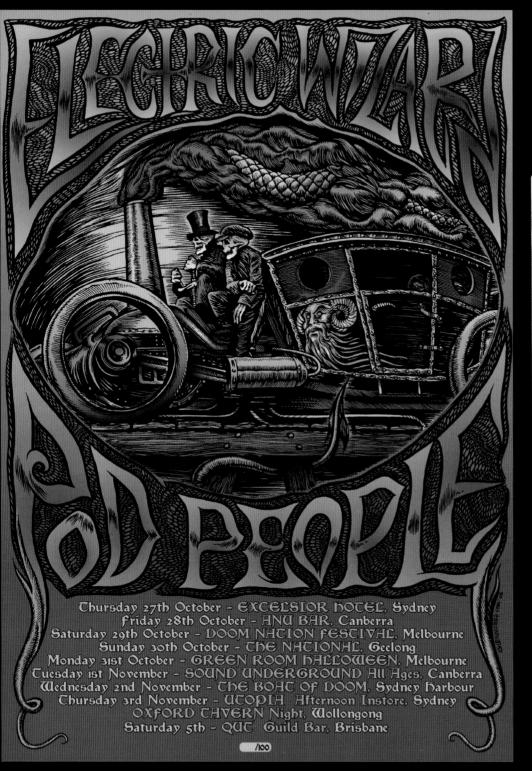

ABOVE LEFT Designed by Australian newcomer Glenn Smith, this poster for Electric Wizard's headlining tour down under suggests that the band should be regarded as a marauding sonic ghost train, hell-bent on dragging everyone screaming into the abyss, and completely unstoppable. Given the Wizard's fearsome live reputation, it's a valid point.

TOP RIGHT Designer Hugh Gilmour says of the artwork for Electric Wizard's *Dopethrone* (Rise Above, 2000): "Jus Oborn did a black-and-white drawing, but the wizards looked a bit too much like Ku Klux Klansmen, so that was shelved! Tom Bagshaw, the brother of bassist Tim, came up with the final cover painting based on Jus's original sketch."

BOTTOM RIGHT Often cited as one of the heaviest albums ever made, Electric Wizard's *Come My Fanatics* (Rise Above, 1997) stood in bold contrast to the boisterous stoner rock scene that was erupting at that time, in both musical and visual terms. A shadowy congregation of indeterminate origin gathers to break bread. And, presumably, to get thoroughly wasted.

SCORPIONICA, SHE IS BORN!

"THE ARTWORK FOR *FREQUENCIES FROM PLANET TEN* WAS DONE BY A FRIEND OF OURS CALLED MARTIN HANFORD, WHO HAD BEEN DOING A LOT OF FLYERS AND PROMO STUFF FOR US. WE WANTED SOMETHING THAT REFLECTED THE BOLD ROCK-MEETS-PSYCHEDELIA VIBE OF THE ALBUM, AND WHAT HE SUPPLIED WAS SPOT ON. IT'S THE PERFECT COMBINATION OF DOOM METAL MEETS SCI-FI AND WAS A BRIGHT, COLORFUL, AND ATTENTION-GRABBING IMAGE FOR A DEBUT ALBUM."

—Ben Ward, Orange Goblin vocalist

TOP LEFT Representing London in the great stoner rock explosion of the mid-'90s, Orange Goblin may have exhibited a more rounded metallic approach to heavy music than most of their heavy-lidded contemporaries, but their debut album, *Frequencies from Planet Ten* (Rise Above, 1997), boasted a cover that exposed the band as surfers of the lysergic slipstream.

BOTTOM LEFT Ben Ward: "We wanted something like the old Tales from the Crypt comics or the *Creepshow* movie poster. All we did was give the artist, Frank Kozik, a theme and the song titles, and he did the rest, delivering the perfect packaging, complete with freaky images and adverts too!" (*Coup de Grace*, Rise Above, 2002).

ABOVE RIGHT Ben Ward: "We commissioned Jimbob Isaac to do this. As well as the main image of the Scorpionica woman, there are nods to our favorite horror movies and bands. Who wouldn't want a poster of a giant scorpion woman with big boobs and zombies wearing Saint Vitus shirts?"

DRUGS, RIFFS & THE ETERNAL QUEST FOR PSYCHEDELIC NIRVANA

With their roots in the Flower Power counterculture of the late '60s and the subsequent reactionary clangor of the protometal bands that emerged from the hippie era's dark denouement, stoner rock and doom metal always had the recreational use of drugs firmly embedded in their sonic and lyrical DNA. Given that Black Sabbath created the fundamental blueprint that continues to provide a stylistic starting point for both genres—and, indeed, for the vast amount of music that exists in the blurred boundary between them and extends into each subgenre's outer limits—the fact that Tony Iommi's heavy metal pioneers frequently touched on the subject has effectively given an entire generation (or two) of bands carte blanche to celebrate bong hits and other hedonistic pursuits with impunity.

One unavoidable truth about stoner rock and doom metal is that both embrace an atavistic mentality, and so the influence of such weed-saluting '70s phenomena as comic strips like the *Fabulous Furry Freak Brothers* and the movies of Cheech and Chong loom large over much of the artwork and lyrics of the genres' most fervently buzz-pursuing protagonists. It is hard to imagine albums like Sleep's *Holy Mountain* (1992) or Monster Magnet's *Spine of God* (1991) existing at all without the allure of the psychedelic experience, and there is a clear correlation between, on the one hand, the often disorientating fuzz and haze of these bands' chosen guitar tones and their penchant for improvisational detours and, on the other, the brain-mangling effects of magic mushrooms, LSD, and, of course, industrial-strength marijuana. Rumor has it that Electric Wizard, clearly the most pot-addled of all modern doom bands, have even manufactured their own hashish, and front man Jus Oborn has always been vocal about his devotion to getting heroically smashed before, during, and after the creative process. Some bands are even more blatant about their enthusiasm for smoking weed—not least sludge crew Bongzilla, whose entire oeuvre is a sustained hymn to the refined art of making bongs bubble. Similarly, unsung stoner rock gems like *Tumuli Shroomaroom* (1997)—from South Wales' finest, Acrimony—simply would not exist without their creators' THC cravings.

There is a dark side to recreational drug consumption, of course; witness both Pentagram founder Bobby Liebling's well-documented struggle with heroin addiction and Eyehategod front man Mike Williams' brief incarceration on a narcotics charge in 2005. The realization that having a smoke with a few friends could be but a few depressed days away from a catastrophic end to the party casts a shadow over the more morose and oppressive end of the stoner and doom catalogs. Ultimately, though, heavy metal in general has an unbreakable bond with all manner of mind-altering substances. Booze plays a significant part, of course, but there is something mundane about the effects of beer, wine, and spirits that fails to connect with stoner rock and doom metal fans with the same remorseless ease that the psychedelic experience does. Heavy metal music need not always be about escapism, but by exploring the otherworldly possibilities of distorted guitars, and by meddling gleefully with notions of time through languorous tempos and seemingly endless freeform jams, these proudly red-eyed takes on that Sabbath blueprint can hardly fail to attract music fans who find the notion of drifting away from this infuriating planet and exploring the inner cosmos of the human mind perennially appealing. Tune in, turn on, spark up a fat one, and bring on the riffs, right?

> "IT IS HARD TO IMAGINE ALBUMS LIKE SLEEP'S *HOLY MOUNTAIN* OR MONSTER MAGNET'S *SPINE OF GOD* EXISTING AT ALL WITHOUT THE ALLURE OF THE PSYCHEDELIC EXPERIENCE, AND THERE IS A CLEAR CORRELATION BETWEEN . . . THE OFTEN DISORIENTATING FUZZ AND HAZE OF THESE BANDS' CHOSEN GUITAR TONES AND PENCHANT FOR IMPROVISATIONAL DETOURS AND . . . THE BRAIN-MANGLING EFFECTS OF MAGIC MUSHROOMS, LSD, AND, OF COURSE, INDUSTRIAL-STRENGTH MARIJUANA . . ."—Dom Lawson

ABOVE Cheech and Chong's weed-obsessed Californian slacker shtick made them a huge hit with hippies, bikers, and other counterculture rebels in the '70s. Stoner rock's prevailing demeanor of benign sociopathy can be traced back to the hapless, pot-befuddled chaos that erupts in *Up in Smoke* et al.

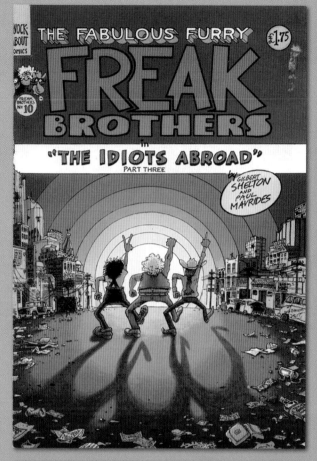

TOP LEFT Stoner rock's penchant for cartoon imagery can surely be attributed to the influence of the *Fabulous Furry Freak Brothers*, Gilbert Shelton's drug-guzzling comic strip heroes. "While you're out there smashing the state," they would proclaim, "don't forget to keep a smile on your lips and a song in your heart!" Stoner rock in excelsis, then.

BOTTOM LEFT South Wales' cosmic doom merchants Acrimony went further into psychedelic orbit than most on their 1997 masterpiece *Tumuli Shroomaroom* (Peaceville), released at the height of stoner rock's first wave during the '90s. Listening to it without some kind of chemical assistance just seems wrong.

ABOVE RIGHT The artist of choice for most avid pot users during the '70s and beyond, Robert Crumb ensured his own immortality in the reddened eyes of stoners everywhere with this iconic *Stoned Agin!* poster, which has since adorned the walls of student residences, squats, and rehearsal rooms around the globe.

"RUMOR HAS IT THAT ELECTRIC WIZARD, CLEARLY THE MOST POT-ADDLED OF ALL MODERN DOOM BANDS, HAVE EVEN MANUFACTURED THEIR OWN HASHISH, AND FRONT MAN JUS OBORN HAS ALWAYS BEEN VOCAL ABOUT HIS DEVOTION TO GETTING HEROICALLY MASHED BOTH BEFORE, DURING, AND AFTER THE CREATIVE PROCESS. SOME BANDS ARE EVEN MORE BLATANT ABOUT THEIR ENTHUSIASM FOR SMOKING WEED—NOT LEAST SLUDGE CREW BONGZILLA, WHOSE ENTIRE OEUVRE IS A SUSTAINED HYMN TO THE REFINED ART OF MAKING BONGS BUBBLE . . ."—Dom Lawson

LEFT Created by the Italian design collective Malleus, the cover image for pot-addled US sludge crew Bongzilla's *Gateway* (Relapse, 2002) amounts to a riotous celebration of the

TOP LEFT Hailing from Nagoya, Japan, you might have expected Eternal Elysium to draw from a more esoteric set of influences than their Western stoner peers, but the cover for their second album *Spiritualized D* (Meteor City, 2000) offers hazy psychedelic abstraction, redolent of many a late-'60s or early-'70s psych rock album sleeve.

BOTTOM LEFT Says artist Arik Roper about *Death Is This Communion* (Relapse, 2007): "I came up with this one entirely on my own and presented it to the High on Fire guys. The art here is meant to convey images of death. It's a postwar scene complete with carnage and carrion, but my intention was also to invoke death in the sense of 'change.'"

ABOVE RIGHT Arik Roper explains the simple thought process behind this monstrous concert poster: "The theme for this poster was SLOW and HEAVY. Hence we see sloths astride tortoises in a swamp. I dare say it doesn't get much slower. Pepper Keenan from Down suggested this idea, and I built on it."

"JOHNNY MORROW IS ONE OF MY FAVORITE LYRICISTS, AND THE TWISTED IMAGERY HE CREATED WAS INTEGRAL TO IRON MONKEY'S DIRT-ENCRUSTED AESTHETIC. I PICKED SOME OF HIS MOST VISUAL LINES IN THEIR ALBUMS AND MASHED THEM TOGETHER. MY OVERALL DRIVE WAS TO CREATE A HOPELESS RAT'S NEST OF SQUALOR AND DEPRIVATION. FETTERED ARMS, BOLTED TO THE FINK DIAL. PIG, PUKE, AND PILLS. FOR JOHNNY. REST IN NOISE." —Jimbob Isaac, artist

MORROWFEST 2012
A DAY TO CELEBRATE THE LIFE OF JOHN PAUL MORROW
NOTTINGHAM ROCK CITY, SUN. MAY 13TH 2012

BREAK IT UP | BLACK FATHOMS | DOOM | DRUNK IN HELL | DRUNKEN BASTARD
ENDLESS GRINNING SKULLS | FUK | GOATSPEED | HARK | JADED EYES | LABRAT
LIFER | ORANGE GOBLIN | RAVENS CREED | I LIKE BUGS | SONTARAN EXPERIMENT
SIGIRIYA | TUSKEN COALITION | WALK THE PLANK | THE X-RAYS

 ALL PROCEEDS GOING TO KIDNEY PATIENT SUPPORT | ILLUSTRATION BY JIMBOBISAAC.COM | POSTERS DONATED BY GIANTIRONFACE.COM

RIGHT The death of former Iron Monkey front man Johnny Morrow in 2002 provoked a huge wave of sadness from the stoner rock, doom, and sludge communities. Morrow was an incredible vocalist, lyricist, and front man and a much-loved figurehead for British brutality. Ten years later, Morrowfest paid tribute to him as noisily and drunkenly as possible.

nu metal

"I THINK FOR THE FIRST TIME IN OUR HISTORY, WE'RE ACTUALLY
OK WITH BEING RECOGNIZED AS A NU METAL BAND."
—Chester Bennington, Linkin Park vocalist

the land of no guitar solos

RAZIQ RAUF

nothing can stay new forever. That was the first major problem with naming the much-vilified genre of "nu metal." Spelling it that way didn't help either. Though its origins can be traced back to the late 1980s via Anthrax's second EP "I'm the Man" (1987) and their 1991 collaboration with the New York hip-hop group Public Enemy on their song "Bring the Noise"—and even to the 1986 duel between Aerosmith and another New York hip-hop group, Run D.M.C.—for the fusion between rap and rock, it is Faith No More's 1990 breakthrough hit "Epic" that is most widely cited as the landmark song in the genre.

Grunge had forced metal to become more "alternative," and Faith No More, along with Red Hot Chili Peppers and Primus, were at the forefront of that bass-heavy scene. Mike Patton's sharp rapping over Jim Martin's chugging metal riffs was the basis of "Epic," the band's only smash hit single, and though the genre was something that many were trying, Faith No More executed it perfectly. The fact that it ended up influencing so many afterward annoyed the front man somewhat.

Those fans he speaks of? They're the ones who would have been Bon Jovi fans had they been born a decade earlier or My Chemical Romance fans a decade later. How did they come to be so exposed to nu metal, though?

One man pinpointed as being behind the proliferation of nu metal is record producer Ross Robinson. Having produced the first two Korn albums, the most successful Sepultura album, *Roots* (1996), and the débuts by Limp Bizkit, Slipknot, and Soulfly by the end of 2000, he was involved in launching the careers of some of the

"NU METAL MAKES MY STOMACH TURN. DON'T BLAME THAT SHIT ON US, BLAME IT ON THEIR MOTHERS! DO YOU THINK I LISTEN TO ANY OF THAT STUFF AT ALL? NO, IT'S FOR THIRTEEN-YEAR-OLD MORONS! BELIEVE ME, WE'LL ALL BE LAUGHING ABOUT NU METAL IN A COUPLE OF YEARS. HECK, I'M ACTUALLY LAUGHING AT IT NOW!"—Mike Patton, Faith No More vocalist, *Metal Hammer*

most prominent bands in the genre and garnered the nickname the "godfather of nu metal." Ross Robinson made this genre what it is. His trademark sound was a lack of guitar solos. The repetitive, down-tuned grunge riffs may be an easy identifier of the genre, but they were far from challenging musically. Easy to replicate at home, this was metal at its base level. Musically, anyway.

Traditional metal artwork didn't really have a place here. The monsters of the New Wave of British Heavy Metal (NWOBHM), the horror of death metal, the monochrome of black metal, and the glitz of glam metal gave way to images that, just like the music, straddled hip-hop and metal imagery without ever really fitting in with either. The artwork, along with the lyrical content, was more often than not based around personal issues such as abuse and disenfranchisement—themes that were easy to relate to for teenagers of the modern era. There were the graffiti-oriented covers of Limp Bizkit's *Three Dollar Bill, Yall$* (1997) and *Significant Other* (1999) (flamboyantly dressed guitarist Wes Borland drew the artwork for both albums, as he is also an accomplished artist), as well as Linkin Park's *Hybrid Theory* (2000), and then there were the childhood-oriented images on the covers of Korn's

first four albums. The spectrum depicted ranged from urban bravado to domestic vulnerability. The general lack of political imagery didn't do much to distance nu metal from the perception that it was a commercially viable genre for meatheads and teenagers.

By the turn of the millennium, it was clear that nu metal was a major concern. Korn had released four multiplatinum-selling albums, and then 2000 saw not only the biggest-selling nu metal album but one of the biggest-selling metal albums of all time. Linkin Park released *Hybrid Theory*. Record labels were falling over themselves to sign the next big nu metal band. There was a slew of bands—such as Spineshank, Coal Chamber, Puddle of Mudd, Papa Roach, and Staind—who added less to the genre than their record sales suggested. With no new ideas in either style or substance, and a base stemming from enormous record sales rather than an underground scene, the radio-friendly genre was quick to stagnate in the twenty-first century.

If nu metal is most readily associated with teenagers, though, it's because they have always been its most visible fans. Along with youth comes a desire to stand apart, and with a genre so popular but so apart from both mainstream culture and the rest of the metal world, true badges of honor are required. No city center was free from a Linkin Park T-shirt, a Limp Bizkit hoodie, or even the odd Slipknot jumpsuit. These bands were well-known enough for everybody to know exactly what they sounded like but distinctive enough to set the wearer apart. Nu metal fashion was the silent voice of a generation.

Along with Faith No More, whose surreal video for "Epic" is vastly at odds with what nu metal came to be, there are other bands included in the catch-all of nu metal that didn't quite fit in. System Of A Down just happened to be around, with their folk influences and particular politics, at the right (or wrong) time— the artwork from their self-titled debut was taken from a poster designed for the Communist Party of Germany during the Third Reich by the German anti-Fascist artist John Heartfield. Continuing the German theme, Rammstein's 1995 debut, *Herzeleid* ("*Heartache*") was labeled Neue Deutsche Härte ("new German hard [metal]"), as the German press described their industrial leanings as dance metal. All these bands can be found situated uneasily under the nu metal umbrella. All of them forged ahead with their own distinct form of metal, but it wasn't just their fans—tribal creatures by nature—who didn't care for being associated with the stigma of nu metal.

With their atmospheric sound, Deftones eventually "qualified" as a nu metal when their DJ, Frank Delgado, joined during the time of *Around the Fur* (1997). They had always had the heavily riffed guitar, but there was a sense that there was more to their music. With a bulb syringe aspirator featured on the cover of *Adrenaline*

"IT'S ALL ON RECORD. WE TOLD MOTHERFUCKERS NOT TO LUMP US IN WITH NU METAL BECAUSE WHEN THOSE BANDS GO DOWN WE AREN'T GOING TO BE WITH THEM."
—Chino Moreno, Deftones vocalist, *Kerrang!*

(1995) and a random photo of a model who was at a party with the band while they recorded *Around the Fur* on that cover, it was difficult to pin the band down. Emerging at the same time as Korn, however, Moreno wasn't happy to be connected to the sports casual of Jonathan Davis, whom he saw as regurgitating the same angst-filled themes in his music.

While Limp Bizkit and Korn have basked in the glow of nu metal, choosing to move their music forward as little as possible, the likes of Linkin Park and Slipknot have sought to transcend the genre in the same way Metallica moved out of straightforward thrash. With their genuine megastar status, Linkin Park were able to collaborate with Jay-Z in 2004 while simultaneously moving away from the hip-hop element of their music. Vocalist Mike Shinoda provided the illustration for *Hybrid Theory*. The winged soldier was meant to be emblematic of the hard and soft elements of their music.

Slipknot, however, had more work to do. With their red jumpsuits and masks, their contrived image—the band was featured on their debut's cover—made them a laughingstock among traditional members of the metal fraternity. Although the presence of a DJ and a keyboardist as well as a full palette of nu metal riffs initially planted their music firmly in the nu metal camp, Slipknot followed their self-titled debut with *Iowa*, a master class in treacherously

heavy metal that was complemented on the cover by that most metal of animals, the goat. The combination both confounded their critics and placed *Iowa* in the Top 10 across the world.

Though nu metal is a distinctly Californian phenomenon, there are a handful of prominent bands from overseas. The aforementioned Rammstein are one of the most successfully enduring ones, and Brazilian bands Sepultura and Soulfly both had exceptional dalliances in the genre. A London quartet, One Minute Silence, and one other notable British band made a splash in the United States as well. A Welsh sextet, Lostprophets, released *Thefakesoundofprogress* in 2000, cementing their position as the premier British nu metal band. The cover of their 2004 follow-up, *Start Something*, was designed by DJ Jamie Oliver, already an acclaimed artist in Wales. The band recorded the album in Los Angeles, and because they saw the artwork as very important, the cover depicted that city.

So what is the ultimate legacy of nu metal? Despite it being widely accepted—even from within its ranks—as the bastard son of metal, the genre not only includes the only Diamond-selling (10 million plus) metal album of the twenty-first century in Linkin Park's *Hybrid Theory* (2000) but it also successfully spawned one of the most iconic metal bands ever to have graced the stage: Slipknot.

"I THINK MUSIC IS SOMETHING THAT EVERY INDIVIDUAL HAS THEIR OWN MEANING TO THE SONG. THEY CAN COME UP WITH WHATEVER THE HELL I'M SAYING, AND THAT'S THE BEAUTY OF IT AND THAT'S WHAT I WANNA KEEP THERE."

—Jonathan Davis, Korn vocalist, regarding the lack of printed song lyrics on their album booklets

ABOVE LEFT Featuring just a simple handprint, this poster design seems equally simple at first glance, but a closer look reveals that Israeli designer Emek Golan has actually made the fingers into a Korn logo. Created for a 1997 show in Pensacola, Florida, it was one of Emek's earlier rock posters. He is now considered one of the most collectible poster artists in the world.

ABOVE RIGHT Staying with Korn's theme of featuring compromised children on their album covers but taking another angle, this poster from a 2011 show in Tulsa, Oklahoma depicts a ghoulish gentleman leering at a girl, yet she appears to have the power, drinking his brains from a tap, while a Venus flytrap is poised to bite his head. Delightful.

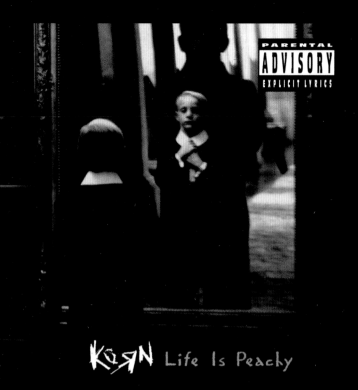

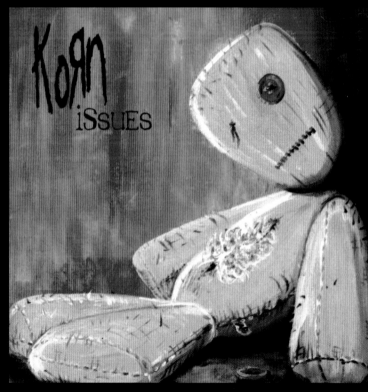

BOTTOM LEFT The music on Korn's debut album (Immortal, 1994) is as iconic today as the album cover. A young girl sitting on a swing shields her eyes from the sun's glare so she can view a menacing figure, depicted only as a shadow in the photograph. "He was a super-nice guy," says Justine Ferrara, no longer six years old. "He was doing me a favor, by blocking my eyes from the sunlight."

TOP LEFT Korn bassist Fieldy had already come up with the album title, which stemmed from his doodling on a popular American school folder. He wrote "Life Is" in front of the brand name, Pee Chee. He said, "I eventually knew my scribbles might someday pay off. I thought that visual would make a really cool album cover." Sadly (but understandably), the manufacturer turned down the band's request to use the folder's image for Life Is Peachy (Immortal, 1996).

TOP RIGHT 1998 was a busy year for cartoon artist Todd McFarlane. Having been nominated for a Grammy for his work on Pearl Jam's Do the Evolution video, the Spawn creator designed the cover artwork for Follow the Leader (Immortal, 1998) as well as the animations that appear in the legendary Freak on a Leash video.

BOTTOM RIGHT After three Korn album covers featuring vulnerable or threatened children, for their fourth album, Issues (Immortal, 1999), the Californian genre pioneers ran a contest on MTV asking their fans to design the cover. In addition to having his design appear on eleven million copies of the album, Alfredo Carlos also received $10,000 for his efforts.

"I WENT TO AN ARTS HIGH SCHOOL AND HAD ALWAYS BEEN INTERESTED IN SCULPTURE AND PAINTING AND DRAWING. GUITAR KIND OF BECAME A HOBBY OF MINE . . . WHEN LIMP GOT SIGNED, THAT CHANGED MY ASPIRATIONS FROM BEING IN FINE ART. BEING A MUSICIAN WAS THE JOB I DIDN'T EXPECT, AND I ENDED UP GOING, 'HOW CAN I INCORPORATE THIS?'"
— Wes Borland, Limp Bizkit guitarist, who designs and paints all the band's artwork

"[WHEN I'M PAINTING] I CAN GET INTO TRANCELIKE STATES [SIC] THAT I FEEL IS BROKEN WHEN I FEEL I HAVE TO COMMUNICATE WITH OTHER PEOPLE ABOUT IDEAS. IT TOTALLY TAKES ME OUT OF THE ZONE. I REALLY LOVE IT BEING BY MYSELF AND NOT EVEN HAVING TO TURN ON THE PART OF MY BRAIN THAT YOU NEED TO INTERFACE OTHER PEOPLE."—Wes Borland

TOP LEFT Wes Borland's style has developed and his work improved over the years, but Limp Bizkit's debut album, *Three Dollar Bill, Yall$* (Interscope, 1997) preserves one of his earliest pieces of artwork. The scratchy design has been likened to the classroom doodles of bored teenagers, which may have contributed to the album's popularity.

BOTTOM LEFT The cover art is as darkly humorous as the origin of the joke that Limp Bizkit's third album, *Chocolate Starfish and the Hot Dog Flavored Water* (Interscope, 2000), is based on. After continually being referred to as an asshole, Fred Durst decided to spoof himself in the title. Wes Borland came up with the rest after mocking all the different flavors of bottled water available for purchase.

ABOVE RIGHT Fittingly for a band that is one of the major players in the nu metal world, the artwork for *Significant Other* (Interscope, 1999) is a graffiti-oriented image, closely associated with the rap scene. This could be seen as a cynical move—or an incredibly smart action intended to maximize the symbiosis of the band's music and their image.

deftones around the fur

"YEARS AGO, I DECIDED TO GO STRAIGHT TO THE BANDS, RATHER THAN DANCE AROUND WITH A PROMOTER WHO REALLY DOESN'T HAVE THE RIGHT TO GIVE YOU PERMISSION TO MAKE A PRINT TO SELL FOR MONEY. I'D WORKED WITH ENOUGH PEOPLE AND FORMED ENOUGH RELATIONSHIPS WITH BANDS AND THEIR MANAGEMENTS THAT I FIGURED I DIDN'T NEED TO MESS AROUND. I WAS LIKE, 'I'VE KNOWN CHINO FOR YEARS, I'M GONNA WORK DIRECTLY WITH THEM.'"—Jermaine Rogers, poster artist

deftones

adrenaline

MAY 19TH RECORD RELEASE

DEFTONES

TOP LEFT The bikini-clad woman on the cover of Deftones' breakthrough album *Around the Fur* (Maverick, 1997) was rumored to be singer Chino Moreno's wife, but the band eventually confirmed that it was simply a photo of a random model taken at a party the band held while they were recording the album. That Rick Kosick captured the perfect "MySpace" angle is pure coincidence.

BOTTOM LEFT There is an ambiguous, abstract theme to Deftones' cover art. Their debut album, *Adrenaline* (Maverick, 1995), features what may appear to be a child's spinning top but is actually a baby aspirator. No explanations have been offered for the band's use of something used to clear mucus from an infant's respiratory passage.

ABOVE RIGHT Poster artist Jermaine Rogers has created the majority of Deftones' concert posters and prints since the 1990s. However, the designer Emek created this poster for Deftones' 2003 tour. Entitled "Space Bug," this is just one of the differently colored versions depicting a giant bug feasting on Earth.

I DIDN'T WANT TO BE A PART OF WHAT THAT CURRENT—I WOULDN'T EVEN CALL IT A MOVEMENT—WAS ABOUT. THERE WAS THAT NU METAL THING. I DIDN'T KNOW ANYTHING ABOUT IT. I DIDN'T UNDERSTAND IT. THE MUSIC I WAS HEARING WAS BASED ALL AROUND DETUNED RIFFS THAT LAID WITHIN ONE OR TWO DIFFERENT KEYS. EVERY RIFF I WAS HEARING WAS THE SAME REGURGITATED CHORD PATTERNS WITH ABSOLUTELY NO MELODY."

—Scott Weiland, former STP/VR vocalist, *Revolver*

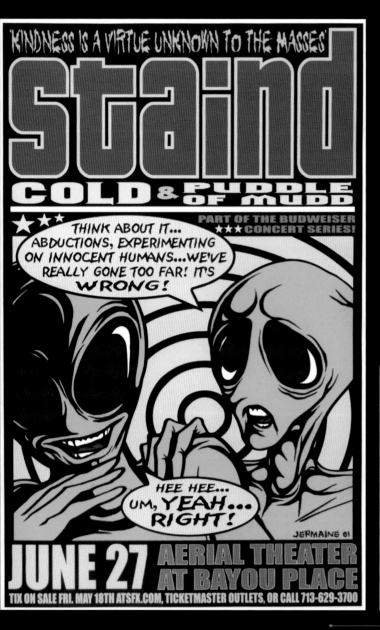

ABOVE LEFT Taken from the 2001 tour headlined by Staind, this poster from Houston, Texas, is by Jermaine Rogers. Featuring one alien battling its conscience and another seemingly happy with their experiments on humans, along with a message that "Kindness is a virtue unknown to the masses," there is an underlying dystopian message at odds

TOP RIGHT Created for the 2013 *Revolver* magazine Road to the Golden Gods Tour headlined by Stone Sour—front man for Slipknot, Corey Taylor's other band—this poster has little to do with anything related to the tour. With a landscape that evokes memories of old-school American entertainment and a car that could either be incredibly old or from the future, there

BOTTOM RIGHT Here's an example of the repurposing that is sometimes done with tour posters. For the same 2013 *Revolver* magazine Road to the Golden Gods Tour headlined by Stone Sour—this time featuring Hell or Highwater instead of Young Guns—it's essentially the same poster; the artist has simply altered the colors and changed a few details.

"SINCE WE FIRST STARTED AND SINCE OUR FIRST ALBUM CAME OUT, THERE HAS BEEN A LOT OF CHANGES IN OPINION AND VIEWS . . . BUT THERE'S STILL DEFINITELY A LOT OF WORK TO DO AND THERE'S DEFINITELY STILL A DOUBLE STANDARD. I THINK, FOR US, OUR PURPOSE IS TO PROVE TO PEOPLE THAT OUR MUSICAL ABILITIES GO BEYOND."

—Morgan Lander, Canadian all-girl band Kittie vocalist, regarding the participation of women in the genre

ABOVE LEFT Another Jermaine Rogers effort, this poster from 2000 is for a Kittie show in Houston, Texas. Continuing his theme of adding a message in his artwork, it declares, "No more asking for respect . . ." As Kittie were a ballsy, young, all-female band, this statement of intent fitted their stance perfectly while also allowing the artist to put his own ideas across.

TOP MIDDLE The cover of Kittie's sixth album, *I've Failed You* (E1 Music, 2011), is an austere affair. Featuring the classic metal icons of a skull, feathers, and roses, it fits with the theme of the album, which vocalist Morgan Lander explains is "An album full of regrets and ill-made choices, of watching those that you love suffer, of that love gone wrong. I've failed myself and those I love; I've failed to protect them."

BOTTOM MIDDLE It wasn't uncommon for nu metal bands to simply feature a photograph of themselves on the cover of their album. Kittie's debut, *Spit* (Artemis, 1999), did just that. However, although Tanya Candler played the bass guitar parts on the album, their newest bassist, Talena Atfield is in the picture. It was a sign of things to come in terms of the band's ever-changing bass guitar position.

ABOVE RIGHT The *Metal Hammer* Trespass America Tour of 2012 featured modern nu metallers Five Finger Death Punch, and this poster, with its decaying image of the Statue of Liberty, does everything it can to convey the feeling that America is in a downward spiral—a feeling that coursed through their third album, *America Capitalist* (Prospect Park, 2011).

shawn crahan: not just clowning around

Slipknot are the most iconic band to have emerged from the nu metal genre. Bursting out of Iowa at the turn of the millennium, in matching bright red jumpsuits and grotesque individual masks, the nine-piece band were peerless both in style and in their music. Their style and their artwork have been formed in large part by founding member and custom percussionist Number 6: the Clown, aka M. Shawn Crahan.

It was Crahan who took a clown mask along to an early Slipknot rehearsal and wore it, thus forming his own persona in the band. He once called it a joke, but there's always been something truly primal about this band. The instinct to dress up while creating the music of Slipknot was a natural one. They wanted to stand out, and they definitely did.

The masks that the nine members wear are changed for every album, becoming more elaborate each time. Initially, the anonymity the masks provided also lent an air of mystique to the band. Coupled with reports that the band was unhinged enough to punch one other in the face before a show to psych themselves up, there was more to Slipknot than just their music right from the start, and that was all thanks to Crahan. He helped to form the bond not only with the fans but, as they all wore the masks together, within the band itself.

"When I put the mask on," he explains, "Clown takes all the pain."

Although the masks were homemade for their debut, from *Iowa* (2001) on the band had the masks made for them. It wasn't until *Vol. 3: (The Subliminal Verses)*

"PHOTO WORK IS MORE INSTANT GRATIFICATION AND IT'S VERY PERSONAL; I DON'T HAVE TO SHARE IT, AND I DON'T HAVE TO GET PERMISSION— WHEREAS I'M ONLY ONE NINTH OF A BAND, AND THERE'S A LOT OF COMPROMISING THERE."—Shawn Crahan, Slipknot percussionist and artist

TOP LEFT Although he is pictured here behind some bars, there is little that holds Shawn Crahan back when it comes to Slipknot. Even when battling a debilitating knee injury, he claimed that putting on his clown mask made him forget about, or even thrive on, the pain. It's the same mentality that he uses in his photography.

(2004) that Slipknot really started taking advantage of the masks. The maggot mask featured on the album cover was designed by Crahan and isn't attributed to any one member. Instead, it is worn by the female protagonist in the video for "Vermilion" while the band members put on their death masks. They wear these masks every time they play "Vermilion" live. It's this continuity and attention to detail that has served the visual art aspect of their music so well.

They took this one step further for the release of *All Hope Is Gone* (2008), however, as they released the purgatory masks—oversized papier-mâché versions of their death masks—which were used in promotional photographs for the album. Another Shawn Crahan idea, the purgatory masks "represent ego," and the ceremonial burning of said masks in the video for "Psychosocial" represents their acknowledgment of their own personas.

All Hope Is Gone also featured the band wearing their latest set of masks— plusher and more clean-cut than ever before—both in the video for "Psychosocial" and on the album sleeve. Full photographs of the band were also featured on the front of their debut album, *Slipknot* (1999), and although it bore all the hallmarks

of what Crahan had envisioned for them, it was not until their second album, *Iowa*, that he could actually call it his own work.

"There were other ideas," Crahan admits, talking of the image of the goat that adorns the cover of the album. "But I was just obsessed with getting the perfect photo of the goat."

One thing is clear—M. Shawn Crahan takes his unofficial role as Slipknot's artistic director very seriously. He lives it. He takes it beyond his band. Take, for instance, the photo book that he released in 2012, *The Apocalyptic Nightmare Journey*. Filled with enlarged images of purposefully mangled Polaroid photographs taken over the past decade on the road with Slipknot and covering some of his home life and incidental moments as well, it's a curious insight into an even more curious mind.

Whether by accident or by intentional design, there is absolutely no doubt that Slipknot would not be held in such high esteem as they are now, within both heavy metal and in mainstream music, without the continued creative desire and vision of the Clown, M. Shawn Crahan.

OPPOSITE, TOP RIGHT This is the maggot mask from the cover of *Vol. 3: (The Subliminal Verses)* (Roadrunner, 2004) in all its glory, being worn by an actress in the video for "Vermilion" in a scene almost halfway through the video. In the scene that follows, Slipknot start placing their death masks over their normal masks and a transformation occurs . . .

OPPOSITE, BOTTOM Slipknot's live performances are one of the reasons that the Des Moines, Iowa band have reached the heights that they have. In early shows, DJ Sid Wilson would launch himself from as high a point in the venue as possible. This feat is less feasible, however, now that the nine-piece usually headline arenas and festivals.

ABOVE Taken from the promotional photographs for their fourth album, *All Hope Is Gone* (Roadrunner, 2008), this is Slipknot evolving. Their masks have retained their identities, but their clothes have taken on a personal individuality that the identical boiler suits could not—and possibly were not meant to, as they exuded a sense of uniformity and togetherness.

TOP LEFT As with Slipknot's debut album on the same label from the same year, the photography for Amen's second, self-titled album (Roadrunner, 1999) was done by Dean Karr. After directing Marilyn Manson's hit video for "Sweet Dreams (Are Made of This)" in 1996, his distinctive, high-contrast style was clearly in great demand with the most popular artists at the time.

BOTTOM LEFT Photographer Dale May talks about the photograph used on the cover of Godsmack's eponymous debut album (Universal, 1998): "I was experimenting with cross-processing color transparency film into a negative, to build saturation. We couldn't use Photoshop because it was predigital, of course. My friend introduced me to a young club kid called Toni Tiller. She was hard to find, but if you're looking for color, she was hard to pass up."

TOP RIGHT Famous mainly for their cover of New Order's "Blue Monday," electronic-oriented industrial metallers Orgy released *Candyass* (Warner Bros., 1998) to some fanfare. Designed by award-winning in-house graphic artist Steve Gerdes, the cover simply featured a digitally manipulated "O." It was basic, but so was everything about the band.

BOTTOM RIGHT The dog featured balancing a lemon on his nose on the cover of Snot's debut album, *Get Some* (Geffen, 1997), belonged to front man Lynn Strait, who called him "the raddest dog alive." Sadly, Dobbs— also the band's mascot—died in the car crash that also killed his master in 1998.

THE GIFT OF GAME

CRAZY TOWN

'WE MAKE A POINT WHEN WE HEADLINE TO PLAY ['THE BLOOD, THE SWEAT, THE TEARS' AND 'BULLDOZER'], BASICALLY AS A WAY TO STICK OUR MIDDLE FINGERS UP TO EVERY ONE OF THOSE FUCKING HATERS AND SAY, 'FUCK YOU!' AS FAR AS THE WAY I LOOKED BACK ON THE VIDEO, WE'VE ALL MADE A FASHION FAUX PAS. [LAUGHS] BUT FUCK IT. IT WAS THIRTEEN YEARS AGO."

—Robb Flynn, Machine Head vocalist-guitarist, on the band's nu metal phase

LEFT A gig poster for a show originally intended for Halloween, it carries the title *Famine*—third of *The Four Sisters of the Apocalypse* series of four posters. Inspired by the biblical connotations of *Unto the Locust* (Roadrunner, 2011), designer Larry West said he was "attempting to bring the Christian concept of the Four Horsemen into a different and more meaningful light."

ABOVE RIGHT In this design for the Texas dates of Machine Head's winter 2012 tour, Rich Knepprath created a dark poster series as part of his Anonymous Ink & Idea side project—he treats it as a hobby. Primarily a multidisciplinary designer, his work "revolves around the creation of limited-edition commemorative posters for touring bands, films, and festivals."

TOP LEFT The art direction, design, and photography for Disturbed's quadruple US platinum debut album, *The Sickness* (Giant, 2000), all were executed by P. R. Brown at Bau-Da Design Lab in Los Angeles. After gaining notoriety with his early work with Marilyn Manson, Brown worked with Godsmack, Korn, Papa Roach, and Coal Chamber as well as Disturbed.

BOTTOM LEFT One Minute Silence's second album, *Buy Now . . . Saved Later* (V2, 2000), featured the band's logo on the front cover —with a devil woman made of dollar bills holding a Bible and a bitten apple— as well as printed on the disc itself. This all fitted with the band's uncompromising antiestablishment stance.

BOTTOM MIDDLE The sleeve for Drowning Pool's debut album, *Sinner* (Wind-Up, 2001), was photographed by the in-house photographer Glen DiCrocco with direction from label exec Ed Sherman. Featuring a sad-looking woman with the album title crudely tattooed across her knuckles, clearly the label was aiming for as much angst in the artwork as there was in the music.

TOP RIGHT When Mushroomhead released *XX* (Universal, 2001), even though it was their fourth album, they were immediately compared to Slipknot, due to the many masked and costumed members in the band rather than to any sonic similarities. Their label—and, presumably, the band too—still seemed happy to capitalize on this fact by featuring the band in all their glory on the cover.

BOTTOM RIGHT Mudvayne were the other nu metal band besides Slipknot to really be noticed for their appearance, yet their label originally chose not to focus on this in marketing the band. As a result, *L.D. 50* (Epic, 2000) was released bearing an image of a chain of particles, relating to the title— a medical term for the median lethal dose required to kill someone.

"HE'S A VERY INTENSE CHARACTER. HE WOULD TALK TO ME ABOUT HIS VISIONS AND IDEAS, AND I LITERALLY WOULDN'T UNDERSTAND A WORD HE SAID, BUT THEN I HUNG UP THE PHONE AND SLEPT ON IT. HE IS THE CREATIVE MIND OF THE BAND. I JUST THINK *IOWA* IS ONE OF THE BEST. IT'S CERTAINLY ONE OF THE FAVORITE ONES I'VE WORKED ON."

—Tom Jermann, designer, on working with M. Shawn Crahan of Slipknot

ABOVE LEFT "With *Iowa* we developed this idea of the mathematical formulas and the goat being the leader of the herd. We wanted to send a positive message to the kids, to the fans."—Tom Jermann on *Iowa* (Roadrunner Records, 2001)

TOP RIGHT Says Tom Jermann, designer on *Slipknot* (Roadrunner, 1999), "I remember the cover [of *Slipknot*] was photographed by a friend of the band, and the other photos were taken by a fairly well-known music photographer called Dean Karr. He had a style where he would mess up the photos when he developed them. Then I came up with the scratchy texture and look."

BOTTOM RIGHT The cover of *Vol. 3: (The Subliminal Verses)* (Roadrunner, 2004) was a photograph of Clown of Slipknot wearing a handmade maggot mask, taken by his son. Appearing also in the video for "Vermilion," the band took their image to the next level, with more elaborate designs and a stronger theme running through the whole album campaign.

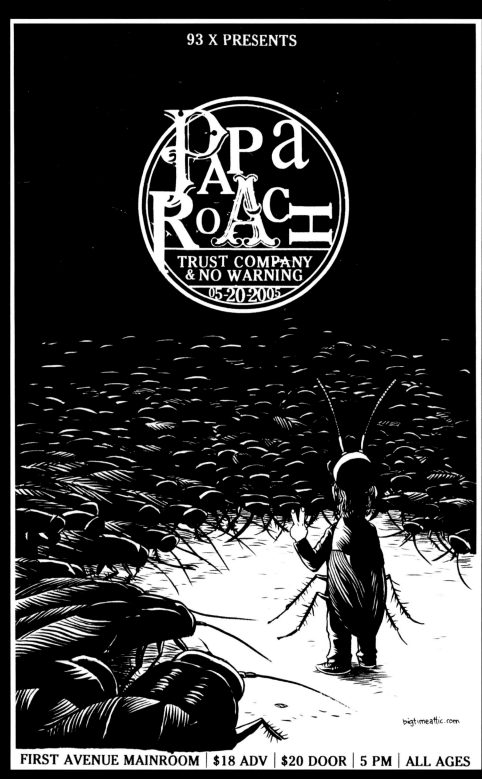

TOP LEFT The artwork for Papa Roach's second album, *Infest* (DreamWorks, 2000), was conceived, designed, and executed by P. R. Brown. The cockroach featured starkly against a white background follows the theme of the album, which also contains songs called "Between Angels and Insects" and "Snakes."

BOTTOM LEFT Over a decade after Papa Roach's rise to nu metal infamy, their seventh album, *The Connection* (Eleven Seven, 2012), resonates much more strongly with hard rock. With a seemingly robotic heart erupting out of an equally robotic skull and DNA strands flying into or out of a pair of headphones, the image seems to be marrying the physical and digital. This was the first Papa Roach album to be released on vinyl.

ABOVE RIGHT Designed by Big Time Attic for a 2005 show in their hometown of Minneapolis, this poster features cockroaches—a whole load of them. With a head roach promoting peace below an ornate band logo, this monochromatic design is as striking as it is fitting.

the phenomenon of wrestle metal

The relationship between metal and professional wrestling is a strong one,
but it's even stronger when the genre is whittled down to nu metal.

i n 1996 the Slam Jam were featured on the compilation album *WWF Full
Metal*—comprising members of Savatage, Anthrax, and Type O Negative—
and then bands such as Metallica, Megadeth, and Slayer appeared on compilation
albums related to both World Championship Wrestling (WCW) and World Wrestling
Entertainment (WWE; formerly the World Wrestling Federation or WWF).

However, it was bands like Drowning Pool and Saliva that really got their
commercial breaks from their inclusion in high-selling albums such as *WWF
Forceable Entry* (2002) and *WWE Wreckless Intent* (2006)—both reached the
Top 10 on the *Billboard* 200 chart—while long-time wrestling fans such as Limp
Bizkit and Insane Clown Posse became involved in a much more hands-on
fashion, but in very different ways.

Limp Bizkit's song "Rollin'" was used as the Undertaker's entrance music from
2000 to 2002, leading to the song's inclusion on *WWF Forceable Entry*; in 2003
the band performed the official theme to Wrestlemania XIX, "Crack Addict," live
at the event. Furthering the band's high-profile involvement in the world's most
visible wrestling network, Limp Bizkit singer Fred Durst was even featured as a
playable character in the 2001 official video game *WWF SmackDown! Just Bring
It*. A regular audience member at WWE events, Durst found himself ejected from
SummerSlam 2012 when he made an obscene gesture to a camera.

Limp Bizkit performed their music at WWE events, and Durst found his way
into the ring digitally, but the hardcore hip-hop duo Insane Clown Posse took their
homage all the way. They are such big wrestling fans that after competing in local
events in Michigan through the 1990s, they actually wrestled professionally for
three months in the WWF in 1998. After leaving for WCW, they created their own
wrestling promotion, Juggalo Championshit Wrestling (normalized to Juggalo
Championship Wrestling in 2007), in which they still wrestle.

The relationship is not a one-way street, as wrestlers often appear at heavy
metal events. For instance, the sixth edition of the California Metal Fest in late
2012, featuring modern fusion metal bands such as Asking Alexandria, was
hosted by legendary wrestler Mick Foley, with appearances from John Morrison,
"Diamond" Dallas Page, and Jimmy Hart, among other pro wrestler names. Just as
metal bands provide the soundtrack to pro wrestling, the overblown personalities
of pro wrestlers fit perfectly into the world of metal.

"I GET GREAT JOY OUT OF BOOKING WRESTLING SHOWS AND BRINGING IN OLD-TIMERS, LEGENDS, AND MAKING IT AS COOL AS I CAN FOR THEM . . . AND PUTTING THEM IN FRONT OF ENTHUSIASTIC JUGGALOS. BECAUSE JUGGALOS ARE LIKE NO OTHER AUDIENCE IN THE WORLD . . . EVEN IF THEY'RE IN FRONT OF ONLY FOUR HUNDRED JUGGALOS, IT FEELS LIKE FOUR THOUSAND."—Violent J, Insane Clown Posse vocalist, the A.V. Club

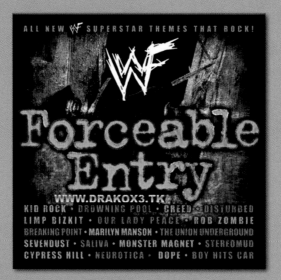

ALL NEW WWF SUPERSTAR THEMES THAT ROCK!

Forceable Entry

WWW.DRAKOX3.TK

KID ROCK · DROWNING POOL · CREED · DISTURBED
LIMP BIZKIT · OUR LADY PEACE · ROB ZOMBIE
BREAKING POINT · MARILYN MANSON · THE UNION UNDERGROUND
SEVENDUST · SALIVA · MONSTER MAGNET · STEREOMUD
CYPRESS HILL · NEUROTICA · DOPE · BOY HITS CAR

TOP RIGHT A collection of covers, remixes,
and some original songs, *Forceable Entry*
(Columbia) reached No. 3 on the Billboard
200 upon its release in March 2002. It was
one of the last products to be released under
the WWF moniker, as the entertainment
company was forced to change its name
to WWE to avoid confusion with the World
Wildlife Fund.

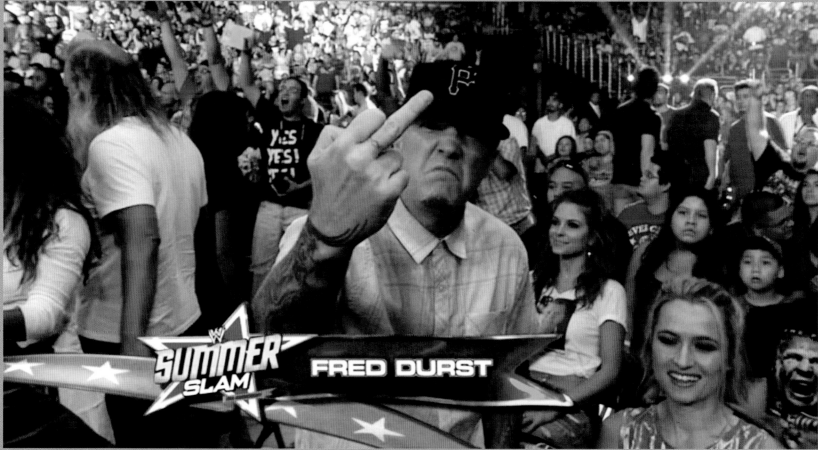

OPPOSITE, BOTTOM Insane Clown Posse were obsessed with wrestling when they were growing up, and Violent J readily admits that he learned a lot about being an entertainer by watching favorite wrestlers on television. "A lot of our early interviews were done like wrestlers do, where we're screaming and yelling all this shit. But we're characters. We'd never be seen without the face paint."

TOP LEFT From December 2000 to May 2002 Undertaker's entry music was "Rollin' (Air Raid Vehicle)"—taken from Limp Bizkit's 2000 album, *Chocolate Starfish and the Hot Dog Flavored Water* (Interscope/ Flip, 2000) and featured on *Forceable Entry*. The band also performed the song live at Wrestlemania XIX in 2003.

TOP MIDDLE Mick Foley, pictured here as Mankind, has previously hosted a podcast for long-time wrestling associates, the Chicago-based hardcore label Victory, and has been interviewed by *Metal Hammer*. A big Twisted Sister fan and a close personal friend of Dee Snider, he is one of WWE's biggest personalities.

TOP RIGHT The platinum-selling Texan quartet Drowning Pool produced a rendition of Triple H's theme song, "The Game," featured as the opening track on *WWF Forceable Entry*. Although "Bodies" remains the band's best-known song to this day, Drowning Pool's strong presence in the wrestling world is widely credited with helping to launch their career.

ABOVE WWE aficionado and frequent contributor to official soundtrack, Fred Durst is seen here "flipping the bird" at SummerSlam 2012, live on pay-per-view television. He vacated his seat very soon afterward but later claimed that he was not ejected from the annual calendar highlight by the WWE; he had actually gone backstage to apologize to the producers. Sure, Fred.

LINKIN PARK

[HYBRID THEORY]

'WE TOOK WHAT WE DID VERY SERIOUSLY . . . SO SPENDING FORTY HOURS ON A PAINTING, THEN PUTTING IT UP IN FRONT OF YOUR CLASS TO HAVE THIRTY PEOPLE CRITIQUE IT WAS BRUTAL. AT SOME POINT, I REALIZED THAT THE CRITICISMS THAT MADE ME THE MOST DEFENSIVE WERE USUALLY THE ONES THAT WERE RIGHT. IT REALLY HELPED ME TO ENJOY THE PROCESS OF MAKING MY WORK BETTER, BY LEAVING EGO AT THE DOOR DURING THE CREATIVE PROCESS." —Mike Shinoda, Linkin Park vocalist, on the process of becoming a graphic designer

ABOVE "I think that the parallel between our music and the art has always been there. With *Hybrid Theory*, the idea of bringing heavy elements and softer elements into the music together was represented in the visual art of the album. The soldier and the dragonfly wings; the really hard, jaded looks with the really soft, frail touches is something that we like to do."—Chester Bennington on the artwork of Linkin Park's twenty-million-plus-selling debut album *Hybrid Theory* (Warner Bros., 2000)

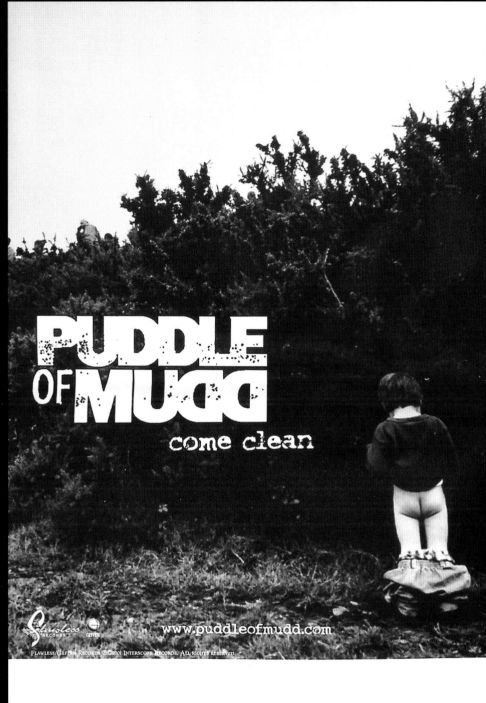

ABOVE LEFT Creating another vibrant poster for the fifth annual Sno-Core Tour featuring System of a Down, this time Jermaine Rogers' message is that Sno-Core may not be a permanent fixture in the metal calendar. Apparently it did have legs, however, as another ten years' worth of tours followed, featuring the likes of Alien Ant Farm, Glassjaw, and Static-X.

ABOVE RIGHT The cover of Puddle of Mudd's debut album, *Come Clean* (Geffen, 2001), immediately sparked controversy when it featured the naked behind of a young boy. Two major American retailers, Walmart and Kmart, refused to stock the album in their stores. The boy is singer Wes Scantlin's son, Jordan, who also appears in the video for "Blurry."

TOP LEFT Dry Kill Logic vocalist Cliff Rigano had the following to say about the cover art for their debut album, *The Darker Side of Nonsense* (Roadrunner, 2001): "We knew we wanted images that would be equal parts intelligent and disturbing. We decided on a freak show theme, but nothing too Crayola or carnival-esque. It had to be something that could mesmerize and repulse you at the same time."

BOTTOM LEFT The art for Spineshank's second album, *The Height of Callousness* (Roadrunner, 2000), was designed by P. R. Brown's Bau-Da Design Lab. It's interesting that there is no real common visual indicator of his influence in the artwork for bands such as Spineshank, Disturbed, and Papa Roach, other than the quality of the work.

TOP RIGHT While Papa Roach featured a photograph of an actual cockroach on the cover of *Infest* (DreamWorks, 2000), *ANThology* (DreamWorks, 2001), by Alien Ant Farm, featured a drawing of their insect of choice. Although the artwork of both albums is designed by P. R. Brown, there is no continuity in style.

BOTTOM RIGHT Vex Red entered a *Kerrang!* competition and won the chance to record an album with "Godfather of Nu Metal" Ross Robinson. S*tart with a Strong and Persistent Desire* (Virgin, 2002) turned out to be their only album. British illustrator David Lupton says of his style, "I love dark and melancholy imagery. I've tried to create something with a more sunny and upbeat nature—something that might appeal to a wider audience—but unfortunately my heart's just not in it."

"THE PICTURES WERE DONE BY GEO AND DANIEL FUCHS, WHO PUT OUT A BOOK IN WHICH ONLY DEAD LIVING THINGS ARE IN IT, DEAD ANIMALS AND PEOPLE WHO ARE PRESERVED IN FORMALIN. THE ENTIRE PHOTO ALBUM RADIATES SUCH A SENSE OF CALM, AS IF THEY HAVE, TO ME, A CONNECTION WITH THE DEAD. THAT IMPRESSED US A BIT; WE THOUGHT IT WAS GOOD, BECAUSE DEATH IS ALWAYS REGARDED AS FRIGHTENING. IN THE BOOK IT'S NO LONGER SCARY, MORE FRIENDLY AND PLEASING."

—Paul H. Landers, Rammstein guitarist, on the artwork for *Mutter* (Motor Music, 2001)

RIGHT Having helped popularize the Neue Deutsche Härte fusion metal genre with *Herzeleid* (Motor Music, 1995) and *Sehnsucht* (Motor Music, 1997), Rammstein set about shocking the world with a photograph of a dead fetus' face adorning the cover of their third album, *Mutter* (Motor Music, 2001). It's their most successful album to date, so their shock tactics clearly worked.

CHAPTER 6

BLACK METAL

"I AM AMAZED AT THE WAY THAT BLACK METAL HAS BECOME SO POPULAR. EVERYTHING ABOUT IT MAKES THIS STYLE OF METAL STAND APART FROM ALL OTHERS. YOU LOOK AT THE ARTWORK SOME BANDS HAVE ON THEIR ALBUM COVERS, AND IT IS STUNNING. SO MUCH WORK HAS GONE INTO IT."

—Cronos, Venom basssist-vocalist

The Black Art of Metal

MALCOLM DOME

Black metal. Perhaps the most misunderstood yet also the most creative area of the whole metal genre. A form of music that has become vilified and feared because of the almost omnipotent violence with which it has long been associated. Yet through the music and also the art that has surrounded it, black metal has long been proven as a creative force, one inevitably propelled by dark forces but also inspired by much that's the very essence of nature and of Mother Earth.

You can suggest that its roots rest uneasily in the birth of Black Sabbath—as does all metal, it must be said—and that it took on board some of the lessons of punk, plus an imagery that owed much to classic and underground horror films. Yet it all coalesced in 1982, when the English trio Venom released their second album, appropriately titled . . . *Black Metal*.

"We got fed up with the way our music was being described," says bassist-vocalist Cronos. "People were always asking us as well what sort of metal we were playing. It was never enough for us just to be heavy metal. Journalists wanted something more descriptive. So one day in an interview Mantas [guitarist] just said, 'Well, we are black metal.' The phrase meant nothing, but it stuck and seemed to fit."

Cronos, under his real name of Conrad Lant, designed the cover for the album, and set a standard and style with use of a satanic image plus black and grey shades. It was classic yet also futuristic, setting the tone for what has come since.

That same year, Denmark's Mercyful Fate released the somewhat shocking *Nuns Have No Fun*. The gruesome and graphic lyrics for the title track were transformed into a startling cover by

"BLACK METAL ISN'T ABOUT BEING OUTRAGEOUS AND SHOCKING PEOPLE. IT'S ABOUT MAKING MUSICAL AND SOCIAL STATEMENTS. THAT'S WHAT WE'VE ALWAYS DONE IN VENOM. WHEN PEOPLE ASK IF WE'RE INTO BLACK MAGIC, I JUST THINK OF THE CHOCOLATES!"—Cronos, Venom bassist-vocalist

Ole Paulson, which depicted a nude nun being subjected to the pains described in the song's story. It wasn't for the sensitive!

King Diamond of Mercyful Fate was an avowed follower of Anton LaVey, founder of the Church of Satan. But the vocalist also had an eye for imagery and detail. He created his own makeup, which, while borrowing from the likes of Arthur Brown, Alice Cooper, and KISS' Gene Simmons, had its own distinctive pattern. This was to become the blueprint (or rather, black-and-white print) for the corpse paint used so freely by black metal bands at the end of the 1980s.

But by the late 1980s, it was clear that black metal bands were taking the imagery and artwork associated with the music a lot more seriously than were those in other metal subgenres. Switzerland's Celtic Frost, who dabbled at the frayed edges of the musical style, even called on compatriot and friend H. R. Giger (the artist who created the look for the celebrated *Alien* movie [1979]) to donate one of his paintings for their 1985 album *To Mega Therion*. This was a true meeting between the art world and extreme metal—a blurring of the lines.

This was a singular collaboration, but an examination of the way bands have since been portraying themselves reveals a deep desire to be seen as more than mere progenitors of noise, as some on the outside would have you believe. In 1994 the Norwegian band

Dimmu Borgir released *For All Tid*. This had a cover drawing inspired by the nineteenth-century French artist Gustave Doré and his depiction of Camelot. The same band showed how color could be used in a distinctive and dark fashion on their 2003 *Death Cult Armageddon*, the perfect showcase for the talents of cross-media artist Joachim Luetke, who helped to transform black metal art into something more elaborate.

Norway's Burzum, a one-man project that was the brainchild of the infamous Varg Vikernes (who spent nearly fifteen years in prison on charges of murder and arson attacks on churches), became celebrated for a form of black metal that was eerily based as much on synthesizers as it was on guitar. Much of the work was inspired by ancient Norwegian folk music, and the covers reflected this approach. The 1996 album *Filosofem* featured a haunting painting by the nineteenth- and twentieth-century artist Theodor Kittelsen: a field and forest scene with a sense of foreboding.

Of course, one enduring theme in black metal is an abiding hatred for Christianity and by implication all organized religions. In Norway at the start of the 1990s this antagonism crossed over into shocking criminal behavior when the movement called the Inner Circle burned down churches in protest of the way the "pure" pagan Norwegian way of life had been usurped. In truth, the Inner Circle was based around an Oslo shop called Helvete ("Hell").

This was run by Mayhem guitarist Euronymous, an insidious individual who persuaded easily led young members of local black metal bands like Mayhem, Emperor, and Darkthrone to go on a rampage of arson attacks on over fifty churches between 1992 and 1996. Euronymous was murdered by Vikernes in 1993.

On a more commercial level, the United Kingdom's Cradle of Filth caused outrage in 1997 when they sold T-shirts bearing the legend *Jesus Is a Cunt*, with a masturbating nun in full view. Some fans have even been prosecuted for wearing the shirts, which are now a collector's item. In the same vein, Sweden's Marduk had used a similar, although less contentious, image on the cover of their 1991 demo *Fuck Me Jesus*, which was finally released in 1997.

Reflecting the influence of the early 1990s Norwegian scene, a copycat musical alliance was started in France during the early part of that decade. Called Les Légions Noires, this featured bands like Mütiilation, Vlad Tepes, and Torgeist. As once stated by Wlad Drakksteim of Vlad Tepes, their intention was a "return to darkness." The bleak, dark, and sadistic artwork used by this conglomeration was definitely a return to the style of Emperor, Darkthrone, and Dimmu Borgir.

One of the most unusual aspects of black metal is its attraction for some Christian musicians. Although it's generally assumed that the satanic sensibility permeates every corner of the subgenre, nonetheless there are bands that use black metal to spread the word of God. Bands of this ilk include Azmaveth, from Puerto Rico; Bealia, from Indonesia; Nazareo, from Ecuador; Wintersoul, from the United Kingdom; and Arch of Thorns and Cabalistic, from the United States. In fact, the United States has become the center for

"WE ARE ABOUT RECONNECTING WITH OUR NORWEGIAN HERITAGE. CHRISTIANITY HAS NO PART TO PLAY IN LIFE OVER HERE. WE NEED TO GET BACK TO OUR ROOTS OF PAGANISM. THAT'S WHAT WE ARE DOING WITH THE MUSIC, AND THAT'S WHY THE CHURCHES MUST BURN!"—Fenriz, Darkthrone drummer

such bands, who usually call themselves "unblack metallers." Cabalistic defended the idea of Christian black metal as follows: "Why darkness in music? Why black metal? God is present even in the darkness. He rules both the darkness and the light. As humans we spend a lot of time in the darkness, with sickness, nasty people, and troubles but this is no vacation from God. He is with us. So while we sit on a pile of dung with nothing left, like the man Job in the Bible, we have this black metal that speaks of the pain of existence but gives us hope, and of course we have God. Justice will come, the light will come."

The artwork and logos of such bands tend to be a little softer than the usual fare in this area of metal. However, in most aspects such bands still reflect the overall power and extremes that must be the calling cards of anyone who claims to be involved in black metal.

The other fascinating aspect of black metal is that, perhaps more than any other branch of metal, not only does it have global fan appeal, but there are bands of this type around the world. Wherever you look, there are black metal musicians delivering their own take on the music and imagery. For instance, there's Orisha Shakpana in Jamaica, whose 2006 debut album *Satanic Powers in Jamaican Hills* has a cover that not only draws heavily from the

works of such designers as the Swedish Kristian Wåhlin (who has collaborated with Emperor, Bathory, and King Diamond) but also has a flavor of the band's locale. Arallu are based in Israel; the oriental influences in their music are also manifest in their artwork. Across the Middle East, Janaza, based in Iraq, is part of the Arabic Anti-Islamic Legion. What makes Janaza even more intriguing is the fact that it's a one-woman solo project, in a country with a history of intolerance toward any female emancipation and also toward any hint of religious criticism.

The spread of black metal over the last three decades shows no sign of slowing down. And bands in diverse countries have managed to instill a flavor of their indigenous art into what they release. This all helps to keep the genre fresh and vital, and although there have been obvious peaks and valleys in its popularity, the fact that it remains steadfastly underground has helped to encourage individuality and creativity.

Everyone associated with black metal—musicians, designers, artists, and fans—has helped to ensure that it continues to evolve. As you can see from the art reproduced here, there is a strand of darkness running through everything, but the true talents take it to a new horizon.

TOP LEFT Band member King Diamond talks about the Mercyful Fate album *Nuns Have No Fun* (Roadrunner, 1983): "I wanted an image that would reflect the song 'Nuns Have No Fun', which was also the title of this record. There's something eerie and nasty about the drawing—and that's the mood I was after. I had a similar drawing on my bedroom door at the time."

BOTTOM LEFT King Diamond says of the artwork for the Mercyful Fate album *Melissa* (Roadrunner, 1983): "For the *Melissa* album cover, we used a human skull that I kept on my satanic altar at home. I stole it from a local hospital in Copenhagen, and I actually gave it the name Melissa. That is where the album title came from."

BOTTOM MIDDLE *Don't Break the Oath* was the second full-length album from Mercyful Fate (Roadrunner, 1984). It was imbued with serious satanic leanings, and this was reflected in a cover that was both demonic yet also a warning. "Your Satan Needs You" is the message in the pointing finger!

TOP RIGHT Band member Cronos says of the Venom album *Black Metal* (Neat, 1982): "We came up with the term 'black metal' almost as a joke. But once we'd done that, it made sense to call our second album *Black Metal*. And if you are gonna represent that sort of thing with an image, then a suitably satanic head is the way to do it."

BOTTOM RIGHT Bathory have long been regarded as one of the pioneers of modern black metal. *Under the Sign of the Black Mark* (New Renaissance, 1987) was the definitive Bathory album. The painting on the cover was by Gunnar Silins and based on something similar at the Royal Swedish Opera in Stockholm. The model was bodybuilder Leif Ehrnborg.

"WE NEVER HAD ANY BUDGET TO DO THINGS PROPERLY. SO, WE HAD TO BE CREATIVE WITH EVERYTHING WE DID. YOU COULD SAY THAT THE ARTISTRY AND ART OF CELTIC FROST WAS BORN FROM A SENSE OF DESPERATION AND DEPRIVATION. BUT WHEREVER IT CAME FROM IT CERTAINLY MADE AN IMPACT!"

—Thomas Gabriel Fischer, Celtic Frost vocalist-guitarist

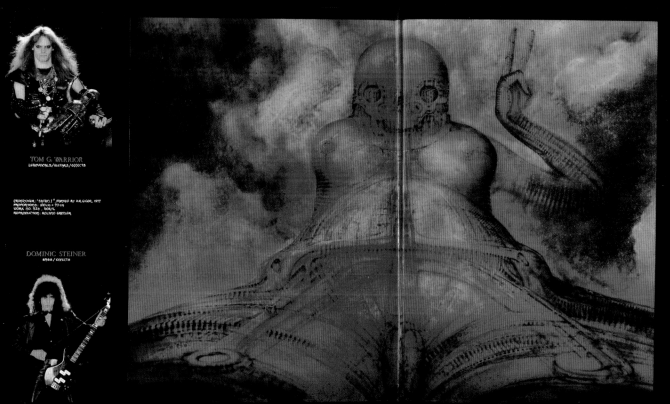

TOM G. WARRIOR
LEAD VOCALS / GUITARS / EFFECTS

FRONTCOVER: "SATAN I", PAINTED BY H.R.GIGER, 1977
PROPORTIONS: 100 cm × 70 cm
WORK NO. 529, ACRYL
REPRODUCTION: ROLAND GRETLER

DOMINIC STEINER
BASS / EFFECTS

REED ST. MARK
DRUMS / PERCUSSION / EFFECTS

BACKCOVER: "VICTORY III", PAINTED BY H.R.GIGER, 1981-83
PROPORTIONS: 70 cm × 100 cm
WORK NO. 710, ACRYL
REPRODUCTION: ROLAND GRETLER

TO MEGA THERION

"BLACK METAL BANDS ARE SO OFTEN DEFINED IN THE FIRST PLACE BY THEIR LOGOS. IN THIS RESPECT, CHRISTOPHE SZPAJDEL HAS SET THE TONE AND STANDARD FOR SO MANY OTHERS. AS SUCH, HE IS ONE OF THE MOST INFLUENTIAL FIGURES IN THE GENRE." —Malcolm Dome

ABOVE All of these logos were designed by Christophe Szpajdel. Born in Belgium, he says his influences come from nature and also from the Art Deco and Art Nouveau movements, which made their impact at the start of the twentieth century. It takes him a minimum of two weeks to create each logo.

OPPOSITE, TOP LEFT There's something altogether erotic yet disturbing about this image. It translates into the ambivalence of a seemingly naked woman, possessed on the spirit of Satanism, being violated by an inverted cross, yet actually enjoying the orgasmic experience. King Diamond of Mercyful Fate once considered using similar imagery on the band's debut EP.

Transilvanian Hunger

Horde

Hellig Usvart

HAIL SATANAS WE ARE THE BLACK LEGIONS

Carpathian Wolves

Dark Medieval Times

BOTTOM LEFT This was the cover of the first EP from French band Mütiilation, "Hail Satanas We Are the Black Legions" (Nightmare Productions, 1994). They had just joined a loose alliance of black metal bands called the Black Legions, and they went for a cover that was bleak and representative of what one should expect from the Black Legions.

BOTTOM MIDDLE The theme of this album from Graveland, *Carpathian Wolves* (Eternal Devils, 1994), is of the Christian sheep being slaughtered by pagan wolves. A pagan warlord prays to the ancient gods, side by side with a wolf. It's all done with a surreal sense of black-and-white starkness.

TOP RIGHT Band member Fenriz comments on the Darkthrone album *Transilvanian Hunger* (Peaceville, 1994): "The photo was taken in 1991 in an abandoned house, in the forest not far from the house I grew up in, but by the time we got round to using it in 1994, the photo was nowhere to be found. I had photocopied [it] to give out to magazines worldwide, but I couldn't find the negative, nor the photo itself, so, devil may care as we were in those days, I just send a photocopy and said, THIS WILL BE THE COVER. Hence the iconic look."

MIDDLE RIGHT *Hellig Usvart* (Nuclear Blast, 1994) was the only album from Australian band Horde. They described their style as unblack metal, and created controversy in the black metal world, because a lot of their lyrics were anti-Satanic. Main man Anonymous was responsible for the artwork, which reflected a desire to shine a light into the doom and gloom of black metal.

BOTTOM RIGHT Band member Satyr says of the Satyricon album *Dark Medieval Times* (Moonfog, 1994): "The mood of Theodor Kittelsen's drawings were a great inspiration for this album, which is why we used one on the cover. We wanted to incorporate a medieval atmosphere into our music. The booklet features another of his drawings, which was titled 'Pesta Drager.'"

"I AM PROUD OF WHAT WE DID IN NORWAY. WHEN WE STARTED TO BURN CHURCHES, WE WERE TAKING BACK THE COUNTRY. WE SHOULD BE WORSHIPPING PAGAN GODS AND IDEALS. CHRISTIANITY HAS CORRUPTED OUR SOULS."—Euronymous, Mayhem guitarist

BOTTOM LEFT Band member Necrobutcher says of the Mayhem EP "Deathcrush" (Posercorpse, 1987): "We set out to find something that fitted with the music; we went to the NTB [Norwegian Telegraf Berau] and went through their picture archive on torture and war. I remember that this picture stood out from the rest. It's from Mauritania, from a marketplace, as a warning to thieves what happens if you get caught stealing there. It's so barbaric that we just had to use it."

TOP RIGHT Necrobutcher on the Mayhem album titled *Dawn of the Black Hearts* (Warmaster, 1995): "It was Euronymous who took that photo, after finding the body of our vocalist Dead [who committed suicide in 1991]. He sent it out to some friends, and this guy from Columbia who called himself Bull Metal released it. When Mayhem went to Columbia in 1999, I went looking for this guy, because he put it out without the band's permission. But he'd also committed suicide."

BOTTOM RIGHT The cover for the Burzum album *Aske* (Deathlike Silence, 1993) is a photo of the Fantoft Stave Church after it was subjected to an arson attack on June 6,1992. Varg Vikernes of Burzum (who then went by the stage name of Count Grishnackh) was strongly suspected of being involved with this attack, and he took the photo on the cover. Vikernes became notorious when, on August 10, 1993, he murdered Mayhem bandmate Euronymous, stabbing him after a major confrontation. Vikernes served almost fifteen years in prison (out of a twenty-one-year sentence), and was released in 2009.

TOP LEFT The artwork for this Burzum album, *Filosofem* (Misanthropy, 1996), was the work of Theodor Kittelsen, a late nineteenth-century–early twentieth-century Norwegian artist known for his illustrations of fairy tales and nature paintings. This painting was titled *Op under Fjeldet toner en Lur* (Up in the Hills a Clarion Call Rings Out).

BOTTOM LEFT The mood of the music in "Through Chasm, Caves and Titan Woods" (Avantgarde, 1995)—the EP issued by Carpathian Forest when the Norwegian band were still a duo—is dark, spooky, and pagan. It's also imbued with the spirit of Edgar Allan Poe. This is reflected in a cover image that has the feeling of dark eeriness, capturing the band's disquieting ambience.

ABOVE RIGHT Another illustration from Theodor Kittelsen, a nineteenth-century–early twentieth-century Norwegian artist. His style was a combination of neoromanticism and a somewhat naïve approach. There's a bleak paganism about his style that appealed to Burzum's desire to promote preChristian Norwegian religious beliefs.

Joachim Luethe: Bringing the Fantastic to Life

One of the most fascinating and idiosyncratic of artists associated with black metal—and with extreme metal in general—Joachim Luetke has established a reputation as a cross-media innovator. Born in Germany and now living in Vienna, he has worked with Dimmu Borgir since 2002 and has also been involved with the bands God Dethroned and Belphegor. His style has been hailed as unique, showing an expressive, incisive manner of visualising music.

For as long as he could remember, Joachim Luetke wanted to be a graphic artist. To this end, he immersed himself in formal training, later discarding this and boldly creating his own visions.

"I went to Switzerland to the Art and Crafts School in Basle, which turned out to be a dead-end street—at least to my eyes. After quitting, I improved my capabilities as a classical painter and sculptor at the Academy of Fine Arts in Vienna. That's where I got introduced to the theories and works of fantastic realism, which is a more 'dreamy' branch of surrealism."

In this respect, one of the biggest influences of Luetke's developing talents was twentieth-century "psychic realist" Rudolf Hausner. Hausner cofounded a group of artists that called themselves the Vienna School of Fantastic Realism, which gave equal weight to both the conscious and subconscious processes involved in the creation of art.

"[Hausner] taught me how to visualize my 'inner cinema,'" Luetke explains. "He once said: 'Whatever imagery—no matter how surreal—you draw or paint, try to make it look as realistic and convincing as possible—otherwise it won't work.' With statements like that he guided me to what I personally wanted to achieve: how to give shape to my nightmares and fears!

"Keep in mind: all of this happened long before the 'dawn' of the first usable Mac, not to mention Photoshop. I'm talking about 'analog work' here."

What attracted Luetke to designing album covers was a desire to combine his love of music with his own artistic tendencies.

"I've always been into music. I always loved looking at cover artworks. Especially on vinyl, which had, due to its size, at the time a big impact on people. The most outstanding artworks always matched the music—a first glimpse of what we nowadays call multimedia products. So, combining my artistic visions with music became self-evident. A love affair, if you will."

Luetke's first commission was to create the cover for German thrash pioneers Destruction's album *Release from Agony* (1988). Since then he has worked with a diverse series of bands, although it is arguable that his most dynamic work has been done in the realm of black metal. And certainly what he has done with Dimmu Borgir has left an impression that both reflects the mood and tone of the music yet also stands alone as having artistic value outside of what is heard by the listener. It is a case of not only having a symbiotic relationship with the band in question but also having the creative spark to go beyond their songs. In this respect, he can be compared to the finest composers of film music. Not only do they enhance what is on the screen, but they also offer self-contained musical canvases.

So, what is it that attracts Luetke to work with a band? Here Luetke describes the critical relationship between the musical and the artistic content, a relationship that can't be compromised by commercial decisions:

"Certain aspects of their music should somehow kick-start my inner cinema. If this doesn't work, I refuse to work for a band, because being able to decipher someone's music in order to understand the mood, the emotion is mandatory—at least as far as I am concerned.

"WHAT ARTWORK PARTICULARLY MAKES ME PROUD? GEE, ALL THOSE ARTWORKS ARE MY CHILDREN; HOW COULD I PREFER ONE OF THEM? NAW, SERIOUSLY— IF YOU WANT ME TO PICK ONE OUT, IT WOULD MOST LIKELY BE [HIS ARTWORK FOR] DIMMU BORGIR'S *Death Cult Armageddon* [2003]."—Joachim Luetke, artist

"Music in this particular case also means the lyrics as well. My task is to visualize what I hear and understand, not just to come up with some catchy images, which are more or less connected to something a little vague. Did I ever refuse [to work] for a band? Yes! Several times, because I wasn't inspired by what they've done. Money is never a deciding factor for me. If I don't feel the music, then I will turn the commission down."

As a multimedia artist, Luetke has worked in the realms of video, sculpture, and painting to come up with his concepts; this makes his work restorative, representational, and revealing. He is a true artist who collaborates with bands and uses music to enter alternate psychic and mentally challenging universes. This makes him an outstanding and crucial part of the metal scene. As influential as any band that carries his art on their album covers.

OPPOSITE, TOP RIGHT Joachim Luetke is known for using modern technology to develop his images and craft. He is very much a cross-media artist, equally at home with painting, sculpture, and cyber activities. But although he has a contemporary approach, in no way does he ignore the traditional values, as can be seen in his striking and diverse work.

OPPOSITE, BOTTOM RIGHT Says Joachim Luetke of his cover for the Dimmu Borgir album *Death Cult Armageddon* (Nuclear Blast, 2003): "It has been a great challenge. How to depict Armageddon in a modern way? Bizarre war machines came to my mind. Like harvesters on an endless field swamped with human remains."

ABOVE LEFT "Joachim Luetke is one artist I really admire. His work really set a new standard for me. I can't say enough good words about his work. It stands out from what so many others are doing. He has a unique vision."
—Samuel Araya, fantasy artist

TOP RIGHT Joachim Luetke says of the cover for the Belphegor album *Blood Magick Necromance* (Nuclear Blast, 2011): "Hell. It's always a great pleasure collaborating with these guys. They really do mean it, in their music and lyrics! And I can assure you that no fake blood's been used in the process at all!"

BOTTOM RIGHT This is a cutout of the first digipak version of Dimmu Borgir's album *Death Cult Armageddon* (Nuclear Blast, 2003). "I view these as being war machines," says artist Joachim Luetke. "They are harvesters, kinda skull-and-bone-crushing mills. I suppose you can say that they were designed to erase the last remnants of mankind."

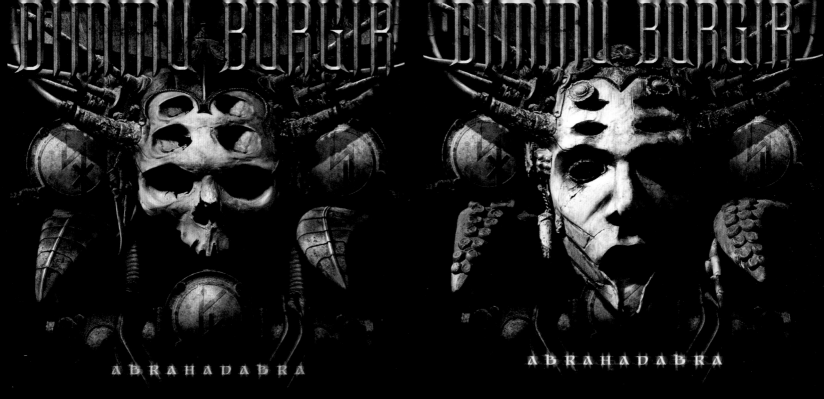

A B R A H A D A B R A

A B R A H A D A B R A

For All Tid

WORLD MISANTHROPY

TOP LEFT Joachim Luetke on the cover for the Dimmu Borgir album *Abrahadabra* (Nuclear Blast, 2010): "The most advanced artwork I've ever created. Dimmu Borgir always trigger my imagination in a very exceptional way. The central figure's mask is representative of H. P. Lovecraft's Elder Gods. The idea was to create something icy, bleak, and wintry."

TOP RIGHT Artist Joachim Luetke says of this alternative cover for *Abrahadabra* (Nuclear Blast, 2010): "Every time I work with the band my challenge is to do something different and more advanced. Here I wanted an image that was eerie and desolate."

BOTTOM LEFT The artwork on the cover for the Dimmu Borgir album *For All Tid* (Nuclear Blast, 1994) was inspired by an illustration of Camelot from nineteenth-century French artists Gustave Doré. The original appeared in *Idylls of the King*, a cycle of twelve poems by Alfred, Lord Tennyson. When released in 1994, the cover was in black and white, but the rerelease three years later had a color version.

BOTTOM RIGHT The cover concept for the Dimmu Borgir live DVD *World Misanthropy* (Nuclear Blast, 2002) is by Joachim Luetke. "I wanted to give the band a sense of the combination of the organic and the machine on the cover. I think this is represented by this image."

"NOW, I FEEL ASHAMED OF WHAT WE DID IN THE EARLY 1990s. BUT WE WERE VERY YOUNG AND IMPRESSIONABLE WHEN WE WERE DIRECTING ARSON ATTACKS ON CHURCHES. NOW IT'S ABOUT THE ART AND THE MUSIC, AS IT SHOULD ALWAYS HAVE BEEN."—Ihsahn, Emperor vocalist-guitarist

TOP LEFT *Cruelty And The Beast* (Music For Nations, 1998) was a Cradle of Filth concept album based on the infamous life of Countess Elisabeth Bathory. She was notorious for believing it was possible to keep herself youthful by bathing in the blood of virgins. The cover photo, by Stu Williamson, depicts exactly this. It's a Hammer Films–style still of the Countess in 'action.'

BOTTOM LEFT Ihsahn on the Emperor album: "By the time we did *Anthems to the Welkin at Dusk* [Candlelight, 1997], we were quite determined to go with an extravagant collage of Gustave Doré–style illustrations on an ongoing basis. So our artwork followed a pattern from here onwards. The more grandiose, the better was basically the motto for our work back then."

ABOVE RIGHT Band member Ihsahn says of the artwork for Emperor's album *In the Nightside Eclipse* (Candlelight, 1994): "[We] wanted to extend the artwork we had on the EP 'As the Shadows Rise' [Nocturnal Art Productions, 1994]. What we did was add in elements from the lyrics. At some point I think we even discussed continuing the artwork further for each album."

"THERE MUST BE A BELIEF SYSTEM SHARED BY ALL MEMBERS OF A BAND. THAT IS A MUST IN ORDER TO DO SOMETHING AS INTIMATE AND PERSONAL AS MUSIC." —Watain

ABOVE Watain say of the cover for the album *Casus Luciferi* (Drakkar Productions, 2003): "The cover and the general graphic vibe of *Casus Luciferi* was an attempt to combine a profound sense of divinity with the raw and cunning aesthetics of the black/death metal cult. The inspirations were an equal amount of Gutenberg and the first releases of Sabbat from Japan. The symbolism of the cover itself is based upon the coming of the Fallen One, with the seven angels of the apocalypse about to blow the trumpets and break the seals."

TOP LEFT *At The Heart of Winter* (Osmose, 1999) from Norwegians Immortal is regarded as the album through which Immortal began to establish their trademark sound. The cover artwork is simple and dignified and reflects the musical aspects, having a spirit of desolation and also of impending devastation. There's also a background of abject loneliness.

BOTTOM LEFT This cover of the original demo from Xasthur, a one-man American black metal project, titled *A Gate Through Bloodstained Mirrors* (Profane Productions, 2001), has a darkness that reflects the philosophy of main man Malefic: "I would tell God that his son is a weak sham, and that what he 'died for' is also a joke. He should have aborted his son from the beginning; we would all be better off today."

TOP RIGHT Enslaved, on the cover for their album *Blodhemn* (Osmose, 1998): "The image on *Blodhemn* was a bit of art by accident. Whereas we had used real-life props on the previous albums, we decided to go with the photographer's idea to post-treat the photo. So the picture of us was taken in the studio and then the rocky beach, the Viking ship and skull in the sky (that one is pretty blatantly obvious)

BOTTOM RIGHT Band member Blackmoon says of Dark Funeral's album *The Secrets of the Black Arts* (No Fashion, 1996): "We wanted the album to be built up like I think an album should: start fast, then slow down a little, then gradually build the speed again to the absolute edge, and then cool down for the very last songs. And the cover has the same impact."

Preludes to Death

SVARGAROTH

Harvest The Last Souls

Black Grave

The Last Exhalation Before The End

Morituri te salutamus

TOP LEFT Krypt are a Norwegian duo whose aims are to promulgate old-school black metal values and to keep the anti-Christian fires stoked. This is the cover for their album *Preludes to Death* (Agonia, 2008). It is certainly reflected in the artwork here, which has the spirit of early 1990s black metal. It's no coincidence that it has a lot in common with Darkthrone. That was the intention.

BOTTOM LEFT *The Last Exhalation Before the End* (Hass Weg Productions, 2011) is a split album featuring the Ukrainian band Nocturnal Amentia and Black Grave, from the UK. As both bands are very much steeped in the underground scene, it was difficult to find an image for the cover that accurately sums up both artists. However, this bleak one is more about capturing the intense atmosphere of the bands.

TOP RIGHT Svargaroth is a black metal band from Egypt. This album cover, for *Harvest The Lost Souls* (self-released, 2011), has nothing to do with local terrain or mythology. The band is steeped in the early Norwegian black metal traditions, and there's a real appreciation of the paganism associated with forests in Norway. So this is certainly going back to the roots.

BOTTOM RIGHT The title of Eyecult's album *Morituri Te Salutamas* (Ewiges Eis, 2009) is Latin for "Those Who Are About to Die, Salute You." This declaration dates back to the year 52 AD, when protagonists ready to enact a mock naval battle declared their allegiance to Emperor Claudius. The artwork, based on this salute, has a dark humor.

"IN MY OPINION, BLACK METAL TODAY IS JUST MUSIC. I'LL TELL YOU THAT NEITHER I NOR THE REST OF THE MAYHEM NEVER REALLY WERE AGAINST RELIGION OR ANYTHING ELSE. WE ARE PRIMARILY INTERESTED IN MUSIC." —Hellhammer, Mayhem drummer

TOP LEFT The face looming out of the cover of the Abazagorath self-titled EP (Negativity, 2012) brings to mind the demon that haunted the climax to the 1957 movie *Night of the Demon*. It has the same disorienting effect here, as the American band show the clearly satanic creature ready to devour all in its wake. A cleverly disturbing image.

BOTTOM LEFT "Of Decay and Decadence/ Zukunftsspruch" (Ván, 2010) is an EP split between German bands Funeral Procession and Abusus. Influenced by Burzum's artwork, this cover doesn't represent each of the bands so much as it offers an overall imagery representing the dark, doomed soul of black metal.

ABOVE RIGHT The imagery in this poster is a combination of Satanism and Christianity. What is invoked by Calth is the duality of an existence that acknowledges both powers. You are never quite sure which has the upper hand, if, indeed, any power does. And the centerpiece is the guitar as the ultimate rock god.

Fanzines: The Voice of the People

The work and influence of fanzines is often overlooked. But in the world of metal, they've had a considerable impact on a global scale. This is where so many bands who later became household names got their first media exposure, and it's also where some of the most important writers in the genre got their first big break.

American fanzines like *Metal Mania* played a huge part in bringing the young thrash scene to life, giving it valuable early exposure at the start of the 1980s. In fact, *Metal Mania*'s founder Ron Quintana, a friend of Metallica drummer Lars Ulrich, is credited with coming up with the band's name. He was thinking of using "Metallica" for his fanzine, until Lars persuaded him to go for *Metal Mania* . . . so that he could have it for his fledgling band!

Some now-established magazines, such as *Rock Hard* in Germany and *Metal Forces* in the United Kingdom, actually began life as fanzines before opening up and becoming professional publications.

What generally differentiates fanzines from their more mainstream cousins is funding (fanzines are run by enthusiasts on virtually no budget), commercial focus (fanzines are free of such constraints, so they can concentrate on the more underground and grassroots scene), objectivity (professional magazines need to be balanced and aware of retaining the largesse of record labels, whereas fanzines can let rip at their leisure, with little or no comeback), frequency (magazines have to adhere to strict deadlines, but many fanzines come out sporadically, when their creators have the time and cash flow), and design (especially in the pre-internet age, many fanzines were typed pages with little or no illustrative content, photocopied and stapled together).

These days, most fanzines have become webzines, which certainly saves on the wear and tear of trying to sell them outside of venues or persuade the occasional specialist shop to stock them. And in an era in which bands use the social network to get their message and profile across, the role of the fanzine has been drastically reduced. Oh, for the halcyon days of such fanzines as *Phoenix* or *Boulevard*, two of the best British ones ever to hit the street!

Comics also had a major impact on metal. The imagery of Marvel and DC Comics was always closely associated with metal music. And the *Watchmen* and *Dark Knight* series of comics heralded an even closer link with the music, in terms of both their more disturbing, ambivalent storylines and their insidious artwork.

And an increasing number of bands are also featured in their own comics. This was started by KISS in 1977 with their Marvel comics special, and it has become part of the way bands market themselves and their product, blurring the already indistinct line between the two disciplines. And let's not forget the American publication *Heavy Metal*, which brings together gothic imagery, eroticism, and fantasy/science fiction, and has been doing so for nearly forty years.

> "I STARTED WITH *SLAYER* BACK IN 1985. WELL, I STARTED IN '84 BUT THE FIRST ISSUE WAS OUT IN EARLY '85. I WAS PREVIOUSLY CONTRIBUTING TO A METAL 'ZINE CALLED *LIVE WIRE*, BUT SINCE THE OTHER GUYS LOST INTEREST, MY AMBITION WAS GROWING BIGGER. I THOUGHT I COULD DO THIS ON MY OWN."
> —Metalion, *Slayer* editor

LEFT "In August of 1981, I xeroxed off copies of the first issue of *Metal Mania* with Lemmy on the cover 'cause Motörhead finally played out here that year. I was pretty excited about it, and it really was a fanzine mainly written by me, and I still don't consider myself a great writer."—Ron Quintana, *Metal Mania* editor

Blood Fire Death

SLAYER Vol. 14

Total Destruktion

SLAYER VOL. II

Metallik Devastation

DEC. 1983   NO. 7 $1.00

THE HEADBANGER

FIRST 50 ISSUES RECEIVE FREE SNOWHITE FLEXIDISC!

IRON MAIDEN
AN INTERVIEW WITH
BRUCE DICKINSON

L. A. METAL
PART 1, OF A 2 PART SPECIAL
FEATURING
W.A.S.P.

BITCH
HELLION
SOUND BARRIER
SLAYER
& MORE

AN INTERVIEW WITH RECORD
PRODUCER-DENNIS MACKAY.
CONCERTS REVIEWS-RAVEN
METALLICA-QUEENSRYCHE.
ALBUM REVIEWS AND MORE

No. 3 $1

THE HEADBANGER

Heavy Metal Fanzine

ARMORED SAINT

features: Armored Saint   Accept

August Redmoon   Randy Hansen Kiss & more!

Euronymous

Never to be forgotten!

OPPOSITE, RIGHT "Obviously the front cover of *Metal Forces* issue one was based on the attention-grabbing headline 'Murray Quits Maiden?' The story had come from a roadie who claimed that he worked for Iron Maiden, and Dave Murray was going to leave the band following their World Piece Tour. Quite naïvely, we went with the headline on the cover without checking the story first." —Bernard Doe, *Metal Forces* editor

TOP LEFT TO RIGHT "For the first issues I didn't really do interviews, just bios on bands I got information [about] in the mail. I'm not sure which was exactly the first band I interviewed, but it was most likely a Norwegian heavy metal band called Road; that interview was never published, but it was an interesting experience." —Metalion

BOTTOM LEFT "This issue introduced part one of my LA metal report, which was one of the first reports on the LA metal scene to have national distribution in the US. Also, contributor Shelly Hammer had recently interviewed Bruce Dickinson and offered us the interview. And seeing that Maiden were one of the hottest up-and-coming metal bands in the US at the time, I thought they should be the cover story." —Bob Nalbandian, *The Headbanger* editor

BOTTOM MIDDLE "I wanted to do a feature on Armored Saint. I saw the band at a small club in Anaheim called The Woodstock and they literally blew me away! This is before anybody really knew who they were, outside their hometown fan base in Pasadena. But I was so into this band that I decided to have them as the cover story." —Bob Nalbandian

BOTTOM RIGHT It is typical of the fanzine philosophy that *Slayer* could dedicate a full page to one-time Mayhem guitarist Euronymous, who was seen as a malevolent force—which only added to his luster in the underground press. "I believe in honesty to myself—that is all that matters. I will never interview anyone just because the label tells me to. I have to like the band. I don't need all those ads anyway." —Metalion

▶
ABOVE Tom Angelripper on the relevance of *In War and Pieces* (Steamhammer/SPV, 2010): "The desire of our society to always be progressive is put into perspective by belligerency. We technically act on a very high level, but we don't think about the fact that those who are at war with one another are sons, fathers, brothers and husbands, who bleed for a country, which they can't identify with properly."

"THE LYRICS DEAL WITH THE DISASTROUS CONDITION OF PLANET EARTH AND THE IGNORANCE OF MANKIND, NOT TO CHANGE THE SITUATION TO ITS OWN WELL-BEING. THE COVER REFLECTS AND DESCRIBES ALL THESE THEMES THAT I USED FOR THIS LYRIC. AND IT IS AN AMAZING ARTWORK, CREATED BY ELIRAN KANTOR."—Tom Angelripper, Sodom vocalist-guitarist

"BENJAMIN HAS MORE THAN MET MY EXPECTATIONS. NOT ONLY DID I GET THE ARTWORK AND EVERYTHING THAT I ASKED FOR, BUT I ALSO GOT A HANDWRITTEN LETTER ON PARCHMENT AND A SKETCH OF THE INTERIOR MEDITATIVE MONK PIECE THAT'S IN THE LAYOUT. I MEAN, HE'S A PROFESSIONAL ARTIST, AND HIS PIECES CAN BE FOUND IN GALLERIES ON BOTH CONTINENTS."
—Aamonael, Avichi solo artist, talks about Benjamin J. Vierling

TOP LEFT Avichi talks about his 2011 album *The Devil's Fractal* (Profound Lore): "Of course the visual aspect is important. Everything is. Most refined black metal bands would tell you this. This music is very personal to both the artist and listener. When I'm holding a release, I want to feel like I'm holding a Beksinski (renowned Polish surrealist painter)."

BOTTOM LEFT Deiphago are renowned for their raw, war-like approach to their music. And this is reflected in the album created by Vierling (*Satan Alpha Omega*, Hell's Headbangers, 2012). It does represent the constant, irresolvable struggle between the powers of darkness and light.

ABOVE RIGHT Vetis Monarch on *From The Devil's Tomb* (The Ajna Offensive, 2010): "The union of great music, great art and great literature is very important to us. Of course, said greatness is subjective, but as far as we are concerned, Benjamin Vierling is one of the few artists of this era who is capable of illustrating in colors and shapes what Weapon conjures via music

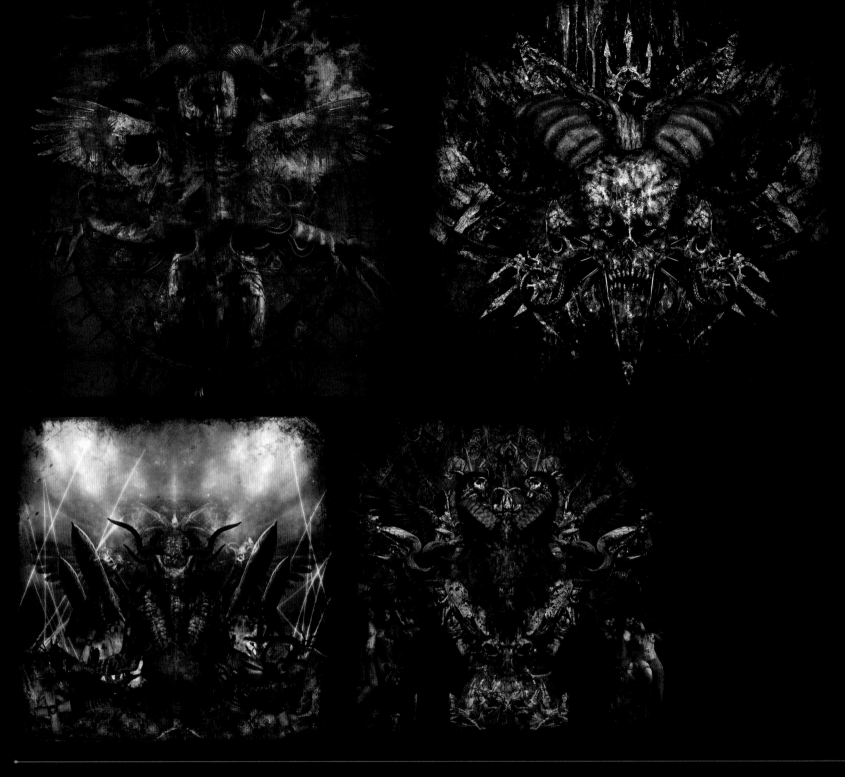

TOP LEFT Bahrull Marta on the artwork for the Belligerent Intent album *Seven Are They* (Sepsis, 2012): "I got a chance to meet the guys of Belligerent Intent from Australia, who worked with me for their first full-length album last year. They had a show in Jakarta before they play[ed] in Bangkok on December 2012; well, it was a good time to meet the band who worked with me."

BOTTOM LEFT Bahrull Marta says of his artwork for the Cosmic Funeral album *Godless War to Eternity* (self-released, 2012): "When I was working with Cosmic Funeral, who are a Turkish black metal [band], they wanted to have an evil image in the center, which was godless, dark, and cosmic surrounded by dark instruments of war."

TOP RIGHT For Daemoni's debut album *Stillborn Redeemer* (Goathorned Productions, 2011), the Colombian band worked with Bahrull Marta to create a complex construction of demonic nuances, as well as something a little more sinister in the background. It has the distinct flavor of old-school—almost 1980s—black metal, but benefits from modern technology.

BOTTOM RIGHT Bahrull Marta created the cover art for the Profanus Nathrahk album *The Second Coming* (self-released, 2011). The title comes from a poem by the twentieth-century Irish poet William Yeats. It deals with the apocalypse, and this is reflected in the imagery, which has a definite feeling of the final war.

ABOVE For the Bane album *The Acausal Fire* (Abyss Records, 2012), the Serbian band attempted to develop a cold, eerie atmosphere with the music, and Bahrull Marta certainly does a similar job with the artwork. This certainly is the sort of image that you can study endlessly and always find something new grabbing your attention.

"WHAT I DO IS SUMMON AND CONSTRUCT THE EQUILIBRIUM BETWEEN DARK AND DARKNESS WHILE CREATING ARTWORK. IT'S A CASE OF LEARNING HOW TO EMPHASIZE AND BRING OUT MY CHAOTIC EXPRESSIONIST DREAMS."—Bahrull Marta, artist

CHAPTER 7

THRASH & DEATH METAL

"THRASH, OR SPEED METAL AS IT WAS ALSO CALLED, STARTED FROM THE UNDERGROUND. A MIXTURE OF PUNK AND METAL ALONG WITH A DIY ATTITUDE, THESE BANDS ALL STARTED BECAUSE OF THEIR LOVE OF THE MUSIC. YOU SEE NOW HOW FRESH AND ORIGINAL THAT WHOLE SCENE WAS."

—Brian Slagel, Metal Blade CEO, the label that "discovered" Metallica

THRASHIN' LIKE A MANIAC

LOUISE BROWN

The dam may have burst in the United Kingdom in the late '70s, ushering in a new wave for heavy metal, but over in America hard rock bands such as KISS, Aerosmith, and Ted Nugent were ruling the airwaves, and punk rock acts like Black Flag and Minor Threat were as extreme as it got. But the new British invasion was about to hit Los Angeles like an earthquake. A small handful of heavy metal obsessives were about to discover a new sound that would become one of rock's biggest selling subgenres —thrash metal.

Lars Ulrich, a young Danish tennis player, who had moved to LA to concentrate on his sporting career, would soon meet record shop clerk Brian Slagel at a concert and over a shared love of the new wave of British heavy metal bands they would start an adventure that led to the formation of one of the world's biggest bands, Metallica, and one of heavy metal's most important record labels, Metal Blade. Arguably, you could say that this led to the creation of a whole new musical movement.

But what was thrash metal and where did it come from? This was 1981. In the United Kingdom, Saxon had just put out their call-to-arms manifesto, *Denim and Leather*, the twin guitar prowess of Iron Maiden had just been laid down on *Killers* and just a year previously Diamond Head had asked the question "Am I Evil?". Venom were busy welcoming us to Hell, and over in Denmark a band called Mercyful Fate were "Burning the Cross". All of these records made their way to LA through shops like Oz Records, where Slagel worked, and made an impact on budding musicians like Ulrich. In 1981 Black Flag were *Damaged* and Minor Threat were "Seein' Red", but more importantly, a man called Ronald Reagan had just been sworn in as the fortieth president of the United States, signaling a shift to conservative politics that would mould a generation of disenfranchised, angry young men.

American punk rock and the European metal imports would collide to create an incendiary weapon of thrash destruction. But there was one thing more repulsive than Reagan, and more catastrophic than the threat of Cold War, and that was glam metal. For our LA music freaks, the spandex-clad, hair-sprayed clans, with their power ballad love songs and metrosexual depravity, was a nemesis to be crushed. To escape the Mötley Crüe crew Metallica would move the 365 miles from LA to San Francisco, where a scene of like-minded heavy metal maniacs were forming bands like Exodus, Legacy (later Testament), Death Angel and D.R.I. (Dirty Rotten Imbeciles). Compared to the over-the-top nature of the

"THRASH METAL WAS BORN OUT OF A NEED FOR SPEED AND AS A VISCERAL OUTLET FOR THEIR RAGE, BUT THOUGH ITS LOW-ART AND LOW-CONCEPT NATURE WAS ORGANIC, THRASH GREW FROM ITS DIY ROOTS AND BECAME AS TURBOCHARGED AS ITS TEMPO. AS THE SUBGENRE GATHERED MOMENTUM, IT GARNERED ATTENTION FROM THE MAJOR LABELS AND IGNITED A PASSION IN FANS THAT EVENTUALLY EARNED THRASH A PLACE AS ONE OF THE MOST CRUCIAL MOVEMENTS IN HEAVY METAL HISTORY."—Louise Brown

LA glam metal scene, the San Francisco scene was stripped down: bands wore the same cut-off band shirts and dirty, ripped jeans as they wore all day; there was no "stage outfit," no gimmicks, and no high art concept. Thrash metal was born out of a need for speed and as a visceral outlet for rage, but though its low-art and low-concept nature was organic, thrash grew from its DIY roots and became as turbocharged as its tempo. As the subgenre gathered momentum, it garnered attention from the major labels and ignited a passion in fans that eventually earned thrash a place as one of the most crucial movements in heavy metal history.

SPREADING THE DISEASE

As thrash evolved into the mid-'80s, it was taken from the garages and dive bars of Oakland, California, to concert arenas and big name record labels like Atlantic and Def Jam. These labels dressed the bands in brand new sneakers; more important, they gave them a budget for new scopes in artwork. Slayer scored the opportunity to work with *Village Voice* cartoonist Larry Carroll for arguably thrash's defining moment, the 1986 album *Reign in Blood*, which continued the Satanic theme of their debut and its follow-up, 1985's *Hell Awaits*, but refined it with a dystopian, apocalyptic, and ultimately more mature design. But the real game-changer in 1986 came from Megadeth, formed by ex-Metallica guitarist Dave Mustaine. Their second opus, *Peace Sells . . . but Who's Buying?* introduced thrash to its artist in residence, Ed Repka. He had already laid paintbrush to canvas for protodeath metallers Possessed and extreme thrash act Dark Angel, but in the *Peace Sells . . .* aftermath, he went on to scribble cover art for Vio-lence, Hirax, and revival thrash bands such as Ravage and Toxic Holocaust.

The art for *Peace Sells . . .* would also mirror another big artistic signifier in thrash. As Reagan's rule of the United States continued into a second term, so too would thrash metal's rallying cry against the status quo, manifesting in an outcry against the threats of

global warming and nuclear war. Armageddon and the destruction of Earth were big themes of mid-period thrash, and this was showcased in much of Repka's artwork. German thrash giants such as Sodom and Destruction gave a nod to these on their albums *Agent Orange* and *Infernal Overkill*, respectively. Nuclear Assault's Ed Repka artwork for their 1986 album *Game Over* would sum up the apocalyptic paranoia of '80s America, while their New York counterparts Carnivore used punk artist Sean Taggart to depict their version of a fallout future.

HAZARDOUS MUTATION

Thrash continued to reign through the '80s, but by the '90s grunge rock was on the rise. The major labels that had championed the metal maniacs were now encouraging them to write radio-friendly ballads and tone down their extreme tendencies. Underground genres like death metal and black metal grew from thrash's ashes, and it seemed that the genre had predicted its own demise with its end-of-the-world artwork. However, by the 2000s the genre had mutated; it seemed as if the alien creatures featured on album covers by Flotsam and Jetsam, Voivod, and Hydra Vein would return to earth in the form of post-millennial thrashers, raised on Slayer and Metallica, who reignited the scene in all its gory glory. Yet far from being fearful of nuclear holocaust, bands like Gama Bomb, Municipal Waste and Evile cracked open the toxic ooze like it was a six-pack of beer and bringing it to a keg party. Thrash was back, and with it the simple, DIY ethics of both its music and its art.

DEATH BY METAL

While thrash was already moshing all around by 1983, no one is quite sure what happened that year to make a group of unconnected heavy metal fiends take their love of bands like Mercyful Fate, Venom, and Slayer and form bands of their own, but nonetheless it was the year that birthed in blood the most depraved, disgusting, and downright dirty genre in heavy metal. Orlando's Mantas wrote the song "Death by Metal" before disbanding and resurrecting themselves as the bands Massacre and Death. Down the road in Tampa, Morbid Angel were starting to conceive their "Unholy Blasphemies" and California's Possessed gave the genre its name with their first demo *Death Metal*. More savage than thrash and more bestial than black, death metal would become heavy metal's uncouth cousin. The genre would ransack the existing extremities of thrash and classic metal and make it slower, deeper, and more decrepit—it was the music of horror and of fear. While thrash wrote about zombies drinking toxic kool aid and going surfing on the ooze, death metal was digging up graves and cutting up corpses—the gruesome slasher flick to thrash's B-movie humor.

In Switzerland thrashing forefathers Hellhammer released their demo *Death Fiend*, but by 1985, Necrophagia claimed that *Death is Fun*, pre-Master mob Death Strike released *Fuckin' Death* and pre-Repulsion misfits Genocide promised us all a Violent Death. Death was everywhere and heavy metal was about to get ugly. This growing music expression was alluring to droves of teenage boys who dissected insects, disembowelled their sister's dolls and filled their school books with doodles of disembodied zombies. As such, they needed an aesthetic to fit. The classic artwork of heavy metal or the lurid, DIY charm of thrash would not do. Death metal needed artwork that would shock as much as its lyrical content—the gorier the better.

Arguably the first "death metal" album, *Seven Churches* by Possessed (1985), was still classed as thrash and with its simple, spiky logo by Vince Stevenson and uncluttered artwork by Donald J. Munz, it did not embrace the gore and guts of the bands it would inspire. Death, one of the genre's undisputed godfathers, were also stuck in the thrash time warp using that genre's go-to artist, Ed Repka, as designer, for 1987's *Scream Bloody Gore*, but his skeletal monks were at least heading in the right destructive direction. The same year Necrophagia's *Season of the Dead* used the zombie motif so famous in thrash, but Drew Elliott used cannibalism, dismembered limbs and a whole lot of red paint to push the theme to the extreme. Not to be outdone by Elliott's ravenous undead depiction, the newly-formed death metal hordes set about a battle of butchery, each band trying to up the stakes of grossness in their artwork and pushing the boundaries of taste and decency. In 1989, California's horror movie obsessives Autopsy put out their debut *Severed Survival* with thrash art veteran

Kent Mathieu getting to unleash his demons on a nightmarish canvas of a man being hacked to pieces on the operating table. Their label, Peaceville, immediately came under pressure to change the graphic artwork and it was finally replaced with a Kev Walker painting of the scene from the point of view of the surgeons, merely hinting at the terrors they were unleashing on their victim. In Britain, Liverpool grinders Carcass had been in similar trouble with the cover of their debut full-length *Reek of Putrefaction* when vocalist Jeff Walker, who had previously provided the artwork for grindcore masterpiece *Scum* by Birmingham's Napalm Death, made a collage of animal and human body parts that was replaced with a more acceptable interpretation of anatomy cross-sections. Also in 1989, Obituary hired Rob Mayworth to pen a decaying corpse for their *Slowly We Rot* debut. Morbid Angel used British artist Dan Seagrave for their debut *Altars of Madness*, which showed a cluttered vortex of ghoulish demons and Cannibal Corpse hooked up with Vincent Locke for the utterly unpleasant *Eaten Back to Life* (1990) cover. It seemed that the nastier the better seemed the way for these death metal legions.

COURTING CONTROVERSY

It wasn't long before the law and the dreaded PRMC (Parents' Music Resource Center), a frightening mob of censorship-crazed warriors, led by Tipper Gore, who were worried for America's youth, stepped in and placed this burgeoning scene firmly in their sights, making sure its horrifying artwork and offensive lyrics would not tempt the innocent into a life of drug-taking and sexual depravity. The PRMC forced the music industry to its knees and made them think twice about their cover art choices as shops started to refuse to stock anything that could be seized by the decency police. It certainly made things very awkward for the death metallers. Fronted by outspoken Satanist Glen Benton, it was no surprise that Florida-based death troop Deicide caught the brunt of the backlash—he did, after all, have an inverted crucifix branded on his forehead and on the cover of 1995's *Once Upon the Cross*, which depicted a bloodied Jesus under a white shroud. This was covered by an advisory sticker by their label, Roadrunner.

Cannibal Corpse's in-house artist Vincent Locke got the band in trouble in Germany, meaning that the band couldn't even tour there until 2006, despite the fact that by today's standards the idea of two zombies caught in the act of oral sex (as seen on the cover of 1992's *Tomb of the Mutilated*), is tame compared to some recent death metal fodder, such as Impaled's 2001 *Choice Cuts*, Cattle Decapitation's *Humanure* (2004), or Putrid Pile's *Blood Fetish* (2012). Perhaps we have simply become desensitized to gore and guts. Where does this leave death metal and its mission to shock and test the boundaries of extremity?

EATEN BACK TO LIFE

Death metal is in rude form today. From its birth in 1983, the genre is flourishing with newer bands inspired by the forefathers and the original architects of the scene still touring and recording. Obituary, Cannibal Corpse, Morbid Angel, Deicide, and Carcass are all still here, spreading the gory gospel of death, and newer bands like Tribulation, Degial, and Chapel of Disease are carrying the torch for the early death metal sounds. The genre has also evolved and mutated, becoming more technical thanks to game-changers such as Opeth, Atheist, and Pestilence. Bands like Autopsy Winter, and Dream Death helped push it into doomier and darker territories, while acts like Darkthone and Dissection paved the way for death metal to merge with its black metal cousins. The genre has had a modern makeover too, and been rebranded as deathcore with groups like Bring Me the Horizon taking the death metal template and regurgitating it for a new generation. Its aesthetic is still evil, disgusting, and horrific, and as the traditional 12" vinyl artwork gives way to the digital MP3, death metal bands are leading the vanguard for new ways to promote their artistic vision. Bands like Job for a Cowboy and Whitechapel are merchandise barons, releasing more T-shirts than records, with their audience hungry for their next, even more brutal design, proudly displaying dismembered limbs and ghoulish monks on their chests. The need for gore is ever-present, and despite starting as a genre that wanted to reject traditional heavy metal aesthetics, death metal has kept the relationship between music and its art alive and still relevant.

"WHILE THRASH WROTE ABOUT ZOMBIES DRINKING TOXIC KOOL AID AND GOING SURFING ON THE OOZE, DEATH METAL WAS DIGGING UP GRAVES AND CUTTING UP CORPSES— THE GRUESOME SLASHER FLICK TO THRASH'S B-MOVIE HUMOR."—Louise Brown

"THE EARLY THRASH METAL ART WAS ALL DONE WITH NO MONEY. IT WAS PRETTY CRUDE, BUT THAT WAS ALSO SO COOL. A FRIEND OF MINE CAME UP WITH THE OVERALL IDEA FOR *METAL MASSACRE* [WHICH FEATURED THE FIRST-EVER SONG BY METALLICA]. I HAD NO MONEY, SO IT WAS SUPER LOW BUDGET. I WANTED TO MAKE SURE WE HAD SKULLS IN WHATEVER ART THERE WAS. I DID SPEND A BIT EXTRA ON THE PRESSING TO GET THE SILVER COLOR."—Brian Slagel, Metal Blade CEO

TOP LEFT After meeting Metallica drummer Lars Ulrich through a mutual love of NWOBHM, record shop clerk Brian Slagel formed Metal Blade. He says, "When I was putting together the *Metal Massacre Volume 1* compilation, Lars asked if [we] put together a band, could he be on it? I guess the rest is history."

BOTTOM LEFT Despite being rejected, the original artwork for *Metal Up Your Ass* has become one of Metallica's most famous images. Featuring a crudely drawn sketch of a hand holding a sword, coming out of a toilet bowl, it sums up the simple style of thrash metal. The band later released the original artwork on a T-shirt, and it was used on a live bootleg.

ABOVE RIGHT Metallica weren't the only band to use a crude, simple design on their early releases. This style became vital to the thrash movement. Anthrax, from New York—who later became one of the Big Four of thrash along with Metallica, Slayer, and Megadeth—adopted this violent, cartoon-like style for their early albums, such as *Spreading the Disease* (Megaforce, 1985), with artwork by David Heffernan.

"WHEN WE DID *HELL AWAITS* WE HAD OUR GUY [ALBERT CUELLAR] AND WE TOLD HIM THE NAME OF THE ALBUM, AND THAT'S WHAT HE CAME UP WITH. WE WERE LIKE 'COOL.' PEOPLE ALWAYS WANT THIS DEEP PHILOSOPHY AS TO WHY WE DID THINGS; WE JUST THOUGHT IT WAS COOL. JUST LIKE EVERYTHING ELSE WITH THIS BAND, IT JUST HAPPENED. THE GUY HAD DONE THE COVER FOR 'LIVE UNDEAD' AND I LOVED IT. IT WAS ON A LITTLE PIECE OF PAPER. THEN BRIAN ASKED HIM TO DO THIS ALBUM, AND HE DID IT OVERNIGHT AND PRESENTED IT THE NEXT DAY. WE DIDN'T SEE IT UNTIL BRIAN SHOWED IT TO US. THIS GUY WAS AN ARTIST AND HE WORKED WITH DIFFERENT MATERIALS, SO HE USED WATER, THEN DREW THESE THINGS OUT AND CUT THINGS OUT."—Tom Araya, Slayer bassist-vocalist

TOP LEFT Slayer are perhaps the definitive thrash band, but instead of the cartoon-like artwork of their contemporaries, they adopted a much darker aesthetic, as shown on the cover of *Show No Mercy* (Metal Blade, 1983). The devil wearing spiked gauntlets was drawn by their friend's father, Lawrence R. Reed; today that style is still associated with the Slayer-inspired subgenre black thrash.

BOTTOM LEFT Sepultura, from Brazil, were part of a legion of bands from around the globe that joined Slayer on the path of thrashing aggression. Sarcofago (Brazil), Nifelheim (Sweden), Destroyer 666 (Australia), and Celtic Frost (Switzerland) were among the many bands bringing the darkness to thrash metal. *Morbid Visions* was Sepultura's debut album and came out in 1986 on Cogumelo with artwork by their friends Alex and Ibsen.

BOTTOM RIGHT Their most famous album and undoubtedly one of the most vital albums of the whole thrash movement, *Reign in Blood*, came out in October 1986 on legendary label Def Jam. The artwork still had the dark, evil motifs but was more mature in execution, thanks to *Village Voice* artist Larry Carroll. Carroll, who also worked for Newsweek and the New York Times, also designed three other Slayer covers: *South of Heaven*

(Def Jam, 1988), *Seasons in the Abyss* (Def American, 1990), and *Christ Illusion* (American Recordings, 2006).

SLAYER

HELL AWAITS

"DAVID ELLEFSON AND MYSELF, AND OUR AGENT AT THE TIME, A GUY NAMED ANDY SUMMERS, HAD GOT TOGETHER IN NEW YORK. WE WERE IN MANHATTAN, AND ACTUALLY ACROSS THE STREET FROM THE UN BUILDING. I DON'T KNOW WHY WE WERE THERE, BUT WE WERE THERE. AND WE TALKED TO THIS GUY, THIS ARTIST, ED REPKA. AND OVER THE COURSE OF THE PERIOD OF TALKING I SAID THAT I WOULD LIKE IT TO BE THE UN, ALL BOMBED OUT. AND THEN SOMEBODY SAID THIS AND SOMEBODY SAID THAT, AND THEN WE WOULD HAVE AIRPLANES COMING IN, AND A 'FOR SALE' SIGN, AND ALL THESE THINGS, AND IT GERMINATED FROM THAT MEAL WITH ANDY SUMMERS."

—Dave Mustaine, Megadeth guitarist

TOP & BOTTOM After leaving Metallica, guitarist Dave Mustaine formed one of the most legendary thrash bands of all time: Megadeth. They hired up-and-coming artist Edward J. Repka to paint the cover for their second album, *Peace Sells . . . But Who's Buying?* (Combat) in 1986, and Repka, with his colorful and apocalyptic style, quickly positioned himself as the go-to guy for thrash art. Among others, he also designed the classic *Hazardous Mutilation* (Earache, 2005) sleeve for Municipal Waste and the *Game Over* (Combat, 1986) cover for Nuclear Assault.

TOP LEFT As thrash metal paved the way for the heavier and more brutal sounds of death metal, many of the early bands of that movement, such as Death and Massacre, opted to use Repka for their cover designs. This ghoulish, colorful piece was for Massacre's debut, *From Beyond* (Earache, 1991). Repka based this design on the H. P. Lovecraft story of the same title.

BOTTOM LEFT The undisputed fathers of death metal, Death formed in Florida in 1983, under the name Mantas. The band was founded by Chuck Schuldiner, Kam Lee (later of Massacre), and Rick Rozz, but it would take five years for the Repka-designed *Scream Bloody Gore* to come out (1987, Combat). The album is called the first true death metal record.

TOP RIGHT Nicknamed the LA Caffeine Machine, Dark Angel were one of the first, and fastest, Bay Area thrash bands. *Darkness Descends* (Combat, 1986) was one of the first designed by thrash artist-in-residence Ed Repka. He also designed their infamous logo. The album featured Gene Hoglan on drums; he later joined the Cartoon Network's Metalocalypse cast.

BOTTOM RIGHT The Bay Area's Possessed coined the term "death metal" on their 1984 demo, but their debut album, *Seven Churches* (Combat, 1985) had simple, thrashy design, and the band were not yet defined as a death metal band. The following year they unleashed *Beyond the Gates* and, in line with its Repka-designed cover, began to push the boundaries of extremity from thrash to death.

TOP LEFT Ed Repka designed the cover for Nuclear Assault's *Game Over* album (Combat, 1986). The songs included "Nuclear War," "Radiation Sickness," and "After the Holocaust." The band was formed by Danny Lilker, previously bass player for Anthrax, as he wanted to pursue a more aggressive form of thrash metal.

BOTTOM LEFT Metallica made their own antiwar statement with the song "Disposable Heroes" on their third album, *Master of Puppets* (Elektra, 1986). The striking artwork of dog tags hanging from soldiers' gravestones was designed by Don Brautigam, who also worked with Mötley Crüe, AC/DC, and Anthrax, as well as James Brown and Chuck Berry.

TOP RIGHT Another big German thrash band was Destruction; their 1985 debut, *Infernal Overkill* (Steamhammer), hinted at planetary disaster and World War III, especially on the song "Antichrist." The ominous mushroom cloud cover painting was by Udo Linke, who later became a celebrated fetish pop artist. Linke himself describes his style as retro pop art. Among his most renowned works is a series called *Suspenstories*.

BOTTOM RIGHT Crossover thrash titans Carnivore began in New York in 1982; their second, and last, album, *Retaliation*, came out on Roadrunner in 1987, with artwork by punk cartoonist Sean Taggart. The lyrics were strongly against religion, war, and nuclear arms. Vocalist Pete Steele went on to play in the very successful goth band Type O Negative until his death in 2010.

"MANY OF THE THRASH BANDS IN THE 1980s USED THEIR ARTWORK TO MAKE STATEMENTS AGAINST NUCLEAR WAR. AGENT ORANGE DEALS WITH INSECTICIDE USED AS A WEAPON IN THE VIETNAM WAR. TOM ANGELRIPPER FROM SODOM SENT ME A PHOTOGRAPH SHOT OUT OF A BOMBER. HE WANTED ME TO USE THIS AS A BASE FOR THE ART, WHICH SHOULD BE COMPOSED LIKE A WIDESCREEN CINEMASCOPE STILL FROM A FILM LIKE APOCALYPSE NOW. IT SHOULD SHOW THE BRUTALITY OF WAR. THE GUY WITH THE MASK IS THE MYSTICAL FIGURE FROM ALMOST ALL OF THE SODOM COVERS, A PERSONIFICATION OF WAR."
—Andreas Marschall, artist

RIGHT "*Agent Orange* is drawn with fine brushes in a very detailed way and finished with airbrush and acrylic colors. The perspective makes you feel like you are on board of the airplane. The aim was to draw the viewer inside the painting and give him the feeling of being present at the brutality of war. When the album was released it was a huge step for the band, from underground cult to the status of a major German thrash band."—Andreas Marschall, on the artwork for Agent Orange (Steamhammer, 1989)

MICHEL "AWAY" LANGEVIN

Who'd have thought that a young daydreamer with fantasies of space travel and a limitless mind, who doodled aliens and mutant creatures on his schoolbooks, would come to define the art of thrash metal? Michel "Away" Langevin, from Jonquière, Canada, certainly never imagined that, but he did imagine much, much more—and he, along with his band, Voivod, would come to push thrash to new boundaries that would rock the genre to its very foundations.

In 1982 Canadian filmmaker Terre Nash made a hard-hitting documentary, *If You Love This Planet*, about the potential consequences of nuclear war. This controversial film was seen as foreign propaganda by the Reagan administration and was actively suppressed, despite its Oscar win for Best Documentary Short Subject. The film, which showed graphic images from the fallout of Hiroshima and Nagasaki, had a huge effect on the twenty-year-old music and art fanatic Michel Langevin. Growing up in Jonquière, an industrial city in the province of Quebec, Canada, the young daydreamer had few prospects other than going to work in one of the town's many factories. But for Langevin there was an escape plan. Scribbling in schoolbooks and on the backs of pizza boxes, Langevin created a fantastical world of evil vampires and alien beings.

"The apocalyptic style of my visuals came around 1980," Langevin recalls. "That documentary about nuclear weapons really opened my eyes, and then very soon after, I discovered punk rock, and that also opened my eyes to nuclear stockpiles, so I integrated that to my art, along with the early cyber punk movies like *Mad Max*, which had a strong influence also."

Langevin's love of punk and progressive bands like Pink Floyd and Faust, along with his artistic tendencies, eventually found a creative outlet in the formation of the thrash band Voivod, who were quickly signed to Metal Blade for their 1984 album *War and Pain*. The nuclear fear and sci-fi fantasies of Langevin, who dubbed himself with the stage name "Away," became the bedrock of Voivod's interstellar overdrive style of thrash, and they quickly became one of the most important, and game-changing, artists of the genre. But it was "Away's" artwork

"I WAS DOING A LOT OF ART THAT WAS BASED ON NIGHTMARES I HAD, BASED ON THE NOISES I HEARD BECAUSE OF THE FACTORIES, SO ART AND MUSIC WAS VERY CONNECTED FOR ME."—Michel "Away" Langevin, Voivod drummer and artist

that cemented the band in the minds of the thrashing maniacs who were hungry for anything fast, wild, and out of this world.

Just as the heavy metal of Britain famously blamed the industrial clank and grind of Birmingham for its birth—the city being home, after all, to Black Sabbath and Judas Priest, among others—the noise and pollution of Jonquière had a similar effect on Langevin. "I was doing a lot of art that was based on nightmares I had, based on the noises I heard because of the factories, so art and music was very connected for me," he remembers.

As Voivod's career trajectory went into hyperdrive, so did his imagination. "Away" created lavish concepts based on chillingly realistic intergalactic terrors from which he designed Voivod's artwork, and their vocalist, "Snake," wrote the lyrics. These simple sketches of alien beasts and B-movie baddies inspired a generation of thrash nuts—including celebrated thrash artists Ed Repka, Sean Taggart, Kent Mathieu, and Andrei Bouzikov—who began to include space and apocalyptic themes in their own lyrics and artwork. From the tank-driving ant overlord on the cover of Voivod's 1983 demo *Anachronism* to the Giger-esque, cyberpunk alien on their 1989 *Nothingface* album, the 1950s robot of their 1993 single "Fix My Heart" to the crude and childlike ant crushing a city on 1995's *Negatron*, the artwork of "Away" and the band it represented became key signifiers of the whole thrash movement. The look wasn't technically proficient; there were no vast canvasses with oil-painted landscapes and jaw-dropping artists' prowess. Rather, it was everything thrash represented: hard, fast, frightening, fun, simple, DIY, and desperate. And that is why Michel Langevin is the ultimate thrash master. Thrash metal was rooted here on earth, but he took it up, up and Away into the stratosphere, where it would finally discover a whole universe of inspiration to tap into.

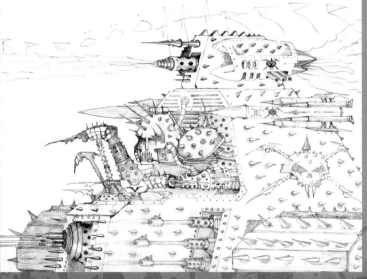

TOP LEFT Michel "Away" Langevin working in his studio in Montreal, Canada. He has provided artwork for all Voivod releases as well as worked with Probot featuring Dave Grohl (Nirvana/Foo Fighters), new thrashers Toxic Holocaust, and hardcore band Ringworm. He has had a book published about his art and exhibited his work at the renowned Roadburn Festival in the Netherlands in 2012.

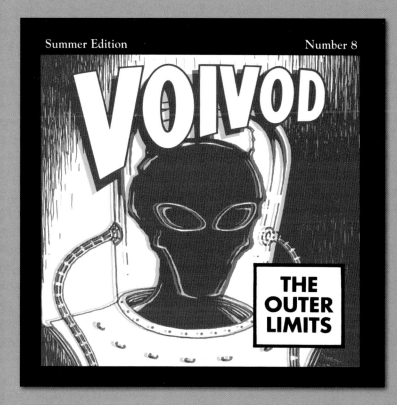

Summer Edition Number 8

VOIVOD

THE
OUTER
LIMITS

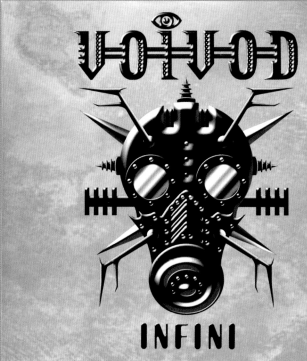

VOIVOD

INFINI

OPPOSITE, BOTTOM LEFT Langevin comments on Voivod's debut album, *War and Pain* (Metal Blade, 1984): "I'm really proud of the first front cover I did for *War and Pain*, a mixture of metal and crust-punk. It's really epresentative of the cold war years, like the music on the album."

OPPOSITE, BOTTOM RIGHT Langevin says, "I started to draw when I was very young, when I saw the cartoon character called Atom Ant. I was not trained in art; later in the mid-'90s I went back to school to study 3-D animation, and the first model I did was an atomic ant!"

TOP LEFT Langevin comments on *The Outer Limits* (MCA, 1993): "TV shows like *The Outer Limits* and *Ultraman* had a huge impact on my art. I also had nightmares because of the sounds of the factory by the family house. It made me dream of mechanical creatures, which I would draw when I woke up."

BOTTOM LEFT Voivod's apocalyptic theme continues well into the modern age, with the cover of *Infini* (Relapse) released in 2009. This is one of Michel's most simple but striking designs. It was the last to feature founding member Denis "Piggy" D'Amour, who died in 2005 of colon cancer. The album was released posthumously.

ABOVE RIGHT Michel "Away" Langevin's unused poster design, 2007. It is featured in the book *Worlds Away: Voivod and the Art of Michel Langevin* (Martin Popoff, 2011) and hints at the style and color schemes of the band's most recent album, *Target Earth* (Century Media, 2013).

At The Gates

Slaughter of the Soul

ABOVE By the mid-1990s death metal was becoming popular in Sweden. At The Gates used Kristian "Necrolord" Wåhlin to design the cover of their landmark album *Slaughter of the Soul* (Earache, 1995). "I talked to him a lot about which kind of cover we were going for, and he responded with a lot of inspired thoughts as well," recalls At The Gates' front man Tomas Lindberg. "I remember that he always painted to music, and that I recorded a special mix tape for him to paint our cover to. I have never worked with someone as dedicated as Necrolord. He put in a lot of extra work into that cover, and I think that really shows."

"NECROLORD WAS ONE OF GOTHENBURG'S TOP GRAFFITI ARTISTS. I STRONGLY REMEMBER HIS PARENTS NOT BEING TOO FOND OF THAT PARTICULAR STYLE OF ART. WE HAD TICKETS TO SEE SLAYER IN STOCKHOLM, BUT THEY FOUND A PHOTO ALBUM WITH NEW PAINTINGS, WHICH GOT HIM GROUNDED."—Tomas Lindberg, At the Gates vocalist, who recalls the legend that is Kristian "Necrolord" Wåhlin. The artist eventually put down the spray can and picked up his paintbrush, painting devilish canvasses for many metal bands such as Emperor, Tiamat, and Bathory. He still provides artwork for bands such as Wintersun, Ensiferum, and the Black Dahlia Murder.

TOP LEFT Necrolord began designing the artwork for his own bands, Grotesque and Liers in Wait, before lending his skill to his friends' bands, such as Cemetery, Morbid, and Nifelheim. The blasphemous "Bröderna Hårdrock" ("The Heavy Metal Brothers") of black thrash collaborated with Wåhlin in 1994 for their self-titled debut on Necropolis Records.

BOTTOM LEFT "When we were about to release our album *Darkside*, we wanted something grand and with impact. A cover with lots of details; a cover that you could be amazed of again and again and again. We knew the works of Necrolord, and we all thought he'd be perfect. I explained what we were looking for and gave him the title of the album and our symbol, the Necrogram. The result is, in my opinion, one of his greater works from that period."—Joakim Sterner, Necrophobic drummer

BOTTOM RIGHT Necrolord and Stockholm death/black pioneers Dissection are synonymous with each other, Wåhlin having penned all their art, from their 1991 demo to their comeback single "Maha Kali" in 2004. Their second album, *Storm of the Light's Bane* (Nuclear Blast, 1995), is both Dissection and Wåhlin's most famous work.

"IF YOU WERE A FAN OF EXTREME MUSIC AT THAT TIME THEN YOU WERE PROBABLY ALSO ATTRACTED TO HORROR MOVIES. OF COURSE, ONLY LATER DID THE IDEAS AND CONCEPTS THE BANDS WANTED TO PORTRAY COME THROUGH, BUT INITIALLY THE SHOCKING IMPACT WAS ENOUGH TO BLOW ANY TEENAGE MIND. IT WAS SHOCKING AND I WAS OPEN TO BEING SHOCKED. I WANTED IT AND NEEDED IT LOOKING BACK."

—Dan Tobin, Earache manager

TOP & BOTTOM LEFT Chris Reifert, of the band Death, formed Autopsy in 1987 as a thrash-inspired death metal band. They later became one of the founding bands of the doom-death movement. The cover by Kent Mathieu of their debut album, *Severed Survival* (1989, Peaceville), was censored for being too violent, and was recommissioned with art by Kev Walker, showing instead the operation from the viewpoint of the patient rather than the surgeon.

ABOVE RIGHT For their second album *Mental Funeral* (Peaceville, 1991), Autopsy returned once more to the intricate artwork of Kev Walker. Walker is a renowned British comic artist and illustrator, who has also worked on such iconic publications as *2000 AD* and Marvel Comics.

TOP LEFT Many death metal bands had their artwork banned for being too violent, blasphemous, or in bad taste. Cannibal Corpse, a band formed in New York in 1988, were victims of the censors for almost all of their early Vincent Locke–designed albums, including the debut *Eaten Back to Life* (Metal Blade, 1990). Locke is most known for his work on the zombie horror comic *Deadworld*. He has also created weirdly erotic art to illustrate stories by dark

BOTTOM LEFT *Tomb of the Mutilated*, Cannibal Corpse's third album for Metal Blade, came out in 1992. It originally featured two zombies in the act of oral sex on the cover, drawn by their long-time collaborator Vincent Locke. Locke later redrew the scene as an earlier snapshot from the same timeline, viewed from an alternate angle, thus hiding the offending act (from all but those in the know), and escaping the wrath of the censors.

TOP RIGHT Obituary began in Tampa, Florida, in 1984 under the name Executioner, before changing their name in 1988. Their debut, *Slowly We Rot* (Roadrunner, 1989), featured a zombified corpse on the cover, painted by Rob Mayworth, who went on to work with them on four further albums.

BOTTOM RIGHT Zombie art was a staple of the thrash movement, but as death metal grew it took the theme and made it less cartoon like and more gruesome. Necrophagia, from Ohio, started in 1983 and were one of the earliest death bands. The cover of *Season of the Dead* (New Renaissance, 1987) was painted by Drew Elliot, who later provided zombie art for Amorphis, Goreaphobia, and Festered.

METAL LOGOS

The heavy metal logo is perhaps the most undervalued art form across the whole genre. There it is, everywhere you look—from album covers to T-shirts and even tattoos—but has it become so ubiquitous that you forget just how much thought, time, and talent has gone into how it is presented? After all, the logo becomes the brand signifier for your band. And in thrash metal particularly, it is the one piece of art that carries you throughout your career. Think of the Metallica "M" or the Slayer "S," the Overkill bat or the Nifelheim trident. How many of those logos have been scribbled on the backs of school books or traced onto jean jackets? The logo is the most essential piece of art a band can have.

Once the band have their logo, often crudely drawn by a band member (for example, the infamous Death logo penned by drummer Kam Lee), only then can they think about releasing albums, T-shirts, and flyers—the logo is where it all begins, and without a key identifier, how can the heavy metal band begin to market itself to like-minded fans? "A band logo could be a deal breaker," admits Radio One rock DJ Daniel P. Carter. "People maybe bought one or two albums a week. When you were in a shop holding a couple of albums without knowing either, a band's logo was as important as the artwork, song titles, and band photo."

And the logo is a surefire way to tell fans, at a glance, what "tribe" of metal you belong to. Death metal bands tend to include gore and horror in their chunky form of typography. Black metal bands go for ineligible, spiky, symmetrical scrawls. Thrash is all about simple, basic, punchy calligraphy—easy to draw on your school books and even easier to embroider onto a patch, because that is where thrash tribalism comes to the fore.

"Patches are where it's at, man," says Canadian thrasher, Jason Decay, of the band Cauldron. "A good logo is definitely important—you want it to stand out. Putting patches on your jacket shows a bit about who you are and what you stand for. It's also a good conversation piece and a great way to meet like-minded people when you're out at gigs or record shops."

Patches have become the calling card of the heavy metal fan. Friendships have formed, bands started, and even lovers wed because of the simple patch.

"I love seeing patched jackets; they are a walking badge of metal honor," says Joel Graham of the British thrash band Evile. "We get loads of fans who get us to sign them, and I always take time to scan over the logos and discuss the bands on show."

Why wear just one band logo T-shirt to display your allegiance to heavy metal, when you can sew up to fifty band names onto your jacket?

"PUTTING PATCHES ON YOUR JACKET SHOWS A BIT ABOUT WHO YOU ARE AND WHAT YOU STAND FOR."
—Jason Decay, Cauldron bassist

OPPOSITE (PATCHES) One item of vital importance, which would become the lifeblood of the scene, was the band logo. Each band wanted the perfect signifier to represent them. Metallica, Exodus, and Testament nailed their brand early on, and that simple lettering would become more important than any thought-out or well-designed album sleeve. These logos were printed on T-shirts, embroidered on patches, and scrawled on school books and jean jackets, acting as a tribal calling that forged friendships and eventually more bands. The simple opener "Is that a Slayer patch?" could find you your best friend, your future guitar player, or sometimes both.

OPPOSITE (JACKETS) The patch jacket is sometimes known as the "battle jacket." It should be worn until it is almost falling apart, held together only by the patches themselves, and the older it is, the more authentic it becomes. It should also never be washed!

ABOVE In the thrash and death metal worlds, the patch jacket has become the telltale sign of how much of a die-hard fan you are. The more obscure the patch, the more respect from fellow thrashers. Just a simple Hallows Eve or Razor patch can promote you from lowly fan to true cult warrior. For a certain group of young American teens, fed up with the widespread popularity of hair metal, the pacts made from the painting of a certain band logo on their leather jacket were priceless. And the bands involved in the scene knew that a good logo could make or break your band. Cronos of Venom once said: "Seeing a fan wearing your patch on their jacket is a real badge of honor. To go to the trouble of sewing your logo onto their jacket—it's a real thrill. Because they identify with you."

TOP LEFT This piece, called *The World Is a Thorn*, was painted by Seagrave and used by metalcore band Demon Hunter on their album of the same name, released in 2010 by Solid State. The style is similar to covers painted for Morbid Angel's 2000 album *Gateways to Annihilation* (Earache) and Horde of Anachron's Aeons of Damnation (self-released, 2009).

BOTTOM LEFT Earache kept Seagrave busy throughout the 1990s; this piece was painted for Swedish grindcore band Carnage for their album *Dark Recollections* (Earache, 1990). Carnage were one of the forerunners of the Swedish death metal scene, becoming the third band to record a full-length at the now-famous Sunlight Studios in Stockholm.

TOP RIGHT Entombed are one of the most important Swedish death metal bands and one of the most important bands in heavy metal history. They pioneered the guitar tone that defined the genre, as well as term "death 'n' roll." *Left Hand Path* (Earache, 1990) is a cult classic, its artwork provided once again by Dan Seagrave.

BOTTOM RIGHT Seagrave has continued to provide artwork for the heavy metal world and is one of the most sought-after artists for upcoming bands. This work was used by Invection, one of many thrash metal revival bands to come out of California in recent years. They hired Seagrave for their debut full-length, *Facet of Aberration* (StormSpell, 2011). Self-taught, Seagrave was hired because his distinctive, detailed style made him one of the most acclaimed extreme metal artists from the early 1990s onward.

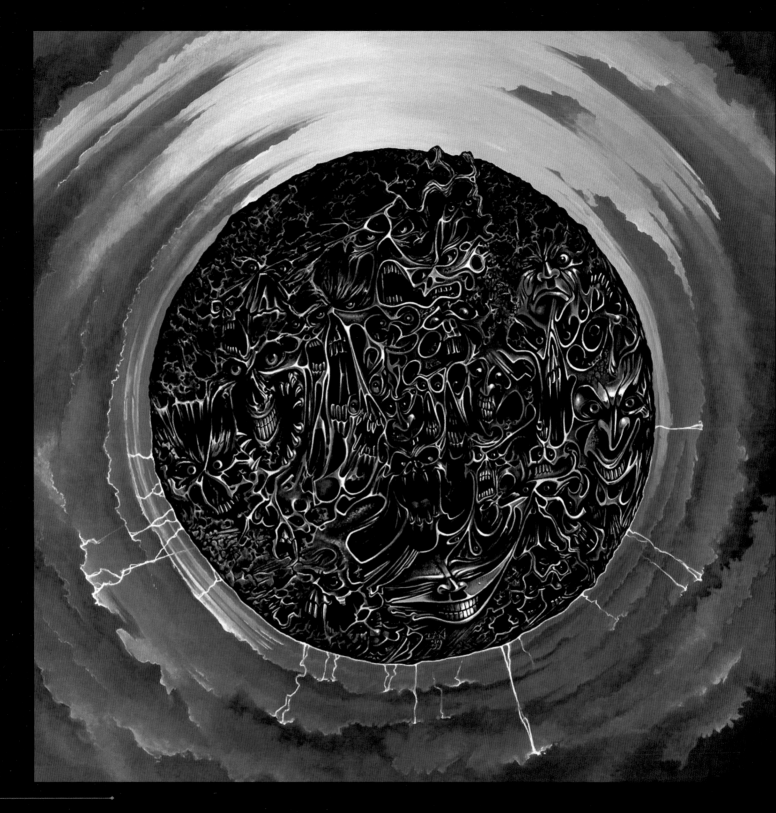

"MY INFLUENCES COME FROM OUTSIDE THE MUSIC BUSINESS. FILM HAS ALWAYS INTERESTED ME, AS SOME OF MY EARLIEST INFLUENCES STEM FROM THERE. AND MY WORK HAS ALWAYS HAD A DARK SENSE OF HUMOR AS WELL."—Dan Seagrave, artist

"THIS WAS INSPIRED BY ANALOG TECHNOLOGY, WHICH IS SOMETHING WE FIND REALLY INTERESTING. I STRUCK UPON THE IDEA OF A TAPE MACHINE AS A SKULL, OOZING TAPE LIKE BLOOD. THE ARTIST WE USED WAS GRAHAM HUMPHREYS. HE CREATED ICONIC POSTERS FOR THE FILMS *A NIGHTMARE ON ELM STREET* AND *EVIL DEAD*. HE'S ONE OF THE FEW ARTISTS OF THAT KIND LEFT, THE TYPE WHO ACTUALLY HOLD A BRUSH." —Philly Byrne, Gama Bomb vocalist

HELL ON EARTH

OPPOSITE By the late 2000s underground death metal was being taken over by the more popular deathcore style. Thrash made its attack and came back stronger than ever, with a wave of new bands such as Evile, Gama Bomb, and Municipal Waste. Graham Humphreys, who had worked previously with grindcore legends Napalm Death, painted this cover for Gama Bomb's 2013 album *The Terror Tapes* (AFM). Humphreys has also designed posters for cult horror movies and magazines and has done the storyboards for such films as *Hardware* and *Dust Devil*.

TOP LEFT Featuring all the trademarks of old-school thrash, including the patch jacket, studded leather, and cartoon-like violence (including a nod to how thrash was back to rid the world of emo, in the same way the band of old had wanted to rid the world of hair metal), California's Fueled by Fire put out *Spread the Fire* (Annialation) in 2006, with artwork by their friend Dez Ambrose.

TOP RIGHT Inspired by old thrash and black metal bands, Toxic Holocaust, from Portland, Oregon, formed in 1999. A solo project of Joel Grind, he hired thrash king Ed Repka for the cover of 2005's *Hell on Earth*, which was released on the cult label Nuclear War Now. When the band signed with the much bigger Relapse three years later, it gave them the chance for greater exposure, once the album was re-pressed.

ABOVE One of the biggest names of the thrash revival was Municipal Waste, of Richmond, Virginia, who used Andrei Bouzikov to design the zombie holocaust–themed artwork for their third full-length release, *The Art of Partying* (Earache, 2007).

"IN 1991 I DISCOVERED THE UNDERGROUND BLACK/DEATH METAL SCENE. THE ONSLAUGHT OF PHOTOCOPIED FLIERS, DO-IT-YOURSELF FANZINES, AND DEMO TAPE COLLECTIONS LEFT AN ETERNAL IMPRESSION ON MY YOUTHFUL PSYCHE. TO THIS DAY, SOME TWENTY-PLUS YEARS LATER, I CONTINUE TO STRIVE TO PRESERVE THE AMBIANCE AND FEELING OF THE EARLY '90s UNDERGROUND METAL SCENE THROUGH MY ARTISTIC VISION. BLACK-AND-WHITE, PENS AND MARKERS ON PAPER, IS HOW I ACHIEVE MY CREATIVE EXPRESSION; NO COMPUTERS OR MOUSE-CLICKING. IMPURE, RAW, AND FOUL . . . JUST LIKE THE MUSIC I ADORE."—Mark Riddick, graphic artist

LEFT Mark Riddick began drawing his trademark demons in 1991 and has become one of the go-to artists for the contemporary extreme metal scene. His pen-and-ink work is key to the underground scene, where shunning the mainstream is vital. This artwork was used by Indian thrash band Kryptos for their 2012 album *The Coils of Apollyon* (AFM).

TOP LEFT Profanatica, from New York, were one of the first American extreme metal bands, forming in 1990 by former members of death metal band Incantation. Vehemently underground and cult, they turned to Riddick to provide the blasphemous artwork for their 2012 EP "Sickened By Holy Host" (Hell's Headbangers).

BOTTOM LEFT As well as being a renowned artist, Riddick plays in various underground death and grind metal bands, such as Macabra, Unburied, Unearthed, Equimanthorn, and Fetid Zombie, a gore-obsessed death metal band, for whom this design was created.

ABOVE RIGHT Rhode Island's Headrot were an unknown early death metal band until Riddick started to shout about their hidden greatness. In 2010 Pathos Productions gathered together their early demos *I Gulp Your Guts* and *Among the Remains* and reissued them with this (un)fresh artwork for "Gulping the Remains", provided by, of course, Riddick himself.

"ALBUM ART HAS TO REFLECT THE NATURE OF THE MUSIC. IT NEEDS TO PROVOKE A REACTION IN THE VIEWER, EITHER OF DISGUST, OR OF EXCITEMENT. THOSE ARE THE ONLY TWO EXTREMES WORTH CARING ABOUT. THE SCUM ARTWORK SPOKE A LANGUAGE I UNDERSTOOD. I WASN'T POLITICAL BUT I HAD VAGUE IDEAS OF RIGHT/WRONG, OF THE 'POWERS THAT BE' CRUSHING THE SOUL OUT OF EVERYDAY FOLK. THE ARTWORK SAID A MILLION THINGS IN ONE HORRENDOUS IMAGE."

—Dan Tobin, Earache manager

ABOVE LEFT Scott Carlson of grind veterans Repulsion on the artwork of their sole full-length album, *Horrified* (Necrosis/ Earache, 1989): "The head was our symbol, but when we did the album, Jeff from Carcass thought that skull should be on the album cover, and he was right. So Jeff did the artwork; he just took my drawing of the head, blew it up, and painted over it."

TOP RIGHT Napalm Death, a favorite of John Peel, formed from the British punk scene in 1981 and were the pioneers of the grindcore sound. Their debut, Scum, was released in 1987 by Earache, with DIY cut 'n' paste artwork by Jeff Walker of the death metal band Carcass.

BOTTOM RIGHT Carcass, who formed in Liverpool in 1995, were in the firing line of controversy when it came to their Walker-designed gruesome and graphic cut 'n' paste album covers. Almost all of their early albums had "alternative" covers, including this one for *Symphonies of Sickness* (Earache, 1989).

OPPOSITE In the late 1980s the British death metal scene pioneered the grindcore sound, a faster and dirtier offshoot of death metal, and radio DJ John Peel became a staunch supporter, promoting bands like Napalm Death, Extreme Noise Terror, and Godflesh on his radio show. In 2009 Earache gathered these lost recordings together for a compilation disc, with art by up-and-coming Belarussian sleeve artist

"I KNEW WE HAD TO KEEP THE SPIRIT OF THOSE EARLY DAYS OF GRINDCORE AND THAT WE NEEDED A PEN-AND-INK GUY TO DRAW SOMETHING, NOT PHOTOSHOP IT. THEY'RE NOT EASY TO FIND THESE DAYS. BUT I SEARCHED THE NET AND FOUND SOME COOL PUNK RELEASES I LIKED, RECENT ONES, AND SET ABOUT FINDING AN ARTIST TO DO WHAT WE HAD IN MIND. THE CONCEPT WAS THE ICONIC BBC BUILDING, CRUMBLING UNDER THE WEIGHT OF EXTREME MUSIC. WE GOT THE AWESOME ANDREI BOUZIKOV TO DO IT. THAT GUY GETS IT, HE GOT THE ERA WE WERE CELEBRATING. IT'S A HOMAGE TO JOHN PEEL, WITHOUT WHOM EXTREME MUSIC WOULD NEVER HAVE GOT OFF THE GROUND."

—Dan Tobin, on the making of *Grind Madness at the BBC* (Earache, 2009)

"THE MORE WE MOVE INTO THE DIGITAL AGE, THE MORE IMPORTANT THE BAND SHIRT BECOMES; IT'S A WAY FOR BANDS TO EXPRESS THEMSELVES THROUGH ANOTHER MEDIUM WHILST PHYSICAL CDs DIE OUT. GROWING UP, I LOVED HAVING A NEW BAND SHIRT; THIS WAS BACK WHEN IT WOULD JUST BE A LOGO OR SOMETHING SIMPLE. IT ALLOWED YOU TO SHOW THE WORLD WHAT NEW BAND YOU WERE INTO. THE LAST TEN YEARS HAS SEEN BAND MERCH JUMP TO AN EXTREME NEW LEVEL, AND IT'S BEEN REALLY FUN TO BE A PART OF THAT REJUVENATION AS ARTISTS PUSH THE BOUNDARIES OF WHAT CAN BE ACHIEVED WITH THE SIMPLE T-SHIRT." —Dan Mumford, designer of death metal merchandise

LEFT With the rise of digital distribution, is the album art at risk of disappearing? Will the 12″ album sleeve become extinct? Modern death metal bands are keeping the art of metal alive through merchandise, hiring key contemporary artists like Dan Mumford, Godmachine, and Funeral French to design a range of must-have T-shirts.

ABOVE RIGHT Named after the area in London where Jack the Ripper committed most of his crimes, Tennessee band Whitechapel are one of the leading bands of the deathcore movement, which mixes death metal, thrash, and hardcore punk. This T-shirt was designed by Dan Mumford, who has also worked with fashion brands like Iron Fist and Nike, as well as bands like Trivium and Bleeding Through.

ABOVE LEFT Funeral French is a London-based artist who has created gruesome pen-and-ink work for bands such as Brutal Truth, Municipal Waste, and Decrepid. This T-shirt design is for American grindcore band Pig Destroyer (Relapse). "They didn't want anything to do with pigs, but they wanted something about the pope being evil, and they liked some of the stuff I'd done with zombied bodies. I detail it in pencil, and once that's okay with the band, I ink that sucker."

ABOVE RIGHT This piece, called *Spider Baby*, is by death metal T-shirt designer Godmachine. He produces his artwork in Photoshop "using a Wacom tablet. The idea behind it was just to create a gnarly skull with spiders' legs and a coffin. I wanted to put a load of ideas, objects, and techniques that I'd been trying lately together in one piece. I produced it for a company whose only brief was 'It has to be skulls.' The name was taken from the film by the same name."

CHAPTER 8

PROG METAL

"WE LIKED A LOT OF REALLY STRAIGHT ROCK METAL BANDS LIKE SABBATH AND UFO, BUT THEN THERE
WAS THE PROG SIDE, WHICH I REALLY ENJOYED TOO—GENESIS, YES, EMERSON, LAKE & PALMER.
SO I GUESS IT ALL STARTS WITH NEVER BEING HAPPY WITH WHAT WE DO, AND HAVING SUCH HIGH
RESPECT FOR PEOPLE WHO INFLUENCED US, AND TRYING TO ATTAIN THAT GOAL OF WRITING SOMETHING
THAT EQUALS, AT LEAST IN OUR MINDS, THOSE CLASSICS THAT WE GREW UP LISTENING TO."

—Jim Matheos, Fates Warning guitarist

A Propensity for Note Density

MARTIN POPOFF

"Heavy metal is the new progressive rock," noted Porcupine Tree's Steven Wilson a few years back, and it's gone more that way ever since, with metal of all stripes becoming the domain of the craftiest, speediest, trickiest playing in rock. Indeed, metal guitarists, drummers, and bassists, once denigrated, are now at the forefront of musical achievement, and our loud 'n' proud format is enjoying a deserved level of near-academic respect.

So it's no surprise that within metal there are armies of bands respectful of what is known as progressive rock, an initially British form blossoming from psychedelia in '69 and populated by the likes of Yes, Genesis, Jethro Tull, ELP, Pink Floyd, and King Crimson—the last being the loudest of this frankly elitist bunch.

Characterized by long instrumental passages, odd time signatures, fantasy lyrics, concepts that spanned entire records, superior musicianship, and at times artful maneuvers borrowed from classical music, prog rock (aka art rock) nonetheless was rarely heavy, like Sabbath or Heep or Deep Purple, even if all of those bands could be proggy at times. For no good reason at all, it took a band from Canada called Rush to marry—deliberately and resolutely—heavy metal and prog rock, drawing on pure prog influences but also on the long-form storytelling tendencies of the Who and the "progressive blues" jammability of Cream.

"I think it was just something we wanted to do," says Rush guitarist Alex Lifeson. "It seemed right, you know? We liked to play hard rock, as a three-piece, but we wanted it to be more challenging, mostly musically, to ourselves."

Unbeknownst to the band at the time, their new direction would prove to be a paradigm shift for metal. Drummer Neil Peart has more to say: "If you look at the late '60s, when I was doing my apprenticeship, what it took to be a rock drummer from, say, 1965 to 1970 [holding his hands at a 45-degree angle] it elevated enormously, in terms of what you were supposed to

"MASTODON DOESN'T REALLY HAVE ANY BOUNDARIES. I'VE ALWAYS BEEN BOTHERED BY THAT WHEN I TALK TO PEOPLE. LIKE, WHEN I PICK MY KIDS UP FROM SCHOOL, THEIR PARENTS ASK ME, 'WHAT DO YOU DO?' 'I'M IN A BAND.' 'WHAT KIND OF MUSIC DO YOU PLAY?' AND AUTOMATICALLY, I'M JUST LIKE, 'I GUESS HEAVY METAL, BUT WE'RE NOT REALLY . . .' AND I TRY TO GET INTO IT, AND THEN IT'S LIKE, NEVER MIND. IT'S DIFFICULT TO EXPLAIN."
—Bill Kelliher, Mastodon guitarist

be able to do. Just consider the difference. To be a drummer in 1965, all you had to do was play one beat. Whereas suddenly, through '67, '68, '69, what happened?! What it took to be a drummer was so daunting as a teenager at the time. 'That's what I have to do to be a good drummer?! I have to play a complicated time signature, exotic percussion instruments, intricate arrangements, inventive drum fills?' All of that was coming at me as a teenager. That became my new benchmark. So I just pursued that goal, and through those years, you'd start hearing different drummers come along—Phil Collins, Carl Palmer, Ian Paice, John Bonham—these people that really had technical ability. The music got really complicated and hard to figure out. The first time I heard somebody say, 'This song's in seven,' I had no idea what they were talking about. So again, that became something I had to learn; it had to become part of what I knew as a rock drummer. But I think there was a real change at that time that's never been equaled in the sudden growth of what the demands were. That happened in jazz, I suppose, as well."

Ergo, prog metal was born, and, almost as if it had been a bad idea, for a number of years it essentially stopped with Rush. Ridiculed for songs like "By-Tor & the Snow Dog," "Xanadu," and a whole side called "2112," Rush were joined in this foolishness (as some would call it) by bands like Styx or Kansas, but that's

about it. Alas, critics found the whole thing pretentious and even juvenile—music for fourteen-year-old sci-fi fans, an exclusively male club. By the late '70s tastemakers were instead embracing peaceful, easy California folk rock as well as the polar opposite of this prog nonsense—namely, punk and new wave.

But prog fans were soon to be satisfied as rapid-fire, note-dense musicianship soon came back into vogue, through bands like Judas Priest—intensely proggy on *Sin After Sin* (1977) and *Stained Class* (1978)—and then Rush-primed purveyors within the New Wave of British Heavy Metal (NWOBHM), most notably Iron Maiden, led by their proghead bassist Steve Harris.

Slightly post-the NWOBHM, a British neo-prog disruption took place: Rush, Yes, and Genesis also enjoyed success with a modern prog sound. From this gumbo emerged metal bands that wanted to push the genre even further, most notably Seattle's Queensrÿche; they tapped James Guthrie, who had worked with Judas Priest and Pink Floyd, to produce their first album, *The Warning* (1984), which became a prog metal staple. Queensrÿche, like Rush before them, were nearly alone in carrying on the prog metal tradition, although Connecticut's Fates Warning soon joined the elite cadre, similarly writing conceptually and immersing their tales in complicated arrangements referencing classical and fusion but mostly the fiery riffs of the NWOBHM.

By the late '80s, inspired by the likes of the super-fast Slayer and the huge prog rock labyrinth of Metallica's . . . *And Justice for All* (1988), bands such as Watchtower, Cynic, Death, Atheist, and Cacophony—and even Megadeth—cranked the intensity and welded prog rock characteristics onto metal of an extreme nature. These reengineered intensifications of what thrash metal and death metal could be set the groundwork for the insanity of today's most radical prog metal "mathcore" bands, including Dillinger Escape Plan, Meshuggah, Protest the Hero, Periphery, Pysopus, and Gojira.

But into the '90s, there was a parallel branch of traditional prog metal as well. Its leader then was, and to this day remains, Dream Theater. Essentially cooked in a lab, Boston's Berklee College of Music, Dream Theater was a rousing success with their second album, *Images and Words* (1992), for much the reason Rush was in the '70s—no one else dared make music like this. Indeed, generations of rock hopefuls had by this point been properly puppy-trained by the rock writing cognoscenti that music should stay behaved and backgrounded so that a singer-songwriter's words of Dylan-derived wisdoms could be clearly parsed.

"Yeah, we embraced it," laughs drummer Mike Portnoy. "Back in the mid-'80s, early-'90s, bands were scared shitless of the term progressive, and we embraced it. We thought there was nothing wrong with writing ten-minute songs and having these long instrumental passages. We wore it on our sleeves like a badge of honor. I wasn't afraid of the term progressive. I was really into it. I thought it symbolized musicianship and integrity."

Portnoy, Petrucci, and crew were essentially Rush on steroids, and their relentless touring and continual record making gave birth to an entire traditional or conservative progressive metal industry; labels like InsideOut, Magna Carta, Sensory Music, Metal Blade, and SPV regularly issued albums whose dramatic musicianship, fantastical lyrics, and meticulously illustrated front covers

> **"THERE'S SOMETHING TO BE SAID FOR THE ALBUM AS A MUSICAL EXPERIENCE. BECAUSE I THINK IN THE SAME WAY, WOULD YOU REALLY WANT TO ONLY EVER READ SHORT STORIES FOR THE REST OF YOUR LIFE? OR WOULD YOU EVER REALLY WANT TO SEE SHORT FILMS FOR THE REST OF YOUR LIFE? THERE'S SOMETHING ABOUT THE TWO-HOUR MOVIE EXPERIENCE OR A COMPLETE NOVEL THAT CAN TAKE YOU ON AN EMOTIONAL JOURNEY. AND I THINK MUSIC IS THE SAME. WOULD *DARK SIDE OF THE MOON* BE SUCH AN ENTITY IF YOU JUST HEARD IT IN BITS AND PIECES?"**—Steven Wilson, Porcupine Tree vocalist-guitarist

combined to celebrate the legacy built by classics such as *Hemispheres* (1978) and *Operation: Mindcrime* (1988).

Surveying prog metal's present robust state, it is clear that the genre is the chosen realm of some of metal's most exciting bands and recordings. In addition to the continued insistent, involved presence of Dream Theater, four bands come to mind that have captured the imaginations of those who love well-executed music, even if the metallic element holds many of them at bay.

Sweden's Meshuggah, with their machine-gun polyrhythms and ethereal Allan Holdsworth stylings, have actually birthed a whole new extreme subgenre called "djent," now explored with fecund bravery by the likes of Periphery, Monument, and Textures. Similarly full-on metal is Mastodon, who could be called a volume knob-crank beyond traditional. Heavy as a sledgehammer, this Atlanta band is nonetheless brainy, virtuosic, and conceptual—and they also wrap their records in some of the most evocative, striking, and memorably colorful art images found in today's metal.

And speaking of art, Sweden's Opeth have also paid as much attention to their visuals as to their quality progressive metal. The band's haunting, photography-based covers come wrapped around records that at first were complicated death metal and later

a unique pastiche of mathematical death and prog. With 2011's *Heritage*, Opeth have come to represent a pure dark prog, evocative of Van Der Graaf Generator and King Crimson circa the mid-'70s.

A collaborator with Opeth mastermind Mikael Åkerfeldt is the aforementioned Steve Wilson, leader of what may well be the flagship band of progressive metal today, Porcupine Tree. If the healthy state of prog metal right now is due to its intense and sincere creativity across all its wildly divergent flavors, one also has to give credit to those who provide a center—those who seem to carry in their DNA the fine features of original British prog. Porcupine Tree, through such classics as *In Absentia* (2002) and *Fear of a Blank Planet* (2007), certainly provide that center around which a scene flies off elegantly in all directions, into doom, neo-psychedelia, neo-prog, ambient, symphonic rock . . .

As for the future? One might look toward one of prog metal's most thriving offshoots, namely the hammer-down white noise heaviness of those subverting death, thrash, and grindcore with a jazz-minded and Mensa-mad ethic of indecipherable mania built on preposterous playing. It's hard to conceive of a prog metal strain more virulent than Psyopus. But then again, we should have learned by now: never underestimate an angry metalhead.

"KING CRIMSON WERE PROBABLY ONE OF THE FIRST EXAMPLES OF PEOPLE THAT COULD REALLY, REALLY PLAY THEIR INSTRUMENTS BEYOND WHAT ANYBODY HAD UP UNTIL THAT POINT AND PUT TOGETHER AGGRESSIVE-SOUNDING MUSIC WITH UNUSUAL STRUCTURE, TO THE POINT OF BEING A LITTLE INDULGENT, YOU KNOW? BUT IN THE EARLY DAYS PEOPLE WERE EXPERIMENTING. THEY WANTED TO SEE HOW FAR THEY COULD GO WITH THIS. HOW MUCH IS TOO MUCH?" —Pete Morticelli, Magna Carta owner

TOP Cover artist Barry Godber died of a heart attack in February 1970, four months after the release of *In the Court of the Crimson King* (Island, 1969). Guitarist Robert Fripp says the screaming figure is the schizoid man of "21st Century Schizoid Man."

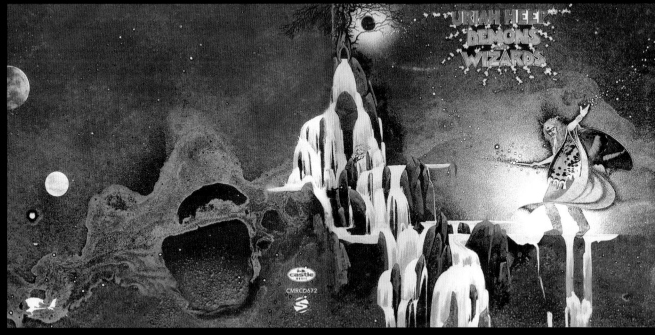

OPPOSITE, BOTTOM Tammo De Jongh's 1967 painting used for King Crimson's *In the Wake of Poseidon* (Island, 1970) is called *The 12 Faces of Humankind*. Depicted (half on the front, half on the back) are the Fool, the Actress, the Observer, the Old Woman, the Warrior, the Slave, the Child, the Patriarch, the Logician, the Joker, the Enchantress, and Mother Nature.

TOP "They were very, very strong covers," noted guitarist Mick Box, "and they were picked up everywhere in the world. *Magician's Birthday* [Bronze, 1972] was just a reflection of—and an obvious move on from—*Demons and Wizards* [Bronze, 1972]. Unfortunately I don't have any of the originals. He was a canny artist— kept them all [laughs]."

BOTTOM Roger Dean's mystical art—as well as the very title *Demons and Wizards* (Bronze, 1972)—helped establish magical themes as recurring lyrical and visual grist for much of the progressive metal to come over the ensuing generations, with sister genre "power metal" indulging heavily as well.

"[*HEMISPHERES*] WAS JUST A BALL-BUSTER TO RECORD! AND I REMEMBER IT
BEING INCREDIBLY FRUSTRATING, YOU KNOW, HAVING HUGE BLOWOUTS DOING
THE VOCALS, WITH TERRY, JUST BECAUSE I WAS SO FRUSTRATED SOMETIMES,
JUST HAVING TO GET OUT OF THE STUDIO AND GO FOR A WALK ON THE STREETS
AND COOL OUT. EVERYTHING TO DO WITH THAT ALBUM WAS LIKE PULLING TEETH.
IT WAS TURNING INTO THE NEVER-ENDING ALBUM, A REAL TEST OF YOUR
PATIENCE AND DETERMINATION."—Geddy Lee, Rush vocalist-bassist

ABOVE As proposed in magazine
advertisements for *Hemispheres* (Mercury,
1978), the dualities suggested by the classic
Hugh Syme–illustrated cover included
reason/emotion, mind/heart, discipline/
freedom, sensibility/sense, love of truth/

"YOU CAN LOOK AT KING CRIMSON AS HAVING A BIT OF A METALLIC ELEMENT TO IT BEFORE THERE WAS EVEN METAL AS WE KNOW IT TODAY, BUT FOR THE REAL ORIGINS OF PROGRESSIVE METAL, I'M LOOKING AT RUSH. I DO CONSIDER EARLY RUSH METAL. I'VE HEARD PEOPLE SAY, 'RUSH IS NOTHING BUT A PROGRESSIVE ROCK BAND.' BUT LISTEN TO 'BASTILLE DAY' AND TELL ME THAT THEY'RE NOT DOING SOMETHING THAT IS VERY EARLY HEAVY METAL RIGHT THERE."—Jeff Wagner, author, *Mean Deviation: Four Decades of Progressive Heavy Metal* (Bazillion Points, 2010)

TOP LEFT Quipped guitarist Alex Lifeson with respect to Rush's enduring pentagram symbol, "If someone gets something else out of that, you know, that's their problem."

BOTTOM LEFT The highly collectible first pressing of *Rush* (Mercury, 1974) on the Canadian Mooncrest label features lettering in red rather than the common pink. In tandem with Neil Peart joining for the band's second album, *Fly by Night* (Mercury, 1975), cover artist Hugh Syme began his long association with the band.

BOTTOM RIGHT Rush found themselves in hot water due to the "boiling" red pentagram adorning their breakthrough album *2112* (Mercury, 1976). In actuality, lyricist Neil Peart meant no satanic inference; rather, the idea was man defending his freedom —and freedom to create—against a future authoritarian regime.

"LOOKING AT MY STYLE, I CAN SAY UNASHAMEDLY, WHOLEHEARTEDLY, THAT I WAS ALWAYS A HUGE ROGER DEAN FAN. SO OBVIOUSLY, MY EARLY '80S COVERS, YOU CAN DEFINITELY TIP THE HAT TO ROGER. BUT I LEARNED MOST OF THOSE TECHNIQUES ON MY OWN—I PAINTED WITH ACRYLICS AND AIRBRUSH AND INK MOSTLY. BUT I MORE SO THOUGHT I WAS GOING TO BE DOING COMIC BOOK COVERS."—Ioannis, cover artist

BOTTOM LEFT Recalls cover artist Ioannis, "I had prepared this huge story for *Heavy Metal* magazine, which was pretty popular in the early '80s, and in fact it had to do with the character on the cover of *The Spectre Within* [Metal Blade, 1985], although it never happened. But when I started doing all these bands for Brian Slagel at Metal Blade, a lot of these paintings had already been done for the story. Brian would look at them and go, 'OK, this would be perfect for Warlord; this would be perfect for Liege Lord.' I think I did all the Lords [laughs]."

TOP RIGHT Crimson Glory's *Transcendence* (Roadracer, 1988) was wrapped in a sleeve that shot the listener into outer space. But as is common within the realm of prog metal, there's a mystical message implied.

BOTTOM RIGHT "*Awaken the Guardian* [Metal Blade, 1986] was a memorable moment for me," says Ioannis, "as it was the first cover that I art directed and designed by myself. At first the band was not that responsive to it, but ten years later talking to Jim Matheos, the band's leader, he told me it was their strongest cover judging by the fans' reactions all these years. The fact that it was also an amazing album helped."

Queensrÿche **Operation: mindcrime**

© ℗ 1988 EMI-Manhattan Records, a division of Capitol Records, Inc.

QUEENSRŸCHE

EMPIRE

QUEENSRŸCHE

HEAR IN THE NOW FRONTIER

TOP "I was living in Montreal, and that's where I came up for the idea for *Operation: Mindcrime* [EMI, 1988]," explains vocalist Geoff Tate. "I launched this idea to the band and none of them were really interested in doing it. I had to fight very, very hard to get them to accept the idea, and it probably took about two months solid of hitting them over the head with it until they finally gave in."

BOTTOM LEFT "We would give the artist an idea and he would go from there," notes Queensrÿche guitarist Michael Wilton on the band's covers. "But our logo, which you see on *Empire* [EMI, 1990], we wanted something ominous to represent Queensrÿche. In the beginning we used some old French font from the middle ages, but then came that symbol and it's ever-changing. It just kind of appeared and we took it by its wings."

BOTTOM RIGHT "That was just a play on words," says Michael Wilton, of the punning cover for Queensrÿche's sixth album, *Hear in the Now Frontier* (EMI, 1997). The richly colored Hugh Syme concoction features ears soaking in clear glass jars embossed with Queensrÿche logos.

The Memory Remains

Very much at the forefront of prog metal—particularly the branch of it that draws heavily from pure '70s prog— is Porcupine Tree and that band's myriad mesmerizing offshoots. And as much as the music that Steven Wilson meticulously crafts is bringing a sense of cachet back to the usually maligned prog metal category, the artwork wrapped around his sonic visions has supported its reputation as well.

"USUALLY, WHAT I DO WHEN I DESIGN, IF THE PHOTOGRAPHY IS STRONG BUT SOMEBODY ELSE HAS BEEN TAKING IT, I STEP BACK—I KEEP MY MOUTH SHUT. I'LL PRESENT IT IN A WAY THAT'S PRETTY NEUTRAL. BECAUSE IT'S HORRIBLE WHEN YOU'VE GOT TYPE COMPETING WITH AN IMAGE. ALL IT DOES IS NULLIFY IT."
—Carl Glover, designer

But it's through the fully eighteen-year-long association with Steven Wilson and his many projects that Aleph Studio has been able to put a design stamp on this difficult-to-define music, evoking in many ways the legacy of Storm Thorgerson and Hipgnosis, particularly the icy cool of that legendary company's industrial photography.

"I grew up in the '70s," begins Glover, "I'm 51, and obviously the Pink Floyd covers had an impact. When *Wish You Were Here* came out, I was at school, and from then on, it was my ambition to do record covers. But with Steven, he's a pretty good friend so working with him is intuitive. He's also very good with titles. He's got a nice way with words—they can put pictures in your head."

In most cases, Porcupine Tree's packaging is the domain of Aleph Studio's Carl Glover, who first thanklessly designed a sleeve for an unreleased New Wave of British Heavy Metal (NWOBHM) album back in '79 by the less-than-forgotten May West. Before long he'd worked his way up through fashion publishing to Mainartery and Bill Smith Studio, where he collaborated with the enigmatic King Crimson, arguably the first prog metal band on the strength of *In the Court of the Crimson King* (1970), again with *Red* (1974), and then fully loud and crunchy on the two that Carl designed, *Vrooom* (1994) and *Thrak* (1995).

As for his romance with industrial sites, Glover says, "It's where I grew up. I lived on the edge of a marsh in a caravan site, a trailer camp—that was my world. We lived near loads of heavy and light industry, and I thought it was beautiful. You'd see these kind of strange alien places on the marshes, and there was still a lot left from World War II. There were all these strange concrete bunkers everywhere; as kids we used to muck around in an old antiaircraft battery, strange concrete buildings with passages and underground tunnels. I'm still very, very partial to them."

king crimson *VROOOM*

King Crimson THRAK

TOP LEFT "The trouble with prog is— especially, to the editors at magazines, the team at *Prog* magazine—they are forever trying to extend its borders, aren't they? One of them talked about how Styx is prog! It's like a Venn diagram, where there's these degrees of overlap. Well, Wagner's prog—definitely, there's no doubt." Carl Glover, Aleph Studios

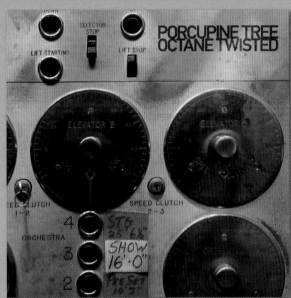

Indeed, there's a wistfulness, a stillness, a powerful nostalgia in Glover's images of mostly forgotten, forsaken industry. And they are usually purely photographic, without much text.

Asked why he rarely uses illustration, Glover protests, "I really do love it. When I started out in college, I tried painting, but I just didn't like the elitism. My dad was an artist, and his dad was too, but ended up a photographer; it was a really hard life for Dad. I really like art and illustration, but I like working photographically, simply because I like dealing with things that are real. And I like to represent them differently—something that is like, for example, a building that

is almost forgotten. On an album cover it takes on a life in itself, and the image could now represent some sort of very layered, dark album." He adds, laughing, "To be played at maximum volume."

"I tend to strip things down," muses Glover, in closing. "But simple things are harder to do than the complex. . . . A good cover should give a clue to the sound, how the thing strikes you. I usually talk to the artist, and that gives me an impression of where they're coming from. I try to work in that space more than anything else. Rather than answering the question that is posed by say, a title, and taking it literally." He laughs again. "It's a shame when it goes that way."

OPPOSITE, BOTTOM LEFT "*Vrooom*'s [DGM, 1994] a weird one," laughs Glover. "That was inspired by a butcher's van down the road. This 3-D effect, but in a 1930s/1940s style; something to do with sausages, I remember. I just liked the lettering and drew it up. There's something beautifully abstract about King Crimson, and it's kind of fun making it crude, grown-up, and complex in equal measure."

OPPOSITE, BOTTOM RIGHT "We wanted something that kind of had a hard exoskeleton and was a bit more interesting inside," says Glover concerning *Thrak* (EG/Virgin, 1999). "In a way, it's a bit like Robert Fripp. You know, I met him about four times, and he can be quite spiky, but really, he's a lovely guy. But also, with King Crimson, I always feel like it's difficult music, and I think intentionally so, and it's a bit like learning a language, really. Once you've cracked it though, it's got something that nothing else has."

TOP LEFT Designer Carl Glover: "*The Incident* [Roadrunner, 2009] was mainly a huge amount of photographs that Lasse Hoile over in Denmark did. He works with Steve a lot, and he does the main photography. His stuff's really beautifully done, very, very good. You can see where it's come from, but he's taking it somewhere completely different. In many respects, he's the David Lynch of Scandinavia."

BOTTOM LEFT Glover, on going retro with Porcupine Tree's *Octane Twisted* (Kscope, 2012): "If it's late Porcupine Tree, I find it quite uncompromising, really, not following the usual vernacular of contemporary prog. It's kind of reaching back into prog's dark ages, and missing out on the whole revival thing, which is kind of fun."

ABOVE RIGHT Notes Glover, "*Blackfield II* [Snapper, 2007] is the word 'Blackfield' in concrete on the side of a building that's torn apart; that was a hospital, funnily enough, the one where my daughter was born. It was bit by bit knocked down, and I'd take her to school, and I walked by the hospital, and every morning photographed it as it was knocked down."

TOP The Hugh Syme–designed cover and booklet artwork for Dream Theater's *Octavarium* (Atlantic, 2005) revolves around the numbers five and eight, for many reasons, one being that on a keyboard, each octave contains eight "naturals" and

BOTTOM Hugh Syme's reputation as prog metal's go-to cover artist is enhanced further with yet another deftly surreal composition, this time for Dream Theater's *Black Clouds & Silver Linings* (Roadrunner, 2009). The muted tones reflect the dark lyrical matter

DREAM THEATER
IMAGES AND WORDS

ABOVE "It was very exciting and my first real album," recalls Dream Theater vocalist James LaBrie of *Images and Words* (Atco, 1992). "There was a really strong exciting bond with the band, and we were all really pumped." The groundbreaking album's cover art reflected the meticulous detailing of the music inside, also introducing us to the band's iconic heart talisman.

"WHEN YOU CONSIDER LATE PROGRESSIVE METAL, THE STUFF THAT IS OUT THERE NOW, THEY ARE THE STARTERS OF THE WHOLE THING, WITH *IMAGES AND WORDS*. THEY CREATED A MONSTER WITH THAT RECORD, WHICH DEFINED THE GENRE AT THAT POINT. FOR THE MOST PART, SINCE THAT RECORD, A GOOD PORTION OF THE BANDS THAT FOLLOWED ARE JUST TRYING TO RE-CREATE WHAT DREAM THEATER CREATED ON THOSE FIRST COUPLE OF RECORDS."—Jim Matheos, Fates Warning guitarist

"ALL OF US BEING HUGE RUSH FANS, IT WAS JUST A HUGE PLEASURE AND A BLAST FOR US TO WORK WITH THESE GUYS WHO WORKED WITH OUR HEROES. HUGH SYME, I LOVE HIS ARTWORK, HE'S DONE SOME AMAZING THINGS, AND IT WAS JUST A PLEASURE TO GET HIM IN THERE. HIS STYLE? I THINK HE CAME FROM THAT KIND OF HIPGNOSIS SCHOOL. THOSE WERE THE ALBUM COVERS BACK IN THE DAY THAT I THOUGHT WERE BRILLIANT. HE JUST TAKES A DIFFERENT ANGLE ON THINGS."

—Jim Matheos, Fates Warning guitarist

BOTTOM LEFT Dug Pinnick on *Gretchen Goes to Nebraska* (Atlantic, 1989): "Whenever we have to make a decision about a name or anything like that, it just ends up turning into comedy. So we were throwing out names, and Kevin our soundman says, 'What if you name it *Gretchen Goes to Nebraska*?' And it was a showstopper for us. We were cracking up so loud. And that cover, the guy who painted it, painted it as just a huge picture, oil painting and everything. And he did our

TOP RIGHT "The idea Hugh came up with for *Perfect Symmetry* [Metal Blade, 1989], you had to think about once or twice, because it was very non-metal, first of all, and secondly, not something that would be the first thing you would think of. There's a little bit more thought put into it."
—Ray Alder, Fates Warning vocalist

BOTTOM RIGHT For their pioneering debut album, *Focus* (Roadrunner, 1993), Florida's Cynic proposed a white-knuckle marriage between death metal and jazz, the result of which could only be called progressive metal. The record's cover art perfectly reflected both the abstraction and the frenzy of such a daring proposal.

ABOVE LEFT This poster celebrates an upcoming show packed with neo-prog talent, featuring Opeth, transformed from a death metal band to prog; Katatonia, from a death metal band to a sort of Radiohead-like alternative prog; and Steven Wilson, whose solo work is just as proggy as that of his bread-and-butter band, Porcupine Tree.

TOP RIGHT Opeth's *Damnation* (Koch, 2003) is significant in the story of prog metal in that it signaled a willingness on the part of Mikael Åkerfeldt to set his grinding Swedish death metal completely aside, for an exploration of mostly acoustic fare. The cover art, however, helps keep it dark like King Crimson.

BOTTOM RIGHT Like the Opeth story on this page, Savatage made a shift toward prog metal with the semi-conceptual *Gutter Ballet* (Atlantic, 1989), the theatrical approach culminating in the penultimate *Streets: A Rock Opera*, the band's next album, from 1991.

Nobody In Particular Presents An Evening With

TOOL

Temple Buell Theatre Wednesday May 10, 2006

ABOVE LEFT Tool, with their heavy yet alternative progressive metal aggression, inspired an avalanche of intensely creative poster art nearly as memorable as the band's convention-shattering album covers.

TOP RIGHT The obese woman, the cow, the forks . . . the actual and innocuous "ribcage" front cover of Tool's debut album, *Undertow* (Zoo, 1993), was about the only image included with the record that didn't create controversy or lead to banning and/or concealment. Design by the band's own guitarist Adam Jones.

BOTTOM RIGHT Tool were able to build formidable mystique around their band through the use of dark, mystical artwork such as this infinite, double helix-styled mind-bender repurposing the third eye thematics from their *Aenima* album (Zoo, 1996).

"TOOL FIND PACKAGING VERY IMPORTANT. ADAM WAS ALWAYS SAYING LOOK, AS MUCH AS ANYTHING ELSE, THE PACKAGING HAS TO BE INTERESTING BECAUSE KIDS LOOK AT A LOT OF THINGS IN A RECORD STORE. IF SOMETHING GRABS THEIR EYE THEY'RE GOING TO BE MORE INTERESTED TO MAYBE HEAR WHAT'S ON THE INSIDE, IF SOMETHING IS INTERESTING STARING AT THEM ON THE OUTSIDE."—David Botrill, Tool producer

TOP For *10,000 Days* (Volcano, 2006), Tool had the digipak CD case for the album built into an old-time invention, namely stereoscopic glasses, to help make the rest of the booklet images come alive in (makeshift) 3-D.

BOTTOM "On *Lateralus* [Volcano, 2001], people are downloading things for free, so you gotta make them want to buy it," remarks Tool producer David Botrill. "And they can't download this. So Adam [Jones] does all that. Adam is very visually creative. He does all the videos and all that stuff, but he's very visually creative, and he feels that's extremely important, the packaging—as

LEFT Coheed and Cambria are a distinguished member of the "alternative" progressive metal subset, led by Tool and also featuring the likes of the Mars Volta, Katatonia, and even Kings of Leon.

S P O C K ' S B E A R D

S N O W

"I THINK ALL OF MY ALBUM COVERS—PORCUPINE TREE, BASS COMMUNION, BLACKFIELD, THE SOLO STUFF—I'M GOING FOR A KIND OF INTELLECTUAL COOL, IF YOU LIKE. I DON'T LIKE THINGS TO BE TOO OBVIOUS. I DON'T LIKE THINGS TO BE PUSHING NECESSARILY THE CULT OF THE PERSONALITY TOO MUCH. I PREFER THINGS THAT ARE MORE THOUGHTFUL AND HAVE AN ELEMENT OF THE SURREAL ABOUT THEM."—Steven Wilson, Porcupine Tree vocalist-guitarist

TOP LEFT InsideOut head Thomas Waber himself designed the very Hugh Syme–like cover for *Snow* (Metal Blade/InsideOut, 2002), one of the most highly regarded albums from LA prog rockers Spock's Beard.

BOTTOM LEFT "Carl's images can be sometimes simultaneously very desolate, but also very beautiful," notes Steven Wilson, on *Fear of a Blank Planet* (Atlantic/Roadrunner, 2007). "And the same is true of Lasse Hoile, who has of course created a lot of the artwork for the album covers, going back to *In Absentia* and *Deadwing*. There's a degree of mystery to it as well."

BOTTOM RIGHT Steven Wilson: "*In Absentia* [Lava/Atlantic, 2002], you see somebody with a hand over their face. And you know, there's a theme that runs through a lot of my album covers, and it is the theme of slightly alienating, depersonalized pictures of human beings. And I think that's always given the album covers a slightly enigmatic, surreal quality."

In Through the Prog Door

Founded by Thomas Waber in 1996, InsideOut Music is a German-based label that has powered the world of progressive metal in both the United States and Europe, as well as the wider realm of progressive rock, helping rejuvenate the careers of establishment artists such as Asia, Saga, and Steve Hackett.

The label's roster, generally speaking, upholds the tenets of traditional prog rock and prog metal, namely virtuosic musicianship, meticulous productions, with many acts addressing the time-honored tradition of the concept album. Interestingly, InsideOut's stable of bands is mostly mainland European, and not so much American or British, even if the United Kingdom is unarguably the birthplace of art rock. Prog metal and its sister genre "power metal" have always been big in countries like Italy, Greece, Spain, and Germany, with many pointing to deep-rooted ties to classical music and theater as part and parcel of the reason.

Still, Thomas points to the Americas with respect to the injection of hard rock into prog. "I think in the beginning, some of the pioneers like Fates Warning or Dream Theater managed to marry different styles of music in a new way. That was exciting and challenging and produced music that had an edge and was still thought-provoking and had depth to it."

Fates Warning indeed recorded for InsideOut, and Dream Theater . . . well, that band of precocious east coasters has been deemed near to a genre in itself, in large part due to the number of European bands worshipping at their altar.

When it comes to the artwork, "You can't force me to generalize," says Thomas, laughing, "as every band has a different sound and needs different artwork. But I will say that I think the best artwork we have has a Hugh Syme style to it. The covers should show that it's not a generic pop or metal album, without being too fantasy and *Dungeons and Dragons*–looking, and Hugh Syme created a perfect look for that."

In that respect, InsideOut covers tend to evoke an almost clinical brightness, the sharpness and detail mirroring the music enclosed, and the recording of that music from a production standpoint.

"Personally, I prefer illustration," says Waber, "because this type of music is supposed to take you out of reality, so photography wouldn't make a lot of sense. But overall, it should fit the band and look professional."

> **"I THINK BACK TO THE IRON MAIDEN ALBUM COVERS, WHEN YOU'D HOLD THE ALBUM IN YOUR HAND, AND YOU'RE LOOKING AT THE DETAILS, AND YOU'RE GOING TO FIND DETAILS THAT YOUR BEST FRIEND DIDN'T FIND. THAT'S KIND OF THE AESTHETIC A LOT OF THESE PROG ARTISTS ARE GOING FOR. THEY WANT THAT. THEY WANT TO HOLD THE ARTWORK IN THEIR HAND, AND EVEN VINYL IS IMPORTANT. YOU'RE NOT BUILDING FOR A DIGITAL AGE; YOU'RE BUILDING FOR A MUSIC FAN."**
>
> —Paul Gargano, InsideOut Music label manager

US label manager Paul Gargano says that progressive metal fans demand nothing less. "Especially with the prog demographic, of all demographics, those people really appreciate packaging. If you look at sales of digital and physical CDs, prog metal fans tend not to buy as much digital. Plus we're also dealing with a demographic that is a bit more affluent. Generally, prog fans have stable jobs, and they like to spend their money on nice products, so we'll put some value into the package. And in terms of design, there's definitely an epic feel to the artwork. For instance, there's the cover for Steve Hackett's 2012 album, *Genesis Revisited II*. It's Venice with a tidal wave sweeping over it.

"I work with other, more mainstream bands here at Century Media/InsideOut, and it's just not the same. When you're dealing with one of those bands, less is more—something very simple, something very plain. Because you've got to jump out from a CD rack. When you're dealing with these InsideOut bands, people think more along the lines of classic LPs, something where there's going to be detail in the artwork. Art is something I think prog fans take a lot more seriously than fans of other genres."

LEFT "It's hard to pigeonhole us," says Symphony X guitarist and founder Michael Romeo, "but at the base of it all, we're a metal band. We have some classical influences, some rock influences, metal, progressive, and all these things go in, but at the end of the day, we're metal guys."

"PEOPLE TEND TO THINK THAT THE PROGRESSIVE METAL GENRE IS MORE ABOUT TECHNIQUE. BUT WHAT PEOPLE USUALLY TELL US IS THAT WE HAVE A REALLY GOOD MIX BETWEEN EMOTIONS AND TECHNIQUE. WE'RE PROGRESSIVE IN THE SENSE THAT WE'RE NOT AFRAID TO TRY ON DIFFERENT MUSICAL STYLES. LET'S JUST SAY THE MUSIC HAS A WILL OF ITS OWN, AND I'M TRYING TO LISTEN TO IT AND SMOOTHLY ARRANGE IT AND PUT IT IN POSITION."

—Daniel Gildenlöw, Pain of Salvation vocalist-guitarist

OPPOSITE, RIGHT Pain of Salvation's *Remedy Lane* (InsideOut, 2002) is a somewhat autobiographical album on which Daniel Gildenlöw writes about the search for identity and the meaning of freedom.

TOP LEFT Asked about Ayreon's preference for illustration, InsideOut America's Paul Gargano responds, "There's definitely more illustration than photography. As you see with *The Dream Sequencer* [InsideOut, 2000], the concepts these guys have are epic. It's not a collection of singles you're going to hear on radio."

BOTTOM LEFT Pictured is compilation *Timeline* (InsideOut, 2008) by Arjen Lucassen and his epic prog metal vehicle Ayreon. "Arjen has the story in his mind before he has the music," notes Gargano. "And he's looking for artwork to match that. And I think it's a lot easier to have someone draw that and design that than to find or take a picture that captures it."

ABOVE RIGHT Germany's Vanden Plas are considered—for better or worse—the leading proponents of the school of note-dense, brisk, metallic, yet traditional prog metal invented and practiced by Dream Theater, as evidenced on the fourth Vanden Plas album, *Beyond Daylight* (InsideOut, 2002).

UR LYRICS ARE PRETTY OBSCURE, AND THEY CAN BE TAKEN DIFFERENT AYS. WE'VE GOTTEN LONG, STRANGE LETTERS ABOUT THEM. SOMETIMES HEY HIT THE NAIL ON THE HEAD AND SOMETIMES THEY ARE WAY OFF BASE. HE SATAN THING COMES UP QUITE A LOT, MOSTLY WHEN JOHN ARCH WAS N THE BAND. IT'S FUNNY; PEOPLE THOUGHT WE WERE EITHER A CHRISTIAN AND OR DEVIL WORSHIPPERS, BECAUSE OF JOHN'S LYRICS, VERY STRANGE, ERY OBSCURE. THE CHRISTIAN THING I CAN UNDERSTAND, BUT THE SATAN HING, NO. MAYBE IT'S BECAUSE WE PUT A WITCH ON THE COVER OF THE IRST RECORD. I THINK IN LATER YEARS PEOPLE REALIZED THAT WE WERE UST A BAND, NOT THESE STRANGE FLOATING PHANTOMS WHO WRITE MUSIC. 'S JUST A COUPLE OF GUYS WRITING MUSIC." —Ray Alder, Fates Warning vocalist

FATES WARNING X

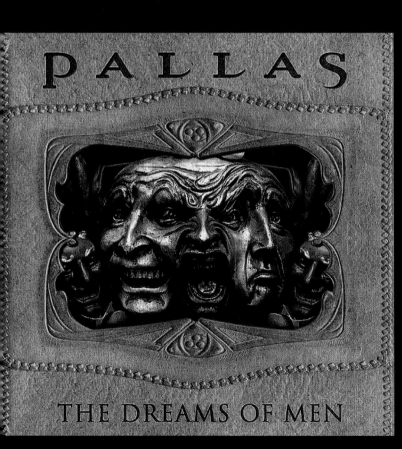

PALLAS

THE DREAMS OF MEN

PROTEST THE HERO
FORTRESS

TOM LEFT Joining Marillion and IQ, llas—all from the UK—have managed survive well past their neo-prog origins the early '80s, issuing top-flight prog oums with a bombastic rock edge, such their sixth record, *The Dreams of Men* sideOut, 2005).

TOP RIGHT Connecticut artist Ioannis turns in one of most impressive offerings, gracing *FWX* (Metal Blade, 2004) with a cover of lush color and Hipgnosis-like surrealism, a technique he's also applied to sleeves for Uriah Heep.

BOTTOM RIGHT Ontario, Canada's Protest the Hero are one of a talented army of extreme metal bands signaling their progressive sensibilities through mystical, nontraditional metal artwork, as seen on the elegant and even feminine sleeve of *Fortress* (Underground Operations/Vagrant, 2008).

OPPOSITE, TOP The disturbing Joachim Luetke–generated image used for Meshuggah's sixth album, *obZen* (Nuclear Blast, 2008), is of an androgynous figure in the full lotus position, the blood signifying, essentially, serenity through gore, with the hand positionings into sixes representing man's implicit evil.

OPPOSITE, BOTTOM LEFT Meshuggah's seventh album, *Koloss* (Nuclear Blast, 2002), took full advantage of the cover's psychedelic, near-humorous artwork, with the label issuing it in standard, digipak, double vinyl, and "magic cube" format—essentially a Rubik's Cube emblazoned with the cover art

BOTTOM RIGHT Meshuggah's Marten Hagstrom on getting across the band's famously difficult music: "I try not to think of people as being unintelligent and not understanding music. I think people are more intelligent about it than people think. So I think, yes, America is very ready for it. They want to have something a little more refreshing. And that's why we're here, to offer an alternative to those who don't want to buy the No. 1 selling album, who don't want to buy the mainstream product."

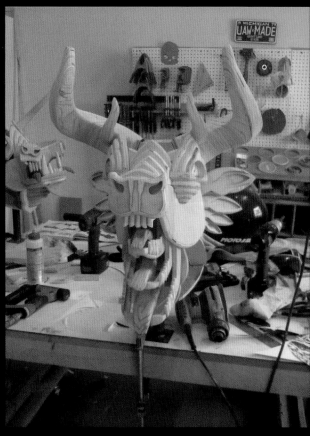

"THE DEPARTURE FOR US, TO ME, IT LOOKS LIKE A RECORD OUT OF THE '70S OR THE EARLY '80S, LIKE A DEVO RECORD OR A JUDAS PRIEST RECORD OR SOMETHING. IT JUST KIND OF SCREAMS TO ME; THE COLORS AND THE SIMPLICITY OF IT, LIKE, 'HEY, I'M LIKE FROM THE NEW WAVE, LEFT OVER FROM THE '70S, EARLY '80S, TALKING HEADS PUPPET THING!' IT'S JUST KIND OF SAYING THAT TO ME."—Bill Kelliher, Mastodon guitarist

TOP LEFT "The album is called *The Hunter* [Reprise, 2011], and it's an ode to Brent's brother, who passed away while hunting," explains guitarist Bill Kelliher. "It's not really a concept, but there are some lyrics there about his brother, being a family, and being a brother and losing family."

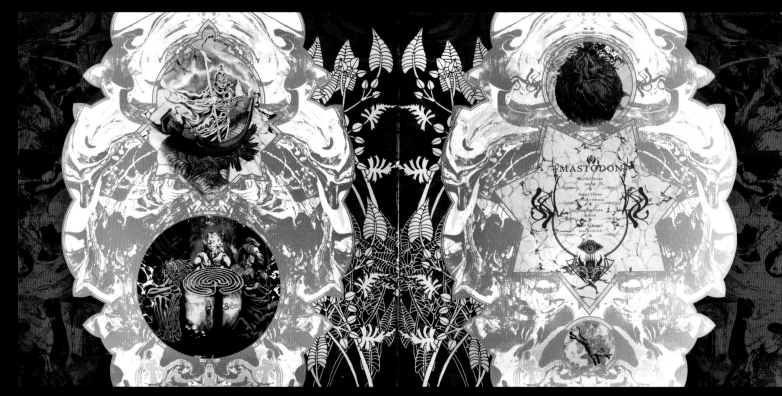

OPPOSITE, TOP RIGHT Kelliher says: "We thought, what's he going to do, make something for us? Just for us? Just for this record? And they were like, yeah. I'm thinking, how long is this going to take? And he actually did it really quickly. And I don't know, for the concept, we kind of figured *crazy animal*. That's all it really is, just a crazy-looking three-mouthed bull."

OPPOSITE, BOTTOM "We looked around for another artist," says Kelliher, "found AJ Fosik, saw some of his sculptures, and we just said, man, this stuff looks really, really awesome. And it's a 3-D piece, a sculpture. And to me, with his head tilted to the side . . . it's cool, because you can photograph it in any different three-dimensional, you know, 360-degree angle, and have something new, which is different

TOP Atlanta's Mastodon arose from the intense, extreme environment of Relapse —"Relapsecore," as it were—to become one of the most highly respected bands on the metal scene, and this despite their grinding, mathematical, conceptual records. In tandem, the band's well-considered artwork was equally intellectually demanding.

BOTTOM LEFT Kelliher on Mastodon cover artist Paul Romano: "He's just a crazy artist, artiste, in every sense of the word. He really gets involved and does so much research. When we did *Leviathan* [Relapse, 2004], he'd take each song and make a painting or a page inside the CD booklet just about that song, and he'll tell our story through his painting."

BOTTOM RIGHT Kelliher on *Blood Mountain* (Warner, 2006): "There's a lot of stuff going on there. Paul had a lot of layers to do and a lot of homework to do with our concept and the methods that we're kind of putting into our lyrics. He translates what we're saying into physical art."

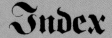

Index

Picture Credits

The publisher would like to thank the following people and organizations. Every effort has been made to acknowledge the pictures, however the publisher welcomes any further information so that future editions may be updated.

© Associated News: 7; 9: TL, CL, BL, R; 11: TR, CR, BR; 12; 16; 17: TL, BL, BR; 18: TL, BL, R; 19: TL, B; 24: TR, BR; 25: TL, BL, R; 26: BL; 27, TL, BL, R; 28: L, TR, BR; 29: TL, B; 30; 31: TL, BL, CR; 33: L, BR, BC; 34: TL, TR, B; 35; 36: BL, TR, BR; 37: TL, TR, BL; 38; 42; 43: L, TR, BR; 44; 45: TL, TR, BL, BC, BR; 46: TR, BL, BC, BR; 47; 48: TL, B; 49: T, BL, BC, BR; 50: TR, BL, BR; 51; 52, 53: TL, TR, BL, BR; 54: TL, TR, BL, BC, BR; 55; 56; 57: TL, TR, BL, BC, BR; 60; 61:TR, BL, BC, BR; 62: TL, TR, BL, BR; 63; 64; 68; 69: TL, TR, BL, BR; 70: TL, TR, BL, BR; 71; 72; 73: T, BL, BR; 74: TL, BL, BR; 75: TL, BL, R; 76: L, TR, BR; 77: TL, BL, R; 78: TR, BR; 79; 80; 81: TL, TR, BL, BR; 82: TL, TC, BL, BC; 83; 86; 87: TL, TR, BL, BR; 88: TL, BL; 89; 90; 94: TL, BL, BR; 95: TL, TR, BL, BR; 96: TL, TR, BL, BR; 97: TL, BL, BR; 98; 99: TL, TR, BL, BR; 102: TL, BL; 103: TL; 104: TR; 105: BL; 106: TL, BL, BR; 107; 108: TR, BR; 109: TL, BL; 110; 111: TL, BL, R; 112; 113: TL, BL; 114: TL, BL; 116; 121: TL, TR, BL, BR; 122: TL, BL, R; 123: TL, BL; 124: L, TL, BL; 125: L, TC, BC, R; 126: TR, BC; 127; 128: TL, BL, TR, BR; 129; 130: L, R; 131: TL, TR, BL, BC, BR; 132: L, TR, BL; 133: TL, BL; 134: B, TR; 135: TL, TC, TR, B; 136; 137: L, R; 138: TR, BL, BR; 139; 140; 144: TL, TR, BL, BC, BR; 145: TL, B; 146: TL, TR, CL, CR, BL, BR; 147: TR, CR, BL, BC, BR; 148: L, TR, BR; 149: TL, BL; 150: BR; 151: L, TR, BR; 152: TL, TR, BL, BR; 153: TL, BL, BR; 154; 155: TL, TR, BL, BR; 156: TL, TR, BL, BR; 157: TL, BL; 158: BL, BR; 160; 164; 168; 169: BL, BR; 170: BL, BR; 171; 172: T, B; 173: TR, BL, BR; 174: TL, TR, BL; 175; 179: TL, BL, BR; 180: TL, BL, R; 181: BR; 184: TL, TR, BL, BR; 185; 186; 187: TR; 188; 189: TL, BL, R; 190: L, BR; 191; 198: T, B; 199: T, B; 200; 201: TL, BL, BR; 202: TR; 203: T, BL, BR; 204: BL, BR; 205: BL, BR; 206: T, B; 207; 208: BL; 209: TR, BR; 210: TL, BR; 211: TL, B; 213: TL, BL, BR; 214: BL, BR; 215: TL, BL, R; 216: BL, BR; 217: T, BL, BR; 218: TL; 219: TC, BL, BR.

Courtesy of Geoff Barton: 59: TL, BL, TC, BC, TR, BR.

Dilek Baykara: 97: TR; 113: R.

© Ernie Cefalu – all rights reserved/Framed, Signed, Numbered, Limited Edition Prints from Ernie's Original Album Cover Art Collection @ PacificEyeandEar.com (Summer 2013): 20: TR, BL, BR; 21: TL, BL, BR, TR; 22: TL, TR; 23: TL, TR, BL, BR; 37: BR.

Metalion: The Slayer Mag Diaries, © 2011 Jon Kristiansen. Courtesy of Bazillion Points: 159: TL, TC, TR, BR.

© Big Time Attic Company: 133: R.

Courtesy of Birmingham County Council: 33: TR.

Corbis Images: 126: TL.

Dave Patchett: 100: TR.

Dudley Archives & Local History Services: 32.

© Earache Records—used with permission: 100: BL, BR; 101; 103: BL; 104: TL; 105: BL; 173: TL; 178. 187: B; 190: TR.

Emek Studios (www.emek.net): 11: L; 102: R; 120: L, R; 123: R; 210: L; 212.

AJ Fosik: 218: TR, B.

Funeral French (www.funeralfrench.com): 193: L.

Carl Glover: 204: TL.

Godmachine: "I produced this for a great company in France. I wanted to do something simple but detailed and with webs.... This is the outcome": 193: R.

Jimbob Isaac: 109: R; 115.

Patrick Klima (photos courtesy of WyCoVintage.com): 84: BL, BC, BR, CR, TR; 85: TL, TC, TR, BL, BC, BR.

Michel "Away" Langevin: 176: TL, BL, BR; 177: TL, BL, R.

Library of Congress Painting by Theodor Severin Kittelsen: 149: R.

Joachim Luetke for Image Eye-Luetke Prod (www.luetke.com): 150: TR.

Carl Lundgren (Detroit Rock Posters): 24: L.

Bahrull Marta of Abomination Imagery, Indonesia (www.abominationimagery.com): 162: TL, TR, BL, BR; 163: C.

© Metal Blade Records, Inc.: 169: TL; 170: TL; 181: TL, BL. 194, 202: BL, BR; 208: TR; 216: TR.

Moon Ring Design: Calth Poster by Moon Ring Design (www.MoonRingDesign.com): 157: R.

Dan Mumford (www.dan-mumford.com): 192: L, R.

Bob Naldanbian: Publisher/editor Headbanger fanzine: 159: BL, BC.

Orphan work: 58: BL, BC, BR; 187: TL. 209: L.

Osmoses Productions © Misha Bass (Illustrator) performed from Herbaut Hervé Sketch: 147: TL.

© Sanctuary/Universal (www.universalmusic.co.uk): 26: R; © UMUSIC: 61: TL.

© Roadrunner Records 105: TL; 106: TL; 138: TL; 174: BR; 181: TR. 205: TL; 208: BR.

Arik Moonhawk Roper: 103: R; 104: BL (collaboration with David D'Andrea): BC; 114: R.

Scrojo: 78: L; 82:R; 88: R.

Glenn "Glenno" Smith (retardmetal@hotmail.com): 108: L.

Photographs by Oran Tarjan/Courtesy of Olivia Airey 182: FL, TL, BL, TR, CR, BR: 183: L, R.

Artwork By Benjamin A. Vierling: 161: TL, BL, BR.

About the Authors

GEOFF BARTON: NEW WAVE OF BRITISH HEAVY METAL
Geoff Barton is a British journalist who founded the heavy metal magazine *Kerrang!* and was an editor of *Sounds*. He joined *Sounds* as a reporter at the age of 19 after completing a journalism course at the London College of Printing. He specialized in covering rock music and helped popularize the New Wave of British Heavy Metal. Barton's articles for *Sounds* on the NWOBHM helped create the sense that an actual movement was taking place, and in a way helped to mold one in the process. He is currently Editor-at-Large for *Classic Rock*, oversees the mag's online presence, and edits offshoot publication *AOR*.

LOUISE BROWN: THRASH & DEATH METAL
Louise Brown is the editor of *Iron Fist*, a magazine dedicated to traditional heavy metal. She was editor of *Terrorizer* magazine from 2007 until 2012, and has contributed to *Metal Hammer*, *Prog*, *The Quietus*, and *Big Cheese*, as well as hosting a regular show on Bloodstock Radio and DJing at some of London's premier rock clubs. She has been a heavy metal maniac since 1990 when her teenage boyfriend stole her a copy of Anthrax's *Persistence Of Time*. Who says crime doesn't pay?

MALCOLM DOME: BLACK METAL
Malcolm Dome started writing about music, and metal in particular, for *Record Mirror* in 1979. He was part of the *Kerrang!* team in the 1980s, co-founded *RAW* magazine in 1988, and now writes for the UK magazines *Metal Hammer*, *Prog*, and *Classic Rock*, among others. Dome has also authored a number of books, including *Encyclopedia Metallica* (from which a certain band got its name), an official book on Bon Jovi, and histories of Van Halen, Aerosmith, and AC/DC. He has presented his own radio shows for Total Rock and has appeared in a number of documentaries, both audio and visual. He even had a cameo role in the award-winning movie *Anvil: The Story of Anvil*. Rumor has it that Dome also enjoys the occasional shot of sambuca!

DOM LAWSON: DOOM & STONER METAL
Since 1999, Dom Lawson has contributed to *Metal Hammer*, *Kerrang!*, *Classic Rock*, and *Prog* magazines, as well as to *The Guardian* newspaper. His regular series of Iron Sandwich video reviews has offended or annoyed almost as many people as it has entertained. He also has his own show on Bloodstock Radio called "The Dompilation Tapes." As a musician, Dom has collaborated with Ginger Wildheart and Devin Townsend and is a bassist/vocalist with prog-punk duo Oaf, whose second album, *Birth School Oaf Death*, will be released in 2013. He lives by the seaside and is an amateur alcoholic.

KYLIE OLSSON: ORIGINS: TRADITIONAL METAL
Kylie Olsson started her career in TV and radio working as a presenter and producer for MTV, ITV, and the BBC. More recently she has authored *Rock: A Life Story*, and works as a journalist for *Classic Rock Presents AOR*. She has also written sleeve notes for the likes of The Allman Brothers Band and FM. Kylie is also a sought-after TV presenter for Sky Arts and VH1 America, specializing in Rock, and she has interviewed some of the biggest names in music. She won a prestigious Sony Radio Award for her documentary about John Bonham for the BBC.

MARTIN POPOFF: PROG METAL
Martin has unofficially written more record reviews—approximately 7,900—than anybody in the history of music writing across all genres. Additionally, Martin has penned 43 books on heavy metal, classic rock, and record collecting. He was Editor-in-Chief of the now web-based *Brave Words & Bloody Knuckles*, Canada's foremost metal publication for 14 years, and has also contributed to *Revolver*, *Guitar World*, *Goldmine*, *Record Collector*, BraveWords.com, Lollipop.com, and HardRadio.com. Martin worked for two years as researcher on the award-wining *Rush: Beyond the Lighted Stage* and on *Metal Evolution*, an 11-episode documentary series for VH1 Classic.

RAZIQ RAUF: NU METAL
A born and bred Londoner, Raziq Rauf has been writing about rock and metal since 1999, and is noted for his work in *Kerrang!*, *Metal Hammer*, and *Prog*, among others. After finding that he was unhappy with the state of music journalism online, he founded the award-winning metal website, ThrashHits.com, in 2008.

BRYAN REESMAN: HAIR METAL
Bryan Reesman is a veteran entertainment journalist and life-long metal fan who has been published in the *New York Times*, *Billboard*, *Inked*, and *Playboy*. He has test-driven a Corvette with Rob Halford, played pool with members of Iron Maiden, had a tour of Lemmy's WWII memorabilia collection, and visited the grounds of the Playboy Mansion. It's a tough job, but somebody has to do it.

Acknowledgments

The authors would like to thank the following collaborators in the development of *The Art of Metal*, without whose valuable advice and support the book would not have been possible: John L. Borowicz, Ian Christe, Kevin Duffy, Ula Gehret, Hugh Gilmour, Godmachine, Steve Hammonds, Steve Horne, Jon "Metalion" Kristiansen, Becky Laverty, Yvonne Maclean, Darrell Mayhew, Jeremy Miller, Dan Mumford, Bob Nalbandian, Will Palmer, Dave Patchett, Mark Riddick, Richard Sayer, Jim Simpson, Brian Slagel, Roslaw Szaybo, Dan Tobin, Andy Turner, and Matt Vickerstaff.

Geoff Barton would like to thank Montalo, Quartz, Cronos, Robb Weir, John and Melanie Gallagher, Brian Tatler, Ian Toomey, Pete Franklin, Lee Payne, and Elixir. Cheers to metal-rules.com for the Garry Sharpe-Young quotes. Extra-special thanks to Stan Lee, Jack Kirby, Steve Ditko, Mike Sekowsky, Jim Mooney, Jim Steranko, and Carmine Infantino.

Malcolm Dome would like to thank everyone at The Crobar, *Metal Hammer*, *Classic Rock*, *Prog*, and Bloodstock Radio.

Dom Lawson would like to thank James Rayment and all friends of the Oaf, Flo and Ozzy, Lee Dorrian and Cathedral, Ben Ward and Orange Goblin, Dave Brock and Hawkwind, all at *Metal Hammer* and *Prog*, all the artists that helped out, John and Frances Lawson for inspiration, and sweet Mary Jane for those magical moments where horticulture and riffs collide. Love and hate are all you need.

Martin Popoff would like to thank Beth, Trevor, Drew Harris, Tim Henderson, Dennis Pernu, the delightful *Art of Metal* team, Ernie Cefalu, Carl Glover, and Blue Öyster Cult.

Bryan Reesman would like to thank Jeff Albright, Ricky C-M, Kevin Chiaramonte, Melissa Dragrich-Cordero, Kim Estlund, Mike Faley, Gail Flug, Jon Freeman, Melissa Kucirek, Tim Mendola, and Ken Sharp.

Elephant Books would like to give special thanks to Ernie Cefalu and the Pacific Eye & Ear team for their images and words.

Thanks to the *Art of Metal* production team, including Olivia Airey, Malcolm Dome, Judith John, Chris McNab, Paul Palmer-Edwards, Martin Popoff, and Joanna St. Mart.